Deprivation and Delinquency

D. W. WINNICOTT

Deprivation and Delinquency

Edited by Clare Winnicott, Ray Shepherd, and Madeleine Davis

TAVISTOCK PUBLICATIONS

London and New York

First published in 1984 by
Tavistock Publications Ltd
11 New Fetter Lane, London EC4P 4EE
Published in the USA by
Tavistock Publications
in association with Methuen, Inc.
733 Third Avenue, New York, NY 10017
© 1984 Clare Winnicott
Typeset by Keyset Composition
Printed in Great Britain at the
University Press, Cambridge

British Library Cataloguing in Publication Data

Winnicott, D. W.
    Deprivation and delinquency.
    1. Juvenile delinquency
    I. Title   II. Winnicott, Clare
    III. Shepherd, Ray   IV. Davis, Madeleine
    364.3'6   HV9069

    ISBN 0-422-79170-9
    ISBN 0-422-79180-6 Pbk

Library of Congress Cataloging in Publication Data

Winnicott, D. W. (Donald Woods), 1896–1971.
    Deprivation and delinquency.

    Includes index.
    1. Juvenile delinquency.   2. Antisocial personality disorders.
3. Deprivation (Psychology).   4. Parental deprivation.   5. Child
psychotherapy—Residential treatment.   6. World War,
1939–1945—Children—Great Britain.   7. World War, 1939–1945—
Evacuation of civilians—Great Britain.   I. Winnicott, Clare.
II. Shepherd, Ray.   III. Davis, Madeleine.   IV. Title.
RJ506.J88W56   1984   616.85'82071'088055   84-8837
ISBN 0-422-79170-9
ISBN 0-422-79180-6 (pbk.)

Contents

Part III
The social provision

Part IV
Individual therapy

Acknowledgements

'The Psychotherapy of Character Disorders' and 'The Development of the Capacity for Concern' are reprinted from *The Maturational Processes and the Facilitating Environment* by permission of Hogarth Press, London and International Universities Press, New York. 'The Antisocial Tendency' is reprinted from *Through Paediatrics to Psychoanalysis* by permission of Hogarth Press, London and Basic Books, New York.

Editors' preface

In selecting the papers for publication in this volume we have aimed to present Donald Winnicott's ideas in a way that will be of practical value and enjoyable to the reader. The papers include some that are hitherto unpublished, some that only appear in journals or are not available, and also, for the sake of clarity and completeness, a very few well-known papers from his own books. The editing of the unpublished papers has purposely been kept to a minimum although we feel that Winnicott himself might well have revised them before presenting them to the public. All this means that there is bound to be some repetition, but this seems a small price to pay for being able to present Winnicott's views on the subject as a whole.

London
March 1983

Clare Winnicott
Ray Shepherd
Madeleine Davis

Introduction
by Clare Winnicott

It does not seem an exaggeration to say that the manifestations of deprivation and delinquency in society are as big a threat as that of the nuclear bomb. In fact there is surely a connection between the two kinds of threat, because as the antisocial element in society rises, so does the destructive potential within society rise to a new danger level. At the present time we are fighting to prevent the danger level rising, and we need to muster all the resources we can for this task. One resource will undoubtedly be the knowledge gained by anyone who has had to come to grips with the problems of deprivation and delinquency by taking responsibility for individual cases. Donald Winnicott was such a person and was precipitated into this position by the Second World War when he became Consultant Psychiatrist to the Government Evacuation Scheme in a reception area in England.

Although the circumstances in which Winnicott found himself were abnormal because of the war time, the knowledge gained from the experience has general application because deprived children who become delinquent have basic problems which are manifested in predictable ways whatever the circumstances. Moreover, the children who became Winnicott's responsibility were those who needed special provision because they could not settle in ordinary homes. In other words, they were already in trouble in their own homes before the war started. The war was almost incidental to them except in those cases (not a few) when it was positively beneficial in that it removed them from an intolerable situation and placed them in one where they might, and often did, find help and relief.

The evacuation experience had a profound effect on Winnicott because he had to meet in a concentrated way the confusion brought about by the wholesale break-up of family life, and he had to experience the effect of separation and loss, and of destruction and death. The personal responses in bizarre and delinquent behaviour that followed had to be managed and encompassed and gradually understood by Winnicott working with a staff team at local level. The children he worked with had reached the end of the line; there was nowhere else for them to go, and how to hold them became the main preoccupation of all those trying to help them.

Up to this point in his career Winnicott had been concerned with clinical practice in hospital settings and in private practice where adults responsible for children brought them to see him. In building up his early clinical experience he had deliberately avoided as far as he could taking on cases of delinquency, because the hospital did not have the resources needed to deal with them, and he himself did not feel ready to be side-tracked into this area of work which is infinitely time consuming and would require skills and facilities that he did not have. He felt he must first gain experience of working with ordinary parents and children in their family and local settings. The majority of these children could be helped and prevented from further psychiatric deterioration, whereas he knew that the children who had gone over into delinquency needed more than clinical help. They presented a problem of care and management.

When the war came Winnicott could not avoid the delinquency issue any longer, and he deliberately took on the Evacuation Consultancy knowing something of what he was in for, and that a whole new range of experience was awaiting him. His clinical experience would have to be extended to include the care and management aspects of treatment.

Soon after the start of the area scheme to which Winnicott was appointed I joined his team as Psychiatric Social Worker and administrator of the five hostels for dealing with children who were too disturbed to be placed in ordinary homes. I saw my first task as that of trying to evolve a method of working so that all of us, including Winnicott, could make the best possible use of his weekly visits. The staff living in the hostels were taking the full impact of the children's confusion and despair and the resulting behaviour problems. The staff were demanding to be told *what to do* and were often desperate for help in the form of instructions, and it took time for them to accept that Winnicott would not, and in fact could not, take on that role, because he was not available and involved in the day-to-day living situation as they were. Gradually it was recognized that all of us must take responsibility for doing the best we could with the individual children in the situations that arose from day to day. Then we would think about what we did and discuss it with Winnicott as honestly as we could when he visited. This turned out to be a good way of working and the only one possible in the circumstances. These sessions with him were the highlight of the week and were invaluable learning experiences for us all including Winnicott, who kept careful records of each child's situation and the stresses put on staff members. His comments were nearly always in the form of questions which widened the discussion and never violated the vulnerability of individual members. After these sessions, Winnicott and I would try to work out what was going on from the mass of detail that had been given to us, and we would form some tentative theories about it. This was a totally absorbing task because no sooner had a theory been formulated than it had to be scrapped or modified. Moreover the exercise was an essential one for me, because during the week I was used as a sounding board by those in charge of the hostels and as a support at any time in difficult moments. I was then in a position to alert the administrator responsible for the scheme when risks that could have led to disaster had to be taken, and to inform Winnicott about what was happening.

There is no doubt that working with deprived children gave a whole new dimension to Winnicott's thinking and to his practice, and affected his basic concepts on emotional growth and development. Quite early on his theories about the drives behind the antisocial tendency began to take shape and to be expressed. His thinking affected what actually went on in the hostels, and how children were treated by individual staff members, and the results were always carefully noted by him. The hostel notebooks still exist, and show his careful observation and attention to detail. Gradually new approaches and attitudes were built up and attempts made to get to the innocence behind the defences and the delinquent acts. There were no miracles, but if crises could be met, and *lived through* rather than *reacted to*, there could be easing of tension and renewed trust and hope.

As it turned out I became the one who held the job together

because I was able to be in daily contact with the staff and children in the hostels. I also saw it as essential to keep communications open and as clear as possible between all concerned in the scheme: committee members, local authority administrators, the parents of the children, and the public bodies who were involved. In this way a wide section of the public was kept informed about the effect of separation and loss on the children, and about the complex nature of the task of trying to help them. It was the dissemination of this kind of first-hand knowledge from evacuation areas all over the country that eventually provided the momentum for the setting-up of a statutory committee of enquiry into the care of children separated from their parents (The Curtis Committee) and eventually led to that landmark in the social history of this country – The Children Act 1948. Winnicott and I both gave written and oral evidence to the Curtis Committee.

With regard to the actual job itself, Winnicott was the person who made it work. He was the central figure who gathered together and held the experiences of us all and made sense of them, thus helping staff living with the children to keep sane in the children's subjective and bizarre world in which they lived for long periods at a time. For us, one of the important lessons of the total experience was that attitudes cannot be taught in words – they can only be 'caught' by assimilation in living relationships.

I have often been asked, 'What was it like to work with Winnicott?'. I have always avoided answering, but I think I would say something like this: it was to be in a situation of complete reciprocity where giving and taking were indistinguishable, and where roles and responsibilities were taken for granted, and never disputed. In this fact lay the security and freedom needed for creative work to emerge out of the chaos and devastation of war. And it did emerge on many levels, and brought satisfaction to all of us taking part in it. We discovered new dimensions in ourselves and in others. Our potentiality was realized and stretched to the limit, so that new capacities emerged. This is what it was like to work with Winnicott.

The papers included in this collection fall into a natural sequence which starts with those written under pressure of Winnicott's clinical involvement in the war and which describe the effects of deprivation as he experienced them. Then follow papers giving his ideas about the nature and origins of the antisocial tendency. The third section is devoted to the kind of social provision needed for the treatment of delinquent children; and finally come three papers about individual therapy and its use in work with the deprived.

Although these writings are of historical interest, they do not belong to history, but to the ever-present encounter between the antisocial elements in society and the forces of health and sanity which reach out to reclaim and recover what has been lost. The complexity of this encounter cannot be overestimated. The point of interaction between the care givers and the cared for is always the focus for therapy in this field or work, and it requires constant attention and support from the professional experts involved, and enlightened backing from the responsible administrators. Today, as always, the practical question is how to maintain an environment that is humane enough, and strong enough, to contain both the care givers and the deprived and delinquent who desperately need care and containment, but who will do their best to destroy it when they find it.

Part I
Children under stress:
wartime experience

Editors' introduction

Behaviour disorders, or what Winnicott often called character disorders, were seen by him as the clinical manifestations of the antisocial tendency. They ranged from greediness and bed-wetting at one end of the scale to perversions and all kinds of psychopathy (apart from brain damage) at the other. The tracing of the origins of the antisocial tendency to more or less specific deprivation in the infancy and early childhood of the individual gave a whole new dimension to Winnicott's theory of emotional development – the theory that he himself described as the backbone of his teaching and clinical work.

The Second World War was a watershed for Winnicott in many ways, but perhaps in none was it more apparent than in the broadening and flowering of his theory of development into something truly original and truly his own. There can be little doubt that his wartime encounter with deprived children contributed to this.

Up to this time psychoanalytic theory had, roughly speaking, attributed delinquency and crime to anxiety or guilt arising from unavoidable unconscious ambivalence: that is to say, they were thought to be the result of the conflict that arises when hate (and therefore the wish to destroy) is directed towards a loved and needed person. The basic idea was that where guilt built up to too great a degree, and found no outlet in sublimation or reparation, something had to be done, or acted out, for the individual to feel guilty about. In other words the aetiology of delinquency was seen mainly in terms of the struggle within the inner world, or psyche, of the individual.

When Winnicott began, in the 1920s, to use psychoanalytic theory to help him with the cases that turned up in his paediatric clinic, and later to write about these, he made it clear that he

believed that many childish symptoms, including behaviour disorders, had their origin in these unconscious conflicts. Nevertheless, though the emphasis here *was* undoubtedly on the inner
world of the child, it is interesting to note that in the snippets of
case histories with which he illustrated his lectures and papers he
often seemed to see an environmental factor as decisive. There
was Veronica, for instance, who at one and a half became a
bed-wetter after her mother spent a month in hospital; Ellen who
stole at school and whose family had broken up when she was
one; and Francis whose violent episodes were linked to his
mother's depression. One feels the common sense behind the
telling of these stories – the common knowledge, stretching back
into history, of the need in childhood for a safe and steady
environment.

For a few years before the war John Bowlby, another psychoanalyst, had also had an opportunity for studying the background
of disturbed children who were referred to the Child Guidance
Clinic where he worked. In a formal study of 150 children with
various complaints he had found a direct link between stealing
and deprivation – particularly separation from the mother in
infancy.[1] This is discussed in the letter at the beginning of this
section.

So the stage was set, so to speak, for Winnicott's experiences in
the war, which, as Clare Winnicott has described in the Introduction to this book, brought home the link between deprivation
and delinquency with almost overwhelming immediacy.
Winnicott never lost sight, however, of the deeper understanding
of these problems that psychoanalysis made possible. Among
other reasons something surely was (and is) needed to make sense
of the seeming irrationality of delinquent behaviour, of its
rigidity of pattern, and of its compulsiveness which can make the
perpetrator seem mad even to himself. Psychoanalytic theory thus
came together with observation and practical experience and
emerged in the statements to be found in the second part of this
volume.

Part I is concerned with Winnicott's experiences in the war, and
begins with the letter already mentioned, written by Bowlby,
Winnicott and Emanuel Miller, pointing out the dangers in the

[1] J. Bowlby, 'The Influence of Early Environment in the Development of Neurosis
and Neurotic Character' in the *International Journal of Psycho-Analysis*, 21, 1940.

evacuation from the cities of children under five years. This is followed by an article entitled 'Children and Their Mothers' (1940) showing the effects of separation from the home environment and from the mother on two such evacuated children. The second chapter is a review of a book containing a statistical survey of the problems of children evacuated to Cambridge in the charge of schoolteachers, written in 1941. By now Winnicott had come to see the whole of evacuation as a 'story of tragedies', though he has much praise for the teachers who had to care for the children. Bowlby's work appears once more as providing the classification of abnormalities according to which the survey was conducted.

These three papers have in common a point of view that subsequently gained wide acceptance among professional workers: namely that where loss is suffered a manifest indication of distress *is to be expected*, and that where no such reaction occurs there may be disturbance of a deeper kind. The letter draws attention to the value of the capacity to mourn – the mature reaction to loss. (The process of mourning is described in the paper entitled 'The Psychology of Separation' in Part II.) It is clear, however, that the *Cambridge Education Survey* found other and less mature reactions, including some degree of antisocial behaviour, not uncommon among schoolchildren. By the time Winnicott came, in 1945, to give his broadcast talks to foster-parents and to parents ('The Evacuated Child' and 'Home Again') it can be seen that he attached a positive psychological value to antisocial behaviour in children, as a reaction both to loss of people who are loved and to loss of security, provided this found an appropriate personal response from those in charge of them. This idea lies at the heart of Winnicott's theory of the antisocial tendency, and it was inherent in all his clinical work as well, for he held that it is the individual who suffers who can most readily be helped.

Apart from the first two chapters the remainder of Part I consists of talks which originally formed a section of Winnicott's book *The Child and the Outside World*, now long out of print. The section was called 'Children under Stress' and we have borrowed its title here. It begins with a talk to teachers about how listening to wartime news bulletins affects children of different ages and types, and here can be seen Winnicott's insistence that the inner world of the individual child needs to be taken into account. Then follow four BBC broadcast talks about evacuation: the first, given in 1939, about the mother's grief on losing her child and the many apprehensions she may feel about what the child is experiencing away from home; the second given in 1945 to foster-parents about the essential part they have played in the evacuation (this was actually the only time Winnicott ever addressed himself specifically to foster-parents); and the other two, also given in 1945, to and about parents concerning the problems as well as the pleasures facing them on the children's return home. It is perhaps especially in these broadcast talks, with their clear and vivid language, that the depth of Winnicott's understanding of the feelings of those involved in painful separations emerges. Not only are the feelings understood, but they are respected in a way that must have brought relief to many of his listeners.

Finally there are two papers, one written in 1947 and one in 1949, about the development of hostels for the children who presented bigger problems in management than could be contained in foster-homes. It was found that these were already deprived children: that is, they had suffered deprivation before being evacuated. The first of these papers tells the fascinating story of the growth of the hostels scheme arising out of a need so urgent that there was a single-minded determination to meet it. It is, taken broadly, a success story – though success in such undertakings must always be relative – and it should be of interest to all those who have contact with any one of the many hostels that have been set up since the war to meet a variety of needs. The last paper urges that the hostels scheme developed in the war be given a place in the peacetime management of difficult children.

1 Evacuation of small children

LETTER TO THE *BRITISH MEDICAL JOURNAL*
(16 December, 1939)

SIR – The evacuation of small children between the ages of 2 and 5 introduces major psychological problems. Schemes for evacuation are being thought out, and before they are completed we wish to draw attention to these problems.

There are dangers in the interference with the life of a toddler which have but little counterpart in the case of older children. Evacuation of older children has been sufficiently successful to show, if it were not known before, that many children over 5 can stand separation from home and even benefit from it. It does not follow from this that the evacuation of smaller children without their mothers can be equally successful or free from danger.

From among much research done on this subject a recent investigation carried out by one of us at the London Child Guidance Clinic may be quoted. It showed that one important external factor in the causation of persistent delinquency is a small child's prolonged separation from his mother. Over half of a statistically valid series of cases investigated had suffered periods of separation from their mothers and familiar environment lasting six months or more during their first 5 years of life. Study of individual case histories confirmed the statistical inference that the separation was the outstanding aetiological factor in these cases. Apart from such a gross abnormality as chronic delinquency, mild behaviour disorders, anxiety, and a tendency to vague physical illness can often be traced to such disturbances of the little child's environment, and most mothers of small children recognize this by being unwilling to leave their little children for more than very short periods.

It is quite possible for a child of any age to feel sad or upset at having to leave home, but the point that we wish to make is that such an experience in the case of a little child can mean far more than the actual experience of sadness. It can in fact amount to an emotional 'black-out', and can easily lead to a severe disturbance of the development of the personality which may persist throughout life. (Orphans and children without homes start off as tragedies, and we are not dealing with the problems of their evacuation in this letter.)

These views are frequently questioned by workers in day nurseries and children's homes, who speak of the extraordinary way in which small children accustom themselves to a new person and appear quite happy, while those who are a little older often show signs of distress. This may be true, but in our opinion this happiness can easily be deceptive. In spite of it children often fail to recognize their mothers on returning home. When this happens it is found that radical harm has been done and the child's character seriously warped. The capacity to experience and express sadness marks a stage in the development of a child's personality and capacity for social relationships.

If these opinions are correct it follows that evacuation of small children without their mothers can lead to very serious and widespread psychological disorder. For instance, it can lead to a big increase in juvenile delinquency in the next decade.

A great deal more can be said about this problem on the basis of known facts. By this letter we only wish to draw the attention of those who are in authority to the existence of the problem.

We are, etc.,

John Bowlby
Emanuel Miller
D.W. Winnicott

London W1

CHILDREN AND THEIR MOTHERS
(Written for *The New Era in Home and School*, 1940)

In a letter from a woman public servant who has done a great deal for toddlers I find this: '. . . from fifteen years' experience I am convinced that for children from 2 to 5, nursery schools with properly trained teachers – and enough of them – are far better than the child being with its mother . . . they need care and companionship from 2 to 5 and most mothers may give too much of one or the other or both . . .' Is this true?

The question of relationship between children and their mothers is one which cannot be too closely studied, and the problems connected with evacuation can be turned to use if they can force us to further study.

The subject is a big one, but certain things stand out clearly, one of which would be that the younger the child the more danger there is in separating him from his mother.

There are two ways of stating this which at first appear to be very different from each other. One is that the younger the child the less his ability to keep the idea of a person alive in himself; that is to say, unless he sees that person or has tangible evidence of her existence within x minutes, hours or days, that person is for him dead.

A boy of eighteen months was just able to tolerate his father's absence because he could take a postcard his father sent him on which he had written some familiar sign and weep over it while going to sleep. A few months earlier he would not have been able to do even this, and his father then on returning would have been as one risen from the dead.

The other way of putting this has nothing to do with age, but has to do with depression. Depressive people of any age characteristically find it difficult to keep alive the idea of those whom they love, even perhaps when they are living in the same room with them. It would be unnecessary here to try to connect up these two different ways of putting the same thing.

Uninstructed parents may intuitively recognize the importance of this and similar human qualities, and yet authorities who are responsible for such big things as the evacuation of children are not incapable of neglecting them.

An ordinary working-class father writes:

'I am replying on behalf of my wife to your letter of 4th December.

'She has evacuated to Carpenders Park with John (age 5), and his younger brother, Philip. She says John appears to be quite happy and healthy.

'I see them every week-end and John seemed completely contented until very recently. Now he is insistent about seeing his grandmother, *i.e.* my mother. She has evacuated to Dorset but may return in the near future. I have promised him he shall see her, if and when she returns. . . .'

Here are notes of a hospital consultation dated December 12th, in the course of which appears the expressed opinion of an ordinary working-class London mother.

Tony Banks: Aged 4½.

Mrs. Banks brought Tony and his sister Anne, aged 3, being glad that I was still willing to share responsibility for decisions with her in spite of the hospital having closed. The main decision at the moment is in regard to evacuation. She and the two children went to Northampton at the outbreak of war. They were unhappy in a small billet where they all had to sleep in one bed. They were as much in the town there as at home and they felt they had all the disadvantages of evacuation without the advantages. After a fortnight they changed to a billet which has proved very satisfactory, except that Tony is in bed with his mother. Anne has her own cot. When the father goes down he sleeps in the bed with his wife and his son.

The Banks family is a very happy one. The father is very fond of his children and they of him. He himself had a happy childhood, the only son of a very lovable mother. Mrs. Banks was one of six and her childhood was happy enough except that she had a very strict father. She feels that she never really knew happiness until she was married, since when she has given herself to her husband and children.

She feels that this present period of her life is the important period where the children are young and respond so much to every detail of good management. Her problem then is to avoid losing what she feels to be the best of life out of fear of something that may never come. She feels that it would be logical to go out of London for a few months but not for three years. She and her husband have the double need of each other, sexual and friendly, and Mr. Banks visits them every week-end, although this leaves him exactly 1/- out of his wages to spend on himself: he neither drinks nor smokes and does not feel badly off. Mrs. Banks says that he must come down and see them once a week *because they are small and if he stays away longer they fret or, worse still, forget.* Once his father had to get into the train quickly and Tony said, 'Daddy didn't cuddle me enough before he went' and sobbed his heart out. Mr. Banks is also upset if he does not see his family regularly.

The children ask such a lot of questions: 'Where is Nanny?' (that is mother's mother), 'Where is Auntie?' so that she decided to bring the children up for a week to take them around to see their relations. This has worked very well, but she felt that if she had left it longer the children would have become puzzled and unable to remake contact satisfactorily. They are all going back to be in the billet by special request at Christmas time, but she feels that it is likely that soon after Christmas on weighing things up she will decide to come home. The billet is obviously almost ideal, but Mrs. Banks says that however nearly ideal it is it is not the same as one's own home.

When I asked her about Tony and his sleeping in bed with both of them when his father visits them, she first of all said that he is always asleep and so never witnesses anything. She says that she always tests him first by talking to him and seeing that he is deeply asleep. Then she said once he woke up – his father must have knocked him – and he said, 'Mum, what is Dad moving up and down for?' and she said, 'Oh, he is just rubbing his legs, he is so cold', whereupon he went to sleep again. But in the day time he asked a great number of questions, chiefly about the real war. He says to his sister, 'Hush, you must be quiet now, it is the news', and then he insists on listening to the news and asking his mother all about the points he doesn't understand. For instance, when a ship sinks how do they let the wireless people know that it is sinking. Doesn't the wireless operator go down with the ship. This interest in the news, of course, involves his learning daily about the death of men and no doubt the mother was right in linking his interest in the news with his interest in the sexual intercourse which he is forced to deal with, at any rate in his fantasy, and perhaps in consciousness.

Going with his forwardness in intellectual development is his inability to dress himself: he cannot do up the back buttons of his trousers or his shoe buttons, and he cannot open the lavatory door. In eating, too, he is very slow, not only with putting food to his mouth but also in completing the act of mastication. He is one of those children who retain food in the mouth, chewing and chewing; sometimes his mother eventually has to take a piece of meat out of his mouth after it has been masticated for an hour or more.

Tony and his sister are happy together and will not hear of being parted. They quarrel if left quite alone, their play is imaginative but tending to deal with present day real affairs such as ambulances and A.R.P. shelters. They play doctors and mothers, and they reconstruct families having tea, and his particular game is doctors and nurses, which he will play endlessly and enjoy.

Father makes it his job to take the children right off their mother's hands on Sunday. This is a treat that they all look forward to. He is very good with them, takes them walking, which they love better than riding in buses and he consults them as to where they want to go and what they want to see, and is clearly at home with children.

This boy has been coming to my department at hospital since three years old. He was well until his sister was born when he was 18 months old, whereupon he became violently jealous, especially when his mother was feeding the baby. He would rush up to his mother and pull down her jumper and try and get the breast for himself, or he would stand by furious when his mother was changing the baby's napkins or preparing her cot. His jealousy of the new baby slowly turned to love of her and great pleasure in playing with her. When he was two he had an attack of diarrhoea. The second big event in his life was diphtheria when he was about 3. Soon after this it was noted that he developed the feeding inhibition which has persisted to the present day, although as a baby he was nice and greedy. He developed liability to definite depression. The social visitor found that he had been made a lot of as a baby, although perhaps not abnormally so, and that when the little girl came his father took him over while his mother was fond of the new one. At present he is in good physical health.

Harm done by separation of child from mother is illustrated by the following case history:

Eddie, aged 21 months, is the first and only child of ordinary intelligent parents, the father being in business and the mother having been till her marriage a professional musician.

At 18 months he slept for the first time in the same room with his parents, when he was away on holiday with them. He would not go off to sleep unless his mother cuddled him. After being lifted out at 10 o'clock he grizzled but went off to sleep fairly easily. On and off during this holiday he had to be cuddled because of being too excited to go to sleep on his own. This was noted as unusual for him and put down to the fact that he had his father, of whom he is very fond, all day. At this stage there was never any difficulty in quietening him, the only thing noted was that he had to be quietened.

After this holiday the family returned home, but in a week war broke out so off he went with his mother to his mother's mother, father being left to look after himself. He now slept in his mother's room. At this stage he started to need more nursing, seeming to be upset by the disturbance in his parents' lives, but he could always be reassured. After ten days it was considered that he knew his grandmother well enough to be left with her, so the mother returned to her home to look after her husband, and for one reason and another stayed away as long as a month. She was then written for, the child had become poorly, cutting teeth, vaguely ill. So his mother went and found him feverish and with painful gums. He is cutting his last four first teeth. She wondered at his being so upset at his cutting teeth since he had never before been upset when his teeth came. The thing which struck her most was that *when she came he did not know her*. This was distressing to him and a real shock to her, but she patiently waited and in the morning was rewarded by his being able to recognize her. At the same time he became very much better in physical health and became able to sleep well; he also enjoyed talking to his mother a great deal in his own way. It seemed that his condition changed as he became able to recognize her, so that it was difficult to believe that he had really been suffering from a purely physical illress. After three or four days he was quite well and happy and travelled home. When he got home he could not at first go to his own room as a friend was using it, so he slept in his parents' room. He knew his father immediately and knew where he was, looking around all the old haunts with squeals of delight and pleasure. He was very happy to be home, and slept well the first night. The next night he slept less well and this sleeplessness increased gradually to a serious symptom. After one week he went back to his own room, which he likes, and for three nights there slept better, but *then started sleeplessness again*. The degree of this symptom eventually brought the mother to me. He would stand up and scream for four hours, the screaming got beyond anger to terror and beyond terror to despair. The mother, who is sensible and motherly, recognized that she must do something about what was evidently not simply a matter of temper. The only way she could manage was to nurse him until he slept, but even if she got him soundly asleep, if *she got up to go he always woke as she reached the door*. Firmness was of no use, nor was verbal explanation that all was well. When the mother in the determination not to be mastered matched her own determination against his the final result was exhaustion on both sides with no improvement in the situation when they had both recovered. When she refused to give in however much he cried he eventually started screaming for daddy, having given up hope of his mother. After half an hour she went in and found him in an awful state, flushed and wet and incontinent of faeces. This developed into sobbing until eventually he sunk into his mother's arms and slept worn out. In an hour or two the tussle started again. A general practitioner was called in and said he was teething and advised aspirin. For three nights this worked like a charm and then suffering started again, only worse. All this time he was happy in the day time, not naughty, affectionate, obedient, and able to play by himself and with his father and mother. A compromise was arrived at by his mother letting him sleep in his pram in the parents' room. This gave him permission to be there but without the implication of permanence. The mother was by this time in a state of indecision and badly needing help. She said: 'I can't always be determined, even if I ought to, because the people in the flat above are badly disturbed by the crying.' There was urgency in the clearing up of this problem because in a month's time the family is due to move to a house in the suburbs, in which case he will lose not only the nursery he has known, but also the woman who helps in the house and who understands him very well, but who at this stage was unable to produce in the child a state of mind which would allow his mother out of the room when he was asleep. The mother said she felt in despair, she felt as if all her training of the child had gone to the wind. If she smacked his head and said 'naughty' he smacked himself, seeming to say that he knew all about it anyway and she need not rub it in, and he had taken to grinding his teeth.

Investigation showed that Eddie could not easily meet his mother again because in the time of separation from her he had hated her without being able to get from her presence and smile the reassurance that she could remain alive and friendly in spite of his hate.

The fact that the trouble was resolved with help does not alter the other fact that the child did not easily recover from the trauma of separation from his mother.

Without in any way denying that physical harm may come to children in air raids, and without minimizing the harm that may result from their witnessing fear in grown-ups, or actual destruction, one can usefully go on putting forward the commonplace that there is more in the family unit than considerations of comfort and convenience. In fact the family unit provides a reassurance that the infant cannot really do without, and the toddler cannot miss it without interference with his emotional development and without impoverishment of his personality and character.

2 *Review of* The Cambridge Evacuation Survey: A Wartime Study in Social Welfare and Education

(Edited by Susan Isaacs, 1941)

Evacuation had to be. In a misguided attempt to lessen the evils inherent in exile, many have tried to make out that evacuation is actually a good thing, something sensible, which it takes a war to bring into effect. But to me evacuation is a story of tragedies; either the children are emotionally disturbed, perhaps more than they can recover from, or else the children are happy and it is the parents who suffer, the implication being that they are not needed even by their own children. For me, the only success the scheme can claim is that it could fail.

However, it has been my job to see the failures and the tragedies, and a personal view has but little value. In *The Cambridge Evacuation Survey* we get the view of a team of workers who made a systematic investigation on the spot and at the time, and this book is definitely worth study. The collective view of the editors and nine authors is not entirely a pessimistic one, although strong criticism is offered here and there.

The amount of thought and work and sifting and sorting that this book represents is enormous. The period covered extends from the outbreak of war to the end of the period that preceded the onset of the bombing of open towns. After this, re-evacuation would have merely complicated any attempt at statistical enquiry. In this book statistics are skilfully used, but somehow we never lose sight of the children, the parents, the foster-parents, and the teachers as whole human beings. This must be the reason for its readability.

Something of the feeling of the book can be got from the following quotations:

'This, then, is our broadest and most general conclusion, namely, that the first great scheme for evacuation might have been far less of a failure, far more of a success, if it had been planned with more understanding of human nature, of the way in which ordinary parents and ordinary children feel and are likely to behave.

'In especial, the strength of the family tie, on the one hand, and the need for skilled understanding of the individual child, on the other, seem to have lain too far outside the ken of those responsible for the Scheme.' (p. 9.)

'. . . it is extravagant not to provide personal service to which individuals can turn for understanding and help.' (p. 155.)

'This sharp lesson in the ineffectiveness and waste of a partial approach to a great human issue, one which from its very nature touches every side of human life, applies by no means only to the temporary crisis of dispersing urban populations during a war.' (p. 11.)

The body of the book must be read to be appreciated, for it is carefully written, and justice would not be done to the conclusions by pulling them out of the pie and offering them as fresh fruit.

A chapter on 'What the Children Say' is illuminating and fun. It was possible to make statistical enquiry into the answers given to the two simple questions: What do you like in Cambridge? What do you miss in Cambridge? Sometimes the answers needed interpreting but they do convey the conscious feeling.

A doctor may perhaps be allowed to express regret that the medical profession was found to be so inadequately prepared for the type of problem evacuation presented, that no one thought of asking help of the doctor except for the management of physical health and preventive treatment for infection and infestation. The whole burden fell on the teachers who, as far as they were allowed, undertook the new task of caring for whole children extraordinarily well. In this Survey one doctor's name appears, that of Dr. John Bowlby, who provided a useful working classification of children into six definite groups of varying abnormality:

'(A) Anxious children, who may or may not be depressed as

well; (B) Children who are "shut-in" and tend to withdraw themselves from relationships with other people; (C) Children who are jealous and quarrelsome; (D) Children who are over-active and aggressive; (E) Children who show alternating moods of elation and depression; (F) Delinquent children.

'The children were classified according to these six ways of responding. They were also ranked according to the degree of disorder shown, in three grades. Grade I indicates a slight difficulty, in some cases not much more than a bare tendency, which with reasonable treatment and understanding in the ordinary course of events, in home and school, will right itself. Grade II indicates a fairly serious maladjustment which calls for clinical treatment, but one which may be expected to yield to skilled care and attention. Grade III indicates deeply-seated emotional disturbance which, unless treated at an early stage, will be likely to lead to serious breakdown later on.'

Dr Bowlby's description of the children in each of these three groups is obviously based on clinical observation and therefore has a value even should experience lead to modification.

There remains plenty of work to be done on evacuation and the disturbances in emotional development that it has caused, as well as the ways in which some had used it to get true and lasting benefit. The unconscious feelings and factors, for instance, have not been directly tackled in this book, and yet they are of great importance, as in every matter of human relationships.

This book, however, represents the sort of work that is needed, because it is objective and unsentimental, and Dr Susan Isaacs and her colleagues are to be thanked.

The name of Miss Theodora Alcock should be mentioned, although it is not on the list of authors, since the survey was the child of Miss Alcock's Child Discussion Group, which many of us have attended with pleasure over a number of years.

3 *Children in the war*

(Written for teachers, 1940)

To understand the effect of war on children it is first necessary to know what capacity children have for the understanding of war and of the causes of war, and of the reasons by which we justify our fighting. Of course, what is true of one age group is not true of another. This may be rather obvious, but it is important, and I will try to put into words what it implies.

What is also important is the variation between one child and another, apart from age differences. This I will also try to describe.

Age group variations

Tiny children are only indirectly affected by war. They are scarcely wakened from sleep by guns. The worst effects come from separation from familiar sights and smells, and perhaps from mother, and from loss of contact with father, things which often cannot be avoided. They may however come into contact with mother's body more than they would ordinarily do, and sometimes they have to know what mother feels like when she is scared.

Quite soon, however, children begin to think and talk in terms of war. Instead of talking in terms of fairy stories that have been read and repeated, the child uses the currency of the adults around him, and his mind is full of aeroplanes, bombs, and craters.

The older child leaves the age of violent feelings and ideas, and enters a period of waiting for life itself, a period which is the teacher's heyday, since ordinarily a child between 5 and 11 years is longing to be taught and told what is accepted as right and good. In this period, as is well known, the *real* violence of war can be very distasteful, while at the same time aggression appears regularly in play and fantasy with romantic colouring. Many never leave this stage of emotional development, and the result may be harmless, and may even lead to highly successful accomplishment. Actual war, however, seriously upsets the lives of adults who have stuck here, and this gives the cue to those who have charge of children who are in this 'latency' period of emotional development to select and enlarge upon the non-violent side of war. One teacher has described how this may be done through the use of war news in the geography lesson: this town in Canada is interesting because of evacuation, this country is important because it contains oil or has a good harbour, that country may become important next week because it grows wheat or supplies manganese. The violent side of war is not stressed.

A child in this age group does not understand the idea of a fight for freedom, and indeed could be expected to see a great deal of virtue in what a Fascist or Nazi regime is supposed to provide, in which someone who is idealised controls and directs. This is what is happening inside the child's own nature at this age, and such a child would be liable to feel that freedom meant licence.

In the majority of schools the stress would be laid on the Empire, the parts coloured red in the maps of the world, and it is not easy to show why children in the latency period of emotional development should not be allowed to idealise (since idealise they must) their own country and kind.

A child of 8 or 9 years might be expected to play at 'English and Germans' as a variation on the theme of 'Cowboys and Indians', or 'Oxford and Cambridge'. Some children show a preference for one or other side, but this may vary from day to day, and many do not much care. Then comes an age at which it is expected that, if the game is one of 'English and Germans', the child shall prefer to identify with his own country. The wise teacher is not in a hurry to find this.

Discussion of the case of the child of twelve and over becomes complex because of the great effects which result from the delay of puberty. As I have said, many people partially retain the qualities that belong to the so-called latency period, or return to these qualities after a furtive attempt to attain a more mature development. For them one can say that the same principles hold as for the real latency child, except that it is with more and more misgiving that we tolerate them. For instance, whereas it is quite normal for a nine-year-old to like to be controlled and directed by an idealised authority, it is less healthy if the child is 14. One can often see a definite and conscious hankering after the Nazi or Fascist regime in a child who hovers on the brink, fearing to launch away into puberty, and such a hankering should obviously be treated with sympathy, or be sympathetically ignored, even by those whose more mature judgment on political matters makes admiration of a dictator an ugly thing. In a certain number of cases this pattern sets in as a permanent alternative to puberty.

After all, the Authoritarian regime has not sprung out of nothing; in one sense it is a well-recognised way of life found in the wrong age group. When it claims to be mature it has to stand the full test of reality, and this brings out the fact that the idealisation in the Authoritarian idea is itself an indication of something unideal, something to be feared as a controlling and directing power. The onlooker can see this bad direction at work, but the young devotee himself presumably only knows that he blindly follows where his idealised leader leads.

Children who are really coming to grips with puberty and the new ideas which belong to that period, who are finding a new capacity for the enjoyment of personal responsibility, and who are beginning to cope with an increased potential for destruction and construction, may find some help in war and war news. The point is that grown-ups are more honest in wartime than in peacetime. Even those who cannot acknowledge personal responsibility for this war mostly do show that they can hate and fight. Even *The Times* is full of stories that can be enjoyed like an exciting adventure story. The B.B.C. likes to link Hun-hunting with the pilot's breakfast, dinner, and tea, and exploits over Berlin are called picnics, though each exploit brings about death and destruction. In wartime we are all as bad and as good as the adolescent in his dreams, and this reassures him. We as an adult group may recover sanity, after a spell of war, and the adolescent, as an individual, may one day become able easily to pursue the arts of peace, though by then he will be no longer a youth.

The adolescent, therefore, may be expected to enjoy actual war bulletins as given to adults, which he can take or leave as he pleases. He may hate them, but by then he knows what it is we are so eager about, and this clears his conscience when he discovers that he has himself the capacity to enjoy wars and cruelty as they turn up in his fantasy. Something corresponding to this could be said of adolescent girls, and the differences between boys and girls in this respect very much need working out.

Variations according to diagnosis

It seems strange to use the word diagnosis in the description of presumably normal children, but it is a convenient word for emphasising the fact that children differ from each other widely, and that differences according to the diagnosis of character types can cut right across differences that belong to classification by age groups.

I have already indicated this by pointing out the great allowance that has to be made at such an age as 14, according to whether or not the child has plunged into puberty dangers, or has shrunk back from them to the more sure, if less interesting, position of the latency period. Here we are reaching the borderline of psychological illness.

Without attempting to distinguish between well and ill, one can say that children can often be grouped according to the particular tendency or difficulty they can be seen to be contending with. An obvious case would be the child with an antisocial tendency for whom war news tends to come, whatever his or her age, as an expected thing, something he misses if it is not there. In fact, such children's ideas are so terrible that they dare not think, and they deal with them by acting out things that are less bad than those they might dream about. The alternative is for them to hear about other people's awful adventures. For them the thriller is a sleeping-draught, and the same may be said of war news if it is sufficiently lurid.

In another group is the timid child, who easily develops a strong passive-masochistic trend, or who suffers from a capacity to feel persecuted. I think that such a child is worried by war news and by the idea of war, largely because of his fixed idea that the good loses. He feels defeatist. In his dreams the enemy shoots down the fellow-countryman, or at any rate the tussle is never ending, with no victory, and developing more and more cruelty and destruction.

In another group is the child on whose shoulders the burden of the world seems to lie, the child who is liable to feel depressed.

Out of this group come those capable of the most valuable constructive effort, whether it take the form of the care of the younger
children, or of the production of what is valuable in one or other
art form. For such children the idea of war is awful, but they have
already experienced it within themselves. No despair is new to
them, nor any hope. They worry about war just as they worry
about their parents' separation or the illness of their grandmother.
They feel they ought to be able to put it all right. For such children I
suppose that war news is terrible when really bad, and exhilarating
when really reassuring. Only there will be times when despair or
exhilaration over their internal affairs will show as moods, irre-
spective of the situation in the real world. I think these children
suffer more from the variability of the grown-ups' moods than
from the vagaries of the war itself.

It would be too big a task to enumerate all the character types
here, and unnecessary, since what I have written suffices to show
how the diagnosis of the child affects the problem of the presentation of war news in schools.

Background for news

It may have become clear from what has been said under these first
two headings that in considering this problem we must know as
much as possible of the ideas and feelings that the child already
and naturally owns, on top of which the war news will be planted.
This unfortunately complicates matters considerably, but nothing
can alter the fact that the complexity does in fact exist.

Every one knows that the child is concerned with a personal
world, which is only to a limited extent conscious, and which
requires a deal of managing. The child deals with personal wars
within his or her own breast, and if his outward demeanour is in
conformity with civilised standards this is only the result of a big
and constant struggle. Those who forget this are repeatedly
bewildered by evidences of breakdown of this civilised super-
structure, and by unexpectedly fierce reactions to quite simple
events.

It is sometimes imagined that children would not think of war if
it were not put into their heads. But any one who takes the trouble
to find out what goes on beneath the surface of a child's mind can
discover for himself that the child already knows about greed,

hate, and cruelty, as about love and remorse, and the urge to make good, and about sadness.

Little children understand the words good and bad very well, and it is of no value to say that to them these ideas are only in fantasy, since their imaginary world can seem more real to them than the external world. I must make it clear at this point that I am talking of largely unconscious fantasy, and not of fantasying or day-dreaming, or consciously operated story-making.

It is only possible to come to understand children's reactions to the giving of war news by first studying, or at any rate allowing for, the immensely rich inner world of each child, which forms the background for whatever is painted in from to-day's external reality bulletin. As the child matures he becomes more and more able to sort out external or shared reality from his own personal inner reality, and to let each enrich the other.

Only when the teacher really knows the child personally is the stage properly set for making the best use of war and war news in education. Since, in practice, the teacher can know the child only to a limited extent, it would be a good plan to allow the children to do other things – read or play dominoes – or to wander off altogether whilst the B.B.C. war news is being given.

It seems to me, therefore, that these reports usefully start us off in a study of an immense problem, and perhaps our first task is just to realise and recognise its immensity. The subject is certainly worth study, for, like many another, it carries us far beyond everyday educational procedure, and reaches down to the origins of war itself, and to the fundamentals of the emotional development of the human being.

4 The deprived mother

(Based on a broadcast talk in 1939, at the time of the first evacuation)

Parents are specially attuned to child care, and, to understand the problems of the mothers of children who have been evacuated, it is necessary first of all to recognise that feelings in general about children are not the same as the special feelings of parents towards their own children.

What makes life worth while for many men and women is the experience of the first decade of married life, when a family is being built up, and while the children are still in need of those contributions to personality and character which the parents can give. This is true generally, but it is particularly true of those who manage their household themselves, without servants, and of those whose economic position, or educational standard, sets a limit to the quantity and quality of the interests and distractions available for them. For such parents, to give up the daily and hourly contact with their children is likely to be a serious trial.

One mother said, 'We would give up our children for three months, but if it is to be for longer, perhaps even for three years, what is the point of life?' And another said, 'All I have to care for now is the cat, and my one distraction is the pub.' These are calls for help which should not go unanswered.

Most tales about parents whose children have been evacuated show no appreciation of this simple truth. For instance, the opinion has been expressed that mothers are having such a good time, being free to flirt, to get up late, to go to the cinema, or to go to work and earn good money, that they will certainly not want to have their children with them again. No doubt there are cases on which this is fair comment, but such an idea does not apply to the majority of mothers; and when such comment is true on the surface it is by no means necessarily true in a deeper sense, for it is a well-known human characteristic to become flippant under threat of a grief that cannot be tolerated.

No one would suggest that the bearing and the bringing up of children is all honey, but most people do not expect life to be sweet without bitter; they ask that the bitter part shall be to some extent of their own choosing.

The city-dwelling mother is asked, advised, and indeed pressed to give up her children. Often she feels bullied into compliance, not being able to see that the harshness of the demand comes from the reality of the danger from bombs. A mother can be surprisingly sensitive to criticism; so powerful is the latent sense of guilt about the possession of children (or of anything valuable, for that matter) that the idea of evacuation first tends to make a mother unsure of herself and willing to do whatever she is told, regardless of her own feelings. One can almost hear her saying, 'Yes, of course, take them away, I was never worthy of them: air raids are not the only danger, it is my own self that fails to provide them with the home they ought to have.' It will be understood that she does not consciously feel all this, she only feels confused or stunned.

For this and for other reasons the initial compliance with the scheme must not be expected to last. Eventually the mothers recover from the first shock, and then a great deal has to happen before the compliance can be said to have changed into co-operation. As time goes on the fantasy changes, and the real gradually becomes clearly defined.

If one makes the attempt to put oneself in the mother's place one immediately asks the question: why, in fact, are children being taken from the risk of air raids at such great expense and trouble? Why are parents being asked to make such big sacrifices?

There are alternative answers.

Either the parents themselves really want their children to be taken out of danger, whatever their own feelings, so that the authorities are merely acting on the parents' behalf; or else the State puts more value on the future than on the present, and has decided to take over the care and management of the children, apart altogether from the feelings and wishes and needs of the parents.

As is natural in a democracy, the feeling has been to regard the first alternative as valid.

For this reason evacuation has been voluntary, and has been allowed to some extent to fail. In fact there has been some attempt, even if a half-hearted one, to understand the mother's side of the question.

It is worth remembering that children are cared for and educated not only to give them a good time, but also to help them to grow up. Some of them will in turn become parents. It is reasonable to hold the view that parents are as important as children, and that it is sentimental to assume that parents' feelings should necessarily be sacrificed for children's welfare and happiness. Nothing can compensate the average parent for loss of contact with a child, and of responsibility for the child's bodily and intellectual development.

It is claimed that it is the vastness of the problem, and of the organisation required to deal with mass evacuation, that limits the share that the parents can be allowed in such things as the choosing of billets. Most parents are able to see this. It is, however, the purpose of this article to point out that however much the authorities may attempt to make rules and regulations intended to be of general application, evacuation remains a matter of a million individual human problems, each different from the others, and each urgently important to someone. As an example, a mother may herself be a student of evacuation problems, and in touch with all its many difficulties, yet she will not be helped by such knowledge to tolerate loss of contact with her own child.

Children change rapidly. At the end of the years that this war may last many children will no longer be children, and all toddlers of the present day will have grown out of the stage of quick emotional development into that of intellectual development and emotional marking-time. It makes no sense to talk of postponing getting to know a child, especially a little child.

Furthermore, mothers appreciate one thing that those who are not so close to the child are apt to forget, that time itself is very different according to the age at which it is experienced. A holiday which the grown-ups hardly noticed may have seemed like a huge chunk of life to the children, and it is almost impossible to convey to an adult the length of time that three years may seem to the evacuated child. It really is a big proportion of what the child knows of life, equivalent perhaps to twenty-five years in the life of an adult of 40 or 50. Recognition of this makes a mother still more anxious to lose nothing of her chance of motherhood.

Investigation, therefore, of any one detail of the whole problem of evacuation uncovers individual problems that are important, even urgent, in their own way.

Working now on the basis that the parents' ultimate wishes are represented by the authorities who are thus acting for the parents, it is possible to see what are the complications that are likely to ensue.

It is commonly believed, even by parents themselves, that all would be well if only their children were to be well looked after; that the children, if they were sufficiently developed emotionally to stand the separation, might actually benefit from the change; surely the children would experience a new kind of home, widen their interests, and perhaps get a contact with country life which is denied to town and even to suburban children.

There is no good in denying, however, that the situation is a complex one and that parents cannot by any means be relied on to *feel* assured of their children's well-being.

This is an old and familiar story, but one that seldom fails to upset and astonish those who have children in their care away from their homes. Parents readily complain about the treatment of their children while away, and easily believe any story a child may invent about ill-treatment and especially about bad feeding. The fact that a child arrives home from a convalescent home in the pink of condition does not prevent a mother from lodging a complaint that her child has been neglected. These complaints, on being followed up, very seldom lead to the discovery of really bad convalescent homes; similar complaints in the case of evacuated children's billets may be expected, and are natural enough if the mother's doubts and fears are taken into account. A mother is expected to dislike any one who neglects her child, but she might quite as reasonably be expected to dislike any one who looks after her child better than she does herself; for such good care rouses her envy or jealousy. It is her own child and, quite simply, she wants to be her own child's mother.

It is not difficult to imagine what happens. A child comes home on holiday and quickly senses an atmosphere of tension when asked some detail. 'Did Mrs. So-and-so give you a glass of milk before bed?' The child may be relieved to be able to answer 'No' and so to please mother without dissembling. The child is in a conflict of loyalties and is puzzled. Which is better, home or away? In some cases the defence against this very conflict has been prepared by a refusal of food at the billet during the first and last days there. If the mother shows quite a lot of relief the child is tempted to add a few details imaginatively. The mother now begins really to feel that there has been neglect, and pumps the child for more information. Tension is now high and rising, and the child scarcely dares look back to see what has been said. It is safer to stick to a few details, and to repeat them whenever the subject is brought up. And so the mother's suspicion is built up until in the end she lodges a complaint.

The difficult situation arises from two sources; the child feels it would be disloyal to report happiness and good feeding, and the mother nurses a hope that the foster-mother compares unfavourably with herself. There are moments when a vicious circle of suspicion on the part of the actual parent, and resentment on the part of the foster-mother, may easily be set up. That moment passed, the way is open for friendship and understanding between these potential rivals.

This may all seem very unreasonable to the outsider, who can afford to be reasonable, but logic (or reasoning that denies the existence or importance of *unconscious* feelings and conflicts) is not enough when a mother has her child taken from her. Even though a deprived mother really wishes to co-operate with the scheme, these unconscious feelings and conflicts must be given their due weight.

In the periods intervening between the moments of suspicion, mothers just as easily tend to over-estimate the reliability and goodness of the billets, and to believe that their children are safe and well cared for without knowledge of the real facts. Human nature works that way.

Nothing is so likely to arouse jealousy in the mother as the provision of exceptional care. She may be able to hide her jealousy even from herself, but if she has cause for worry lest her child be neglected, she has no less cause for worry lest her child shall get accustomed while away tc standards which cannot be maintained after his or her return. This is especially likely to be true when this standard is only a grade higher than that in the home, for if the billet is a castle the whole experience is lifted into the realm of a dream.

The way in which little points can become magnified is illustrated by the following incident.

A mother complained about a foster-mother, and it turned out that the complaint was little more than this, that the foster-mother was generous and owned a sweet shop, whereas the mother herself not only could not afford to give the child a lot of sweets, but also withheld them because she felt they were bad for the child's teeth.

These problems are not different from those of everyday life. When a relation or a friend is indulgent to a child the mother suffers by being forced into the role of strict and even cruel parent, and the home situation is frequently eased when a child meets firmness elsewhere.

It will be appreciated that it is not wise to advertise to a mother the wonderful food the child is getting, and all the other special advantages that the billet may have over the child's home. Nor is it wise to say (especially when it is true) that the child is happier in the billet than at home. There can be, in fact, quite a lot of triumph hidden behind such reports.

Yet parents expect and should surely receive reports, written without triumph, and with the object of enabling them to continue sharing responsibility for their children's welfare. If contact is not maintained, imagination is apt to fill in details *on a fantastic basis*.

In a further study of the deprived mother, it is necessary to go beyond what she can be expected to know about herself. An important thing to be reckoned with is that a mother not only wants children, she also *needs* them. In setting out to bring up a family she organises her anxieties, as well as her interests, so as to be able to mobilise as much as possible of her emotional drive to that one end. She finds value in being continuously bothered by her children's crying needs, and this holds good even if she openly complains of her family ties as a nuisance.

She may never have given thought to this aspect of her motherhood experience until, when the children have gone, she first finds herself the possessor of a quiet kitchen, the captain of a vessel with no crew. Even if her personality has sufficient flexibility to allow her to adjust to such a new situation, this change-over of interests requires time.

She can perhaps take a brief holiday from her children without any rearrangement of her vital interests; but there is a period of time beyond which she can no longer do without someone or something that she feels to be worth while caring for, and wearing herself out for; she also begins to seek some alternative way of exercising power usefully.

In the ordinary way a mother gradually accustoms herself to new interests as the children grow up, but mothers are asked in the present time of war to accomplish this difficult process in a few weeks. It is not to be wondered at that they often fail, either becoming depressed, or else illogically insisting on the children's return.

There is another side of this same problem. Mothers may have a similar difficulty in taking their children back after they have reorganised their interests and anxieties to deal with the experience of peace and quiet in the home. Again, the time factor must be allowed for. This second reorganisation may easily be more difficult than the first, for there will be a period, however brief, on the children's return, in which the mother will have to pretend to her children that she is ready for them, and pretend that she needs them as she did before they went away; she will have to pretend because, at first, she will not feel ready for them. Time is required for her to adjust her inner thoughts, as well as the outer arrangement of the home, to their reception.

For one thing, the children really have changed, they are older and they have had new experiences; and also she has had all sorts of thoughts about them while they have been away, and she needs to live with them a little while before she can get to know them again as they really are.

This fear of having to make a big and painful adjustment, with risk of failing in the attempt, drives mothers to go and snatch their children from their billets, regardless of the feelings of those who, as likely as not, have done everything in their power for the children's good. It is as if the mothers are in a play in which they have been robbed, and in which their clear duty is to rescue the children from ogres; as rescuers they reassure themselves of the existence and strength of their own parental love.

Special attitudes of more abnormal mothers ought also to be described. There is the mother who feels her child is only good when personally controlled by herself. Being unable to recognise the child's innate positive qualities she warns the prospective foster-parents to expect trouble, and cannot understand when the child is found to behave normally. Then also there is the mother who runs down her child, just as an artist depreciates his picture and is therefore the worst person in the world to sell it. She, like the artist, fears both praise and blame, and she forestalls criticism by her own undervaluation of her belongings.

Summary

Within the limits of this article I have tried to show that when a child is taken from parents the very strongest feelings are aroused.

Those who are concerned with the problems of the evacuation of children must see the mothers' problems as well as those of the foster-mothers if they are to understand what they are doing.

To look after children may be hard and exacting work, it can feel like a war job. But just to be deprived of one's children is a poor kind of war work, one which appeals to hardly any mother or father, and one that can only be tolerated if its unhappy side is duly appreciated. For this reason it is necessary really to make the effort to find out what it feels like to be a mother stranded without her child.

5   *The evacuated child*

(A broadcast talk to foster-parents, 1945)

It seems a long time since the first evacuation, and it can be assumed that the acute problems belonging to evacuation have mostly solved themselves by now. But I want to remind you of some of your experiences, talking especially to foster-parents.

A great spread of much-needed understanding of child care could follow as a consequence of all that people have been through. Almost every household in Great Britain was affected by evacuation, and indeed every woman has her own evacuation story that sums up her experience and her view of the whole matter. It seems to me that it would be a pity if all this experience were to be wasted. I shall talk chiefly to those who succeeded in keeping their evacuee over a period of years, because I think it is you who stand to gain most by any attempt to put into words what you have been doing.

I suppose that when there was success you will agree that you were fortunate in the child sent to you. The boy or girl had a certain degree of belief in people. You had material to work on; it really is impossible to succeed in this work if the child cannot contribute because of being too ill, too mentally unstable, or too insecure to find goodness in what you have to offer.

A child was billeted on you who had already started satisfactorily in his emotional development. This was going on well before you received the child into your home, and, if you have kept him over a long period, it means that you have enabled the growth of his personality to continue, just as you have enabled his body to go on growing by providing food.

The bodily care of a child is a big thing in itself. To keep a child in health and free from bodily illness is something which needs constant watching, and in the course of a long evacuation period there must have been times when you had to take responsibility for bodily illness, something which is much more difficult to do when the child is not your own than when the child is yours. You cared for the child's body; but the evacuation brought home to many who had not realised it before that this is only part of that larger thing: the care of the whole child, the whole child who is a human being with a constant need for love and imaginative understanding. The point is that you have done so much more than provide food, clothes, and warmth.

But even this was not enough. The child came from home, and you have taken the child into your home. And home seems to get behind the idea of love. It might be possible for someone to love a child and yet to fail because a child got no feeling that he was at home. I think that the point is that if you make a *home* for a child you provide a little bit of the world that the child can understand and can believe in, in moments when love fails. For love must fail at times, at least superficially. There must be times, every now and again, when a child irritates and annoys and earns an angry word, and it is at least equally true that grown-up people, even the best, have moods and times of irritability, when for an hour or so they cannot be relied on to deal with a situation with fairness. If there is a feeling of homeliness, the relationship between a child and the grown-ups can survive periods of misunderstanding. So I think we can assume that if you have kept your evacuee for a long time you have taken the child into your home, which is such a different thing from letting him into your house, and the child has responded and has used your home as a home. The child in your home came to believe in you, and gradually became able to transfer some feelings from his mother to you, so that in a sense you did become temporarily the child's mother. If you have succeeded you must have found some way of dealing with the very tricky relationship between you and the real parent, and something like the George Medal ought to be struck for the parents and foster-parents who have managed to come to terms, and even to form friendships, when there has been so much cause for mutual misunderstanding.

And now what about the child who has suddenly been up-rooted, seemingly turned out of his own home and dumped down among strangers? No wonder he needed special understanding.

At first, when the children were sent away from the danger zones, there was usually with them the teacher who already knew them well. This teacher formed a link with the home town, and in most cases a bond developed between the children and the teacher much stronger than that of the ordinary teacher-pupil relationship. It is indeed scarcely possible to think of the first evacuation scheme without these teachers, but the full story of those exciting, and in some ways tragic, first hours and days of evacuation has yet to be written.

Sooner or later every child had to look the fact fully and squarely in the face, to realise that he was away from home, and lonely. What happened at that point depended on the age of the child, as well as on the kind of child he was, and the kind of home he came from, but essentially the same problem had to be met by all: either the child had to settle down and accept the new home, or else he had to hang on to the idea of his own home, treating the foster-home as a place where he was to stay for rather too long a holiday.

Many children settled in and seemed to present no problem at all, but perhaps more can be learned from the difficulties than from the easy successes. For instance, I should say that the child who settled in right away, and who never seemed to worry about home at all, was not necessarily in a good way. There could easily be an unnatural acceptance of the new conditions, and in some cases this lack of home-sickness proved in the end to be a snare and a delusion. It is so very natural for a child to feel that his own home is best, and that his own mother's cooking is the only good cooking. More usually you found the child in your care took a long time, perhaps a very long time, to settle in. I am suggesting that this was good. Time had to be taken. He remained frankly anxious about his home and his parents, and indeed he had good cause to be anxious, since the danger to the home was real and well known, and as the stories of bombing began to go the rounds the justification for worry grew. Children from bombed areas did not just go about looking exactly like the local children, and joining in all the playing; they tended to keep apart, and to live on letters and parcels from home, and the occasional visits, visits that often led to so much upset that foster-parents wished them rarer still. It was not so pleasant for foster-parents when the children behaved in this way, and refused food, and moped about most of the time wishing to be home sharing the parents' dangers instead of enjoying the benefits of a stay in the country. All this was not really an unhealthy thing, but to understand it we must look deeper. The real worry about bombs was not all.

A child has only a limited capacity for keeping alive the idea of someone who is loved when there is no opportunity for seeing and talking to that person, and that is where the real trouble lies. For days or even weeks all is well, and then the child finds he cannot feel that his mother is real, or else he keeps on having the idea that father or brothers or sisters are coming to harm in some way. This is the idea in his mind. He has dreams with all sorts of frightening struggles which point to the very intense conflicts in his mind. Worse than that, after a while he may find that he has no strong feelings at all. All his life he has had live love feelings, and he has come to rely on them, taking them for granted, being buoyed up by them. Suddenly, in a strange land, he finds himself without the support of any live feelings at all, and he is terrified by this. He does not know he will recover if he can wait. Perhaps there is some teddy or doll or piece of clothing rescued from the home towards which he continues to have some feelings, and this then becomes tremendously important to him.

This threat of loss of feelings, which comes to children who are too long away from all that they love, often leads to rows. The children start milling around looking for trouble, and when someone gets angry there is genuine relief; but this relief is not lasting. In evacuation, children have just had to endure these distressing periods of doubt and uncertainty, being unable to go home, and it must be remembered that they were not just away at a sort of boarding-school, coming home for holidays. They had to find a new home away from home.

You, as guardians of the children, had to deal with all sorts of symptoms of this distress, including the well-known bed-wetting, aches and pains of one kind and another, skin irritations, unpleasant habits, even head-banging, anything by which the child could regain the feeling of the sense of reality. If one recognises the distress that underlies these symptoms one easily sees how futile it must be to punish a child for them; a better treatment always lies at hand, namely, to help the child by your demonstrative love and imaginative understanding.

It was at such a time, surely, that your evacuee looked to you and your home, which was at any rate real to him. Without you, as we know from all the failures, he either would have gone home to real danger, or else he was liable to become disturbed and distorted in his mental development, with a strong likelihood of getting into trouble. It was just then that you did him a great service.

Up to this point the child had been getting to know you, and had been using your house, eating your food. He now looked to you for love and for the feeling that he was loved. In your new position with the child you were not only the person who worked for him, but you were also there to understand him and to help him to keep alive the memory of his own people. You were also there to receive his attempts to give you back something for what you were doing, and you were needed to protect the child in his frightening relationship to the rather strange world around and at school, where the other children were not always friendly. Sooner or later, I suppose, he gained the necessary confidence in the house and the home, and the way you ran it, to enable him to take it for granted, and then, at last, became like one of the family, a village child with the village children, even talking in the local dialect. Many even came to gain through their experiences, but this came as a climax to a complex series of events, and there were many points at which there might have been failure.

And so here you are with a child in your care who has made use of the best you have had to offer, and you ought to know that it is well recognised that what you have done has not been simple or easy, but has been a matter of careful building. Has all this no value beyond the actual good done to one child? One certain value to be got out of evacuation (itself a tragic thing) is that all of you who have succeeded in keeping an evacuee have come to understand the difficulties, as well as the rewards, that belong to caring for other people's children, and you can help others who are doing the same thing. There have always been destitute children, and there have always been foster-parents who have done the sort of work you have been doing, and doing it well. When it comes to the total care of a child, experience is the one thing that counts, and if each one of you who has succeeded with an evacuee is enabled thereby to become an understanding neighbour of a foster-parent of the post-war period, then I think your work will not have ended with the return of your foster child to his real parents.

6   *The return of the evacuated child*

(Broadcast talk, 1945)

I have already spoken about the evacuated child, and tried to show that where evacuation has been a success this has not been a matter of chance, but in every case something of an achievement. You will have guessed already that I am not likely to say that the return of the evacuated child is a simple and straightforward matter. Indeed I can't say it because I don't believe it. The home-coming of the child who has had a long period from home is well worth thinking out, because careless management at the critical moment can so easily lead to bitterness.

Let me say first, however, that I do respect the feelings of those who do not much like thinking things out. They act best on intuition, and when they talk about what they are to expect to have to deal with next week they become self-conscious, if they do not actually become scared by all the possible snags that they see. Besides, if talking is a substitute for feeling or action, then it is indeed worse than useless. But undoubtedly some people do like to widen their experience by talking and listening, and it must be for such that I speak.

As usual, the trouble is to know where to start, since there are so many different kinds of children, kinds of billet, and kinds of home. At one extreme are the children who will just come home, and settle down easily, and, at the other extreme, there will be children who have settled so well in their foster-homes that the return home order will come as a real shock. In between come all the problems. I cannot describe everything, so I must try to get to the heart of the matter.

Of course the end of evacuation has come already for a great number of children. Whatever I shall have to say could be said better by those who have lived through the experience. My idea is to pass on some of the results of these experiences to those who have yet to welcome their children home. I think I am right in saying that it is not all plain sailing, this renewing acquaintance with one's own children.

The problem has been simplified if mothers and fathers have been able to get, and keep, on friendly terms with the foster-parents. This can never be easy. It is almost as bad to have one's own children well cared for by someone else as it is to have them neglected. In fact it is maddening if you have been a good mother, and then you see your own child wanting to stay with a woman who is a stranger to you, and actually liking the food she cooks. But, in spite of all this, some parents did manage to make friends with their representatives in their child's affections in the country. And if this has meant that the child has often been reminded of you, and of his brothers and sisters and other relations, your work has been made much easier. I come across children who cannot remember what their mothers are like, and who only remember with difficulty the names of their brothers and sisters. Perhaps for whole stretches of years no one has ever troubled to speak to them of those who are nearest and dearest to them, and the past life of those children, as well as the memories of their home, become tucked away somewhere right inside them.

In some cases a sort of preparation for the return home may have been going on all the time, but in others there has been none. In any case the main difficulties are the same, and depend on the fact that when people are separated from one another they don't just go on for ever living for the reunion, and indeed no one would wish for this. If they had not the capacity to recover from painful separation at least to some extent, people would be paralysed.

I have said that there is a limit to the ability of a child to keep alive the idea of someone he loves without contact with that person. The same can be said of parents too, and of every human being to some extent. Mothers had almost as much difficulty as their children in this respect. They soon began to feel doubts about their children, to have feelings that they were in danger, or that they were ill or sad or even being ill-treated, quite apart from any justification for thinking these things. It is quite natural for people to need to see and be near those whom they love, or else to worry about them. In the ordinary course of events, with the children at home, when a mother is worried she can just call out, or can wait till the next meal time, and the child she is worried about comes up and gives her a reassuring kiss. Close contact between people has its use, and when it is suddenly broken up people (children or adults) have to suffer fears and doubts, and to go on suffering till recovery occurs. Recovery means that in time the mother ceases to feel responsible for her child, at any rate to a large extent. That is the hateful thing about it: evacuation forced parents to give up their concern for their own children. If they hung on to a child, and tried to keep their responsibility when the child was a hundred or more miles away, they probably lived in hell, and moreover they weakened the sense of responsibility that was developing in the foster-parents, who had the advantage of being on the spot. Imagine the conflict in the minds of the average good parent at this time!

There was nothing for it but for the mother to fill her mind with other interests; perhaps she went to work in a factory or took on civil defence responsibilities, or developed a private life that enabled her to forget from moment to moment her deep grief. In addition to worrying about her children she was often worried about her husband in the forces, and she had to find out how to manage her instincts with a husband forced to be away for an indefinite period. Compared with all this, what a little thing seems the blast of a bomb!

So the children went, and when they went they left a great hole, but in the course of time the gap closed over, and the hole began to be forgotten. Even from a broken heart most people mend up in time, and reluctantly they find new interests where old interests have failed. As I have said, many women went to work, and some had new babies. I even know some who have difficulty in remembering where their children are. If you do not easily write letters it is quite a job to keep track of half a dozen children who are scattered all over the place, each probably changing from billet to billet.

What I want to say now is that when the children come home they are not necessarily going to fall into and fit nicely into the holes they made when they went away, for the simple reason that the hole has disappeared. Mother and child will have become able to manage without each other, and when they meet they will have to start from scratch to get to know each other. This process must take time, and time must be allowed. It is no use mother rushing up to the child and throwing her arms round his neck without looking to see whether he is going to be able to respond sincerely. They can be brutally sincere, can children, and coldness can hurt. Given time, on the other hand, feelings can develop in their natural way, and suddenly a mother may be rewarded by a genuine hug that was worth waiting for. The home is still the child's home, and I think he will be glad to be there in the course of time, if mother can wait.

In two or three years of separation both mother and child have altered, more especially the child out of whose life three years is a big chunk. It is tragic to think that so many parents have had to miss that fleeting thing, the childhood of their own children. After three years he is the same person, but he has lost whatever characterises the six-year-old, because he is now nine. And then, of course, even if the home has escaped bomb damage, even if it is exactly as it was when the child left, it seems much smaller to him, because he is so much bigger. Added to this, he may have been billeted where there was much more room than there is in his own home in the city, and there may have been a garden, or a farm even, over which he could run about as long as he didn't frighten the cows during milking. It must be difficult to come back from a farm to a room or two in a block of flats. Yet I do believe most children prefer to be home, and they will fit in gradually given time.

During the period of waiting there may be complaints. It must always seem to a mother that when her child makes complaints he is making a comparison between her and the foster-parents. A child shows by his tone of voice that he is disappointed in something. I think it is well to remember that usually he is not comparing home with the foster-home so much as comparing home as he finds it with that which he had built up in his mind while he was away. In a period of separation a good deal of idealisation goes on, and this is the more true the more complete the disunion. I find that boys and girls who have such bad homes that they have to be given care and protection quite regularly imagine they have an absolutely wonderful home somewhere, if only they could find it. That is the main reason why they tend to run away. They are trying to find home. Do you see that while one of the functions of a real home is to provide something positive in the child's life, another function is to correct the child's picture by showing the limitations of reality? When the child comes home

with his rather fantastic expectations he has to suffer disillusion-
ment at the same time as he rediscovers that he really has a home
of his own. Again, all this takes time.

So when children complain after they come home, they are often
showing that they had constructed a better home in their
imaginations while they were away, a home that denied them
nothing, and that had no monetary problems and no lack of floor
space, in fact a home that only lacked one thing – reality. Real
home also has its advantages though, and the children have everything to gain if they gradually come to accept it as it is.

The return of the evacuated child is a big part of the evacuation
experience, and nothing would be more disheartening to those
who have taken trouble to make evacuation work than carelessness at the end. Surely each child ought to be 'shoe-horned' home,
and for this there should be someone responsible who knows the
child, the foster-parent, and the real home. Sometimes it will be
found that the return home on Monday would be disastrous,
whereas on Wednesday all would be well. Perhaps mother is ill, or
there is a new baby in the offing, or the builders have not yet quite
finished repairing the roof and the windows, and a month or two
would make all the difference. In not a few cases a child will come
home, but will need skilled supervision for a while, and even so
may need to return to a hostel for a time where experienced
management is available; especially as the children's fathers are
not yet home, and a home without father is no place for a spirited
boy, or an adolescent girl.

Lastly, we must not forget that for children with difficult
mothers evacuation has been something of a godsend. For these
children the return home means a return to strain. In an ideal
world there would be some help for these children after their
return.

It will be a wonderful thing to know that the children of the big
cities are back home again, and I for one will be glad to see the
streets and parks full again of children who go home to dinner and
tea, and who sleep in their own parents' houses. Education will
then start to pick up, and when the men and women come back
from the fighting there will be Boy Scouts and Girl Guides, and
there will be holiday camps and picnics. But in every case there is
the moment of return, and I should like to feel I have made it clear
that the renewal of contact takes time, and that the management of
each return needs to be personally supervised.

7   Home again

(A broadcast talk to parents, 1945)

A little boy I know is 9 years old, and he has spent a great deal of his young life away from his London home. When he heard about the return of the evacuees because of the end of the war, he started thinking things out, getting used to the idea and making plans. Suddenly he announced, 'When I am home in London I shall get up early every morning and milk the cows.'

Just now, with the official end of evacuation, and with mothers returning to the care of their own homes from factories, many parents are welcoming their children back to the big cities. This is the moment families have been waiting for over a period of years, and how good it would be if at the same time all the fathers were able to come home too.

If I am right, many just now are looking at their children, wondering what they are thinking and feeling, and wondering, too, whether they are able to provide all the children want and need. I should like to think round those problems with you for a few minutes.

Here are the children home again, filling our ears with sounds that had long been almost dead. People had forgotten that children are noisy creatures, but now they are being reminded. Schools are reopening. Parks are spreading themselves for the reception of their old customers: mothers and prams, and children of all sizes, shapes, and colours. Back streets have become cricket pitches, with the children gradually adapting themselves to town traffic. Round the street corners come bands of Nazis or other kinds of gangsters, complete with guns improvised out of sticks, hunters and hunted alike oblivious of the passer-by. Chalk marks re-appear on pavements, to let little girls know where to hop, and when the weather is good, and there is nothing else afoot, boys and girls can be seen standing on their heads or on their out-stretched arms, with their feet up against a wall.

The most exciting thing of all, according to my way of thinking, is that at meal-times these children run into their own homes to eat meals prepared by their own mothers. The meal at home means so much, both to the mother who takes the trouble to get the food and to prepare it, and to the children who eat it. And then there is the evening bath, or bedtime story, and the good-night kiss; all these things are private and we do not see them, but we are not ignorant. This is the stuff of which home is made.

Indeed, it is out of the seemingly little things in and around home that the child weaves all that a rich imagination can weave. The wide world is a fine place for grown-ups looking for an escape from boredom, but ordinarily children are not bored, and they can have all the feelings they can stand feeling inside their own house, or within a few minutes from the doorstep. The world is mainly important and satisfactory if it grows for each individual out of the street outside the front door, or the yard at the back.

There are some curious people – optimists, I suppose – who heralded evacuation as something that would bring new life to the poor children of the cities. They could not see evacuation as a great tragedy, so they looked to it as one of the hidden blessings of war. But it could never be a good thing to have to take children from their ordinary decent homes. And by home, you know, I do not mean a lovely house with all the modern conveniences. By home I mean the room or two that has become associated in the child's mind with mother and father, and the other children, and the cat. And there is the shelf or cupboard where the toys are kept.

Yes, a child's imagination can find full scope in the little world of his own home and the street outside, and in fact it is the actual reassurance provided by the home itself that frees the child to play, and in other ways to enjoy his ability to enrich the world out of his own head. There is a serious complication here, when we try to think things out, and I will try to explain what it is. I do say that when a child is home he can have the full range of his feelings there, and this can only be good. At the same time, I am not at all happy about the ideas that come into the child's mind about home when he is away from it for a long time. When he is home, he really knows what home is like, and because of this he is free to pretend it is anything he wants it to be for the purposes of his play. And play is not just pleasure – it is essential to his well-being. When he is away, on the other hand, he has no chance to know from minute to minute what his home is like, and so his ideas lose touch with reality in a way that easily frightens him.

It is one thing for a child at home to fight battles round the wall of the house, and then at one o'clock to go in and have dinner. It is another thing to be evacuated, and out of touch, and to be dreaming of murder in the kitchen. It is one thing to stand on one's head in the street for the pleasure of seeing your house upside down before turning in, and it is quite another to be two hundred miles away, feeling convinced the home is on fire, or falling to pieces.

If you are upset when your child complains that home is not as good as he expected it to be, you can rest assured it is not as bad either. If this is true, you will see how much more free a child is when he is home than when he is away. His home-coming can open up a new era of freedom of thought and imagination, provided he can take time to get to feel that what is real *is* real. This does take time, and you must allow for a slow dawning of confidence.

What happens as a child begins to feel free, free to think what he likes, to play what comes into his head, to find the lost parts of his personality? Surely, he also begins to *act* freely as well, to discover impulses that had lain asleep while he was away, and to show them. He begins to be cheeky, to lose his temper, to waste your food, to try to worry you and to interfere with your other interests. He may very likely try out a little thieving, testing how true it is that you are really his mother, and so in a sense what is yours is his. These can all be signs of a step forward in development – the first stage of a sense of security, although maddening from your point of view. The child has had to be his own strict mother and father while away, and you may be sure that he has had to be over-strict with himself to be on the safe side, unless he has failed to stand the strain, and has got into trouble in his billet. Now, however, at home with you, he will be able to take holidays from self-control, for the simple reason that he will leave the business of control to you. Some children have been living in artificial and over-done self-control for years, and it can be assumed that when they begin to let mother take over control once more they are going to be a bit of a nuisance from time to time. That is why it would be so good if father could be home just now.

I believe that some mothers are genuinely wondering whether they can give as good in Paddington and Portsmouth and

Plymouth as the people could give who were looking after their child in the heart of the country, where there were fields and flowers, cows and pigs, fresh vegetables and eggs. Can home compete with the hostels run by experienced wardens, where there were organised games, carpentry for wet days, rabbits increasing their numbers in home-made hutches, Saturday expeditions into the surrounding country, and visiting doctors caring for the children's bodies and minds? I know that things were often done well both in foster-homes and in hostels, but there are not many who would claim that an ordinary good home can be supplanted. I am sure that, by and large, a child's home, however simple, is more valuable to that boy or girl than any other place to live in.

It is not just the food and shelter that counts, and not even the provision of occupations for spare moments, though, heaven knows, these things are sufficiently important. They may be provided in abundance, and yet the essential must be missing if a child's own parents or adoptive parents or guardians are not the people taking responsibility for his development. There is the matter which I have mentioned of the need for holidays from self-control. Shall I say that, for a child to be brought up so that he can discover the deepest part of his nature, someone has to be defied, and even at times hated, and who but the child's own parents can be in a position to be hated without there being a danger of a complete break in the relationship?

On the return of the children, those who have managed to keep a home together over these years of bitter separation can now start as father and mother to repair the damage done in their children's development by lack of continuity in their management. You took joint responsibility for their coming into the world, and now I believe you are longing to take up this joint responsibility once more, but this time to enable them to develop into citizens.

As we have seen, this home and family business is not all smiles and kisses; the return of your boy does not mean that you now have someone who will want to do the shopping for you (except as the impulse takes him) and the return of your daughter does not mean that you have someone who will do your washing-up (except, again, as the impulse takes her). Their return means that your life will be richer, but less your own. There will be few immediate rewards. At times you will wish all of them back again in billets. We all sympathise with you, and at times things may be so difficult that you will need help. You see, some of the children have been so hurt by evacuation that it is beyond the power of parents to manage them. But if you come through, and your children do develop into citizens, you will have done one of the best jobs that can be done. I am told on good authority that it is a wonderful feeling to have one's own children growing up into independence and setting up their own homes, as well as doing work that they enjoy, and enjoying the riches of the civilisation that they must defend and carry along. You will have to be able to be strong in your attitude towards the children, as well as understanding and loving, and if you are going to be strong eventually you may as well start strong. It is rather unfair suddenly to develop strength when it is late, when the child has already begun to test you and try you for reliability.

And now, what about the boy who said he would go home to London and milk the cows? It is easy to see he did not know much about towns and town life, but I do not think that matters much. What I thought when I heard what he said was that he had an idea in mind, quite a good one. He associated going home with something direct and personal. He had watched cows being milked in the farm near his hostel, but he had not been able to go and milk them himself. Now the war is over, home we go, away with the middle-men! Let us milk the cows ourselves! Not a bad motto for returning evacuees. Let us hope that there were a mother and father waiting for Ronald, ready, as he was, for direct affectionate expression, ready with an easy hug to give him the beginning of a new chance to come to terms with a hard world.

8 Residential management as treatment for difficult children

(Written with Clare Britton for *Human Relations*, 1947)

It fell to the lot of the authors to play a part in a wartime scheme that grew up in a certain county in Britain around the problems presented by children evacuated from London and other big cities. It is well known that a proportion of evacuated children failed to settle in their billets; and that whereas some of those went back home to the air-raids, many of them stayed on and were a nuisance unless given special conditions of management. As visiting psychiatrist and resident psychiatric social worker, we formed a small psychiatric team employed to make a scheme of this kind work in our county. Our job was to see that the available resources were actually brought to bear on the problems that arose: one of us (D.W.W.), as a paediatrician and child psychiatrist whose main work had been in London, was able to relate such problems as were specifically related to the war situation to the corresponding problems of peacetime experience.

The scheme that developed was necessarily complex, and it would be difficult to say that one cog in the wheel was more important than any other. We are, therefore, describing what happened, because we have been asked to do so and without claiming to be specially responsible for its good points; the views expressed are our own and are given without reference to the other participants in the scheme.

It could perhaps be said that in our job of seeing that the children concerned actually did get cared for and treated we also had to keep the total situation in view; because in every case there was a need for much more to be done than could, in fact, be done; and in each case, therefore, the assessment of the total situation had an important practical bearing. It is this relationship between the work done with each child and the total situation that we especially wish to describe.

It should be mentioned that there was no attempt to make this particular scheme a special case or a pilot model. No grant from a research organisation was sought or accepted. It is not claimed that the scheme with which we happened to be connected was specially good or successful, or that it was better in our county than in other counties. Probably, indeed, the arrangement that grew up in this particular county would have been unsuitable for any other county; and what occurred can be taken as an example of natural adaptation to circumstances.

In fact, a significant feature of such wartime schemes as a whole was the lack of rigid planning, which made it possible for each Ministry of Health Region (indeed, of each county in each region) to adapt to local needs; with the result that at the end of the war there were as many types of scheme as there were counties. This might be thought to be a failure of over-all planning, but in this matter we suggest that opportunity to adapt is of more value than prevision. If a rigid scheme is devised and put into operation, there is an uneconomic forcing of situations where local circumstances do not admit of adaptation; more important still, the people who are attracted to the task of applying a set scheme are very different from those who are attracted by the task of developing a scheme themselves. The attitude of the Ministry of Health, which was responsible for dealing with these matters, seems to us to have called for a creative originality, and therefore for a live interest on the part of all those who had to produce work, and work schemes, according to local needs.[1]

In all work that concerns the care of human beings it is the worker with originality and a live sense of responsibility that is needed. When, as in this task, the human beings are children, children who lack an environment specifically adapted to their individual needs, then the worker who loves to follow a rigid plan is unqualified for the task. Any large plan for the care of children deprived of adequate home life must, therefore, be of a type which allows for the fullest degree of local adaptation, and which attracts free-minded people to work it.

---

[1] It could be said that the Ministry of Health threw a task at a county, watched results, and acted accordingly – a situation which recalls the principle of 'leaderless groups' tasks employed in British Army Officer Selection.

The developing problem

Children evacuated from the big cities were sent to ordinary people's homes. It soon became evident that a proportion of these boys and girls were difficult to billet, quite apart from the complementary fact that some homes were unsuitable as foster-homes.

The billeting breakdowns arising in these ways quickly degenerated into cases of antisocial behaviour. A child who did not do well in a billet either went home and to danger, or else changed billet; several changes of billet indicated a degenerating situation, and tended to be the prelude to some antisocial act. It was at this stage that public opinion became an important factor in the situation: on the one hand there was public alarm, and the activities of courts which represented the usual attitudes towards delinquency, while on the other there was the organising concern of the Ministry of Health, with the developing local interest in providing, for these children, an alternative management designed to prevent their reaching the courts.

The symptoms, in the evacuation breakdown cases, were of all kinds. Bed-wetting and faecal incontinence had first place, but every possible kind of difficulty was encountered, including stealing in gangs, burning of hay-ricks, train wrecking, truancy from school and from billet, and consorting with soldiers. There were also, of course, the more obvious evidences of anxiety, as well as maniacal outbursts, depressive phases, sulky moods, odd and insane behaviour, and deterioration of personality with lack of interest in clothes and cleanliness.

It was quickly discovered that the symptom-pictures were diagnostically useless, and were merely evidence of distress as a result of ecological failure in the new foster-home. Psychological illness, in the sense of deep endopsychic disturbance apparently unrelated to the current environment, could hardly be recognised as such in the abnormal conditions of evacuation. This situation was complicated by the natural process of mutual choice which led psychologically healthy children to find the good billets.

The initial reaction of the authorities to the emergence of a problem-group of children was to give such children individual psychological treatment, and to provide facilities where they could be placed while receiving treatment. Gradually, however, it became clear that success in providing accommodation of this kind demanded residential management. It emerged, moreover, that such management in itself constituted a therapy. Further, it was important that proper management, as a therapy, should be practical; for it had to be given by relatively unskilled persons – that is, by wardens untrained in psychotherapy, but informed, guided, and supported by the psychiatric team.

As a basic provision, therefore, hostels became organised for residential care of difficult evacuated children. In our county a big disused institution was first used; but from the difficulties of this initial experience the local authority developed the idea of setting up several small hostels, to be run on personal lines,[2] while the appointment of a Psychiatric Social Worker (P.S.W.) who was to be resident in this county arose out of the need to co-ordinate the work of the several hostels, and to build up a body of experience by which the whole scheme could benefit.

In the early stages it was thought that treatment could be given which would enable each child to be re-billeted in a foster-home, but experience showed that this idea was based on an under-estimate of the gravity of the trouble. It was, indeed, the psychiatrist's task to direct attention to the fact that these children were seriously affected by evacuation and that nearly all had personal reasons why they could not find good billets to be good; to show, in fact, that these evacuation breakdowns occurred for the most part in children who had originally come from unsettled homes, or in children who had never had in their own homes an example of a good environment.

Therapy by management in residential hostels necessitated a long-stay policy, and the original intentions in regard to hostels had to be modified to allow children to stay for indefinite periods, up to two, three, or four years. In the majority of cases children who were difficult to billet had no satisfactory home of their own, or had experienced the break-up of home, or, just before evacuation, had to bear the burden of a home in danger of breaking up. What they needed, therefore, was not so much substitutes for their own homes as *primary home experiences* of a satisfactory kind.

By a primary home experience is meant experience of an environment adapted to the special needs of the infant and the little child, without which the foundations of mental health

[2] Cf. the Curtis Report on the Care of Children (1946), H.M.S.O., London.

cannot be laid down. Without someone specifically orientated to his needs the infant cannot find a working relation to external reality. Without someone to give satisfactory instinctual gratifications the infant cannot find his body, nor can he develop an integrated personality. Without one person to love and to hate he cannot come to know that it is the same person that he loves and hates, and so cannot find his sense of guilt, and his desire to repair and restore. Without a limited human and physical environment that he can know he cannot find out the extent to which his aggressive ideas actually fail to destroy, and so cannot sort out the difference between fantasy and fact. Without a father and mother who are together, and who take joint responsibility for him, he cannot find and express his urge to separate them, nor experience relief at failing to do so. The emotional development of the first years is complex and cannot be skipped over, and every infant absolutely needs a certain degree of favourable environment if he is to negotiate the essential first stages of this development.

To be of value these primary home experiences belatedly provided in the hostels had to be stable over a period measured in years and not in months; and it can be well understood that the results could never be as good as the ordinary results of good primary homes would have been. Success in hostel work, therefore, is to be thought of in terms of lessening the failure of the child's own home.

A corollary of this is that good hostel work must make use of every ounce of value that may still remain in the child's own home.

The task

There are various ways of describing the actual problem:

(1) The protection of the public from the 'nuisance' of children who were difficult to billet.
(2) The resolution of conflicting public feelings of irritation and of concern.
(3) The attempt to prevent delinquency.
(4) The attempt to treat and cure these 'nuisance' children, on the basis of their being ill.
(5) The attempt to help the children on the basis of their hidden suffering.

(6) The attempt to discover the best form of management and treatment for this type of psychiatric case, apart from the specific war emergency.

It will be seen that these various ways of stating the task have to be considered when the question is asked: What were the results? In reply, we might say, in respect to these different formulations of the task:

(1) As far as diminishing the 'nuisance' of difficult children was concerned, 285 children were housed and managed in hostels; and this was a success except in the case of about a dozen who ran away.

(2) With regard to public irritation, many people felt frustrated at times by the fact that 'offences' of the children were treated as distress signals, instead of indications for punishment; for example, a farmer whose rick had been burnt down would complain that the culprits seemed to have gained rather than lost by their antisocial act. As to public concern, a great many people who were genuinely concerned by the state of affairs that had developed were relieved by the knowledge that the problem was being tackled. The work of the hostels developed news-value.

(3) Delinquency, in a proportion of cases, was definitely prevented; as when a child obviously bound for the Juvenile Court before admission into the scheme was seen through to adolescence and a job, without major incident and without Home Office control. In other words, the difficulty was dealt with as a matter of individual and social health, and not merely as a matter of (unconscious) public revenge: the potential delinquency was treated, as it should be, as an illness.

(4) If we regard the problem as one of illness, a small proportion of the children were restored to health, and a fair proportion were brought to a much improved psychological condition.

(5) From the child-patients' point of view, intense suffering was discovered in many of them, as well as hidden or, indeed, open madness; and in the course of the routine work a great deal of suffering was shared and to some extent relieved. In a few cases personal psychotherapy could be added, but only enough to show the great need (on the basis of actual suffering) for more personal therapy than can ever be available.

(6) From the sociological angle, the working of the whole scheme gave an indication of the way to deal with potentially antisocial children and insane[3] children, suffering from disorders not produced by war, though evacuation made public the fact of their existence.

The scheme grows

Thus the scheme grew out of the acute local needs, and out of the wartime feeling that any cost could be borne, provided the working of the scheme solved the problem in hand. Because of the war, houses could be requisitioned; and in a few months there were five hostels in the group, as well as friendly relations with many others. 'Sick bays' for treatment of physically ill evacuees had, of course, been provided, even in excess of need, and these were available for some of the psychologically ill among the child population of the hostels.

The arrangement was as follows:

The national authority, the Ministry of Health, gave 100 per cent grant to the County Council – that is, accepted full financial responsibility – for this work. The County Council appointed a committee of county residents of standing (with a Deputy Clerk to the Council as Secretary) which was empowered to act as well as to report and recommend to its parent body. A full-time P.S.W. was appointed to work with the visiting psychiatrist, who paid a weekly visit to the county. From then on, the small psychiatric team could undertake to pay that attention to personal matters which is essential in this work; and at the same time, through the regular meetings of the committee, could retain contact with the broad administrative aspect of the situation. In fact, when this stage was reached, the central wide vision of the Ministry became focused on detail.

When this arrangement is examined it will be seen that a circle had been established.

The problem children, because of their nuisance value, had produced a public opinion that would support provision for them which, in fact, catered for their needs.

---

[3] The word insane is here used deliberately, for no other word is correct, and the official word 'maladjusted' begs the whole question.

It would be wrong to say that demand produces supply in human affairs. Children's needs do not produce good treatment, and now the war is over it is very difficult to get such things as hostels for the same children whose needs were met in wartime. The fact is that in peacetime the nuisance value of the distressed children is lessened, and public opinion regains a sleepy indifference. In wartime, evacuation spread the problems of such children over the countryside; it also exaggerated them at a time when the general emotional tension of the community, and the shortage of goods and of manpower, made prevention of damage and theft imperative, and made extra police work unwelcome.

It was not that childhood distress produced child care, but rather that society's fear of the antisocial behaviour from which it suffered at an inopportune moment set in motion a train of events, events that could be used by those who knew of the children's suffering to provide therapy in the shape of long-term residential management, with personal care by an adequate and well-informed staff.

The psychiatric team

Because of the situation described, the task of the psychiatric team turned out to have two aspects: on the one hand, the will of the Ministry had to be implemented; and on the other, the needs of the children had to be met and studied. Fortunately, the direct responsibility of the team was to a committee which liked to be informed about all the details.

In this war experience the voluntary committee remained constant in membership and so developed with the scheme. By being itself stable the committee shared with the psychiatric team a gradual 'growth in the job', so that each success or failure helped to build up a body of experience which had general application and which benefited all the hostels.

To illustrate this, specific instances can be given, even although the main development was in a general way and not capable of illustration.

(1) Gradually, the idea of appointing joint married wardens was adopted. At first this was an experiment, which could only be made in an atmosphere of mutual understanding, because of

the complications arising out of the problems of the wardens' own family and its relation to the hostel children.

(2) The question of corporal punishment was brought up for discussion in the committee, at the appropriate moment, by means of a memorandum; and this led to the formulation of a definite policy.[4]

(3) The idea was put forward, and gradually adopted, that it was better to have one person (in this case the P.S.W.) in the centre of the whole scheme, rather than to have shared responsibility in the administrative office of the scheme, with consequent overlapping and waste of experience because it would not be integrated with total experience.

(4) The psychiatrist was originally appointed to give therapy. This was changed, and he was directed to classify cases before their admission, and to decide on the choice of hostel. Eventually he became the indirect therapist of the children through his regular discussions with the wardens and their staffs.

In these and countless other ways the committee, and the psychiatric team employed by them, retained flexibility and together developed an adaptation to the job.

The importance of this cannot be overestimated and can clearly be seen if we compare this situation with direct relation to a Ministry. In the British Civil Service it is essential that the officials get experience in each of the various departments of government. The consequence is, that if one enters into a personal and understanding relationship with the head of the appropriate department in a Ministry, when the inevitable reshuffles of training and promotion occur, one has to start again with another man. When this has happened several times one finds that whereas one has

---

[4] *Author's note* – With regard to corporal punishment, the ruling was that the committee trusted the warden who was appointed, and left to him the right to give corporal punishment. If the committee did not like the way a warden worked the remedy was to get a new warden, and not to interfere directly. A restriction on corporal punishment is quickly found out by the children, and in practice it is a severe handicap to a warden to be curbed by the committee.

In one case, when the committee had doubts, a warden was told to enter each such punishment in a book, which was inspected weekly.

Along with this general policy, there was a drive towards the education of the staff, so that corporal punishment was avoided as much as possible. Through an understanding of the personal difficulties of each child, punishable outbreaks could often be prevented, and in some groups over long periods of time corporal punishment was, in fact, rare.

grown in the job oneself one can no longer feel that the head of the department has grown too; nor can one expect understanding of the details of the work. Since this situation must surely be accepted as an unavoidable phenomenon in large central organisations, one must look to such bodies to give general direction, but to abandon any attempts to keep in touch with detail. And yet in no work is detail more important than in work with children; and so there must always be a 'liaison' committee of interested people who represent the large parent body, and are yet able and willing to stoop to the detail which is the main preoccupation of the actual worker in the field.

It was important that the P.S.W. could take heavy responsibility, and this was made possible by her knowledge that she had the support of the clerk to the Council and the psychiatrist. The latter, by living away from the immediate problems, could discuss the local details without deep emotional involvement, and at the same time, being a medical man, he could accept responsibility for the risks that had to be taken if the best was to be done for the children.

Here is an example of the benefits of technical support and responsibility. A warden rings up the P.S.W. and says, 'A certain boy is on the roof, what shall I do?' He dare not take full responsibility as he is not psychiatrically trained, and he knows the boy has a suicidal tendency. The P.S.W. knows she has the psychiatrist's backing when she says, 'Ignore the boy and take the risk'. The warden knows this is the best treatment, but without backing would have had to give up whatever he was doing, ignore the needs of the other children, perhaps call the local fire brigade, and so do harm to the boy by putting the limelight on him and his escapade. In fact, the result of the advice given to the warden was that at the next meal-time the boy was in his place and no fuss had been made.

The P.S.W. and the visiting psychiatrist provided a psychiatric team that avoided clumsiness by being small, and yet could take responsibility over a wide field. Swift decisions could be made and action be taken within the framework of the powers of the committee by whom they were appointed, and to whom they were directly responsible.

Here are some further examples of detail which proved important:

(1) We found it necessary to take the trouble to gather together the fragments of each child's past history, and to let the child know that one person knew all about him.

(2) No member of the hostel staff could be unimportant. A child might be getting special help from his relationship to the gardener or to the cook. For this reason the staffing of the hostels was very much a matter of concern to us.

(3) It might happen that quite suddenly a warden could not tolerate a particular child any longer, and that the objective assessment of this problem required a very intimate knowledge of the situation. We acted on the principle that a warden should be able to express his feelings to someone who could, if necessary, take action, or who could prevent the matter from developing into an unnecessary crisis.

Classification for placing

In different types of psychiatric work different ways of classifying patients are appropriate. For the purposes of placing these children satisfactorily in hostels, classification according to symptoms was useless, and was set aside. The following principles were developed and followed.

1. In many cases no adequate diagnosis can usefully be made till a child has been watched, in a group, over a period of time.

In regard to the length of time needed a week is better than nothing, but three months is better than a week.

2. If a history of the child's development can be obtained, the existence or non-existence of a fairly stable home is a fact of prime importance.

In the former case the child's experience of home can be used, and the hostel can remind the child of his own home and extend the existing home idea. In the latter case, the hostel has to provide a primary home, and the child's idea of his own home then gets mixed up with the ideal home of his dreams, compared with which the hostel is a pretty poor place.

3. If a home of any kind does exist, then it is important to know of abnormalities there.

Examples of these are a parent who is a psychiatric case, certified or uncertifiable, or a dominating or antisocial brother or sister, or housing conditions that are in themselves a persecution. Hostel life can offer some correction of these abnormalities in the course of time and very gradually enable the child to view his own home objectively, and even sympathetically.

4. If further details are available, it is of great importance to know whether the child did or did not have a satisfactory infant-mother relationship.

If there has been an experience of a good early relationship, even if this has been lost, it may be recovered in the personal relation of some member of the hostel staff to the child. If no such good start in fact existed it is beyond the scope of a hostel to create this, *ab initio*. The answer to this important question is often one of degree, but it is nevertheless worth seeking. In many cases a reliable early history is unobtainable, in which case the past has to be reconstructed through observation of the child in the hostel over a period of months.

5. During the period of observation in the hostel there are certain specially valuable indications – ability to play, to persevere in constructive effort, and to make friends.

If a child can play, this is a very favourable sign. If constructive effort is enjoyed and persevered in without undue supervision and encouragement there is even greater hope of useful work being done through the hostel life. The ability to make a friend is a further valuable sign. Anxious children change friends frequently and too easily, and seriously disturbed children can only achieve membership of a gang – that is to say, a group whose cohesion depends on engineered persecution. A majority of the children drafted to evacuation hostels were at the outset incapable of play, or of sustained constructive effort, or of friendship.

6. Mental defect has obvious importance, and in any group of hostels for difficult children there should be separate accommodation for children with low intelligence.

This is not only because they need special management and education, but also because they wear out the hostel staff to no purpose, and cause a feeling of hopelessness. In such difficult work as that with problem children, there must be some hope of reward, even if reward does not actually come.

7. Bizarre or 'scatty' behaviour, and odd characteristics, distin-

guish some children who are on the whole unpromising material for therapy by hostel management.

Such children puzzle the hostel staffs and make them feel mad themselves. In any case children of this kind need personal psychotherapy; although, even if it can be provided, their treatment is often beyond present-day understanding. They are, in fact, research cases for enterprising analysts, and there are but few satisfactory institutions for these children.

The classification outlined above formed the basis for placing; but the main consideration must always be: what can this hostel, these wardens, this group of children, stand at this particular moment? It was soon found to be a bad thing to decide to put a child in a hostel just because he was needing care and the hostel had a vacancy. Every new child, disturbed in the way that these billet-failures were disturbed, cannot help being, at first, a complication, and no asset to a hostel community. These children (except possibly in the first deceptive and unreal week or two) contribute nothing, and they absorb emotional energy. If they become accepted in the group they then start to be able to contribute to some extent, under supervision; but this is the result of hard work on the part of staff and the established children.

There is no one thing that is more helpful to the wardens of a hostel than this: that on introducing a new child one should present that child to the wardens before the issue of placing the child is settled. If this course is followed, a child is suggested for the hostel, but the wardens can accept or refuse. If the wardens think they can absorb this new child, then they have begun to want him. By the other method, of simply drafting children without prior consultation, wardens cannot help starting with negative feelings towards the child, and can only find other feelings in the course of time, and with luck. This joint consultation over admission to a particular hostel was very difficult to put into practice, but every effort was made to avoid exceptions to the rule, because of the vast practical difference between the two methods.

The central therapeutic idea

The central idea of the scheme was to provide stability which the children could get to know, which they could test out, which they could gradually come to believe in, and around which they could play. This stability was essentially something that existed apart from the ability of the children, individually or collectively, to create or maintain it.[5]

The environmental stability was passed down, from the community in general, to the children. The Ministry provided the background, helped by the County Council. Against this background there was the committee, which in this scheme was, fortunately, made up of a group of experienced and responsible people who could be relied upon to continue to exist. Then there were the hostel staffs, as well as the buildings and grounds, and the general emotional atmosphere. It was the task of the psychiatric team to translate the essential stability of the scheme into terms of emotional stability in the hostels. Only if the wardens are happy, and satisfied, and feeling stable, can the children benefit from their relations to them. Wardens in these hostels are in so difficult a position that understanding and support from someone is an absolute necessity for them. In the scheme we are describing it was the job of the psychiatric team to supply this support.

The most essential thing, then, was the provision of stability, and especially of emotional stability, in the hostel staff; although, of course, this could never be completely achieved. Nevertheless, work was done all the time with this aim. To help in the creation of a stable emotional background for the children the policy of employing married wardens – mentioned earlier – was recommended to the committee, and adopted. Joint married wardens may have children of their own, and then immense complications ensue. Nevertheless, these complications are outweighed by the enrichment of the hostel community through the existence of a real family within it.

It was once said in criticism, 'The hostel looks as if it were made for the staff'; but we felt that this was not a criticism. The staff must be living a satisfactory life, must be allowed time off, proper holidays, and, in peacetime, proper financial reward, if work with antisocial and mad children is to be done at all. It is not enough to provide a beautiful hostel with a nice staff. To do good by residential management the staff of the hostels must 'stay put' for a

[5] Surely, experiments in getting children to create their own central government should always be made first, if they have to be made, with those who have had a good early home experience? With these deprived children it seems to be cruel to make them do the very thing they feel hopeless about.

period of time – long enough for them to see children through to school-leaving age, and to the age of going to work; for the work of the staff is not finished until they have gradually launched the children into the world.

1

There is no particular training for hostel wardens, and even if there were, their selection as suitable people for the work would be of more importance than their training. We find it impossible to generalise about the type of person who makes a good warden. Our successful wardens have differed from each other widely in education, previous experience, and interests, and have been drawn from various walks of life. The following is a list of the previous occupations of some of them: elementary school teacher, social worker, trained church worker, commercial artist, instructor and matron in an approved school, master and matron at a remand home, worker in a public assistance institution, prison welfare officer.

We find that the nature of previous training and experience matters little compared with the ability to assimilate experience, and to deal in a genuine, spontaneous way with the events and relationships of life. This is of the utmost importance, for only those who are confident enough to be themselves, and to act in a natural way, can act consistently day in and day out. Furthermore, wardens are put to such a severe test by the children coming into hostels that only those who are able to be themselves can stand the strain. We must point out, however, that there will be times when the warden will have to 'act naturally' in the sense that an actor acts naturally. This is particularly important with ill children. If a child comes and whines: 'I've cut my finger', just when the warden is in the middle of making Income Tax returns, or when the cook has given notice, he or she must act as though the child had not come in at such an awkward moment; for these children are often too ill or too anxious to be able to allow for the warden's own personal difficulties as well as their own.

We therefore try to choose as hostel wardens those who possess this ability to be consistently natural in their behaviour, for we regard it as essential to the work. We would count as important also the possession of some skill, such as music, painting, pottery, etc. Above and beyond all these things, however, it is, of course, vital that the wardens possess a genuine love of children, for only this will see them through the inevitable ups and downs of hostel life.

Brilliant people who organise one hostel well, and pass on to another to do the same there, would be better if they had never existed as far as the children are concerned. It is the permanent nature of the home that makes it valuable, even more than the fact that the work is done intelligently.

We do not expect the wardens to carry out any prescribed type of regime, or even to carry out agreed plans. Wardens who have to be told what to do are of no use, because the important things have to be done on the spot in a way that is natural to the individual concerned. Only thus will the warden's relationship become real and therefore of importance to the child. Wardens are encouraged to build up a home and community life to the best of their ability, and it will be found that this is along the line of their own beliefs and way of life. No two hostels will therefore be alike.

We find that there are wardens who like organising large groups of children, and others who prefer to have intimate personal relationships with a few children. Some prefer abnormal children of one type or another, and some like true mental defectives.

The education of the wardens in the work is important, and has been discussed earlier as part of the work of the psychiatrist, and of the psychiatric social worker. This education is best done on the job, by the discussion of problems as they arise. It is a great help if wardens are confident enough in themselves to be able to think along psychological lines and discuss problems with other wardens and experienced people.

The staffing of hostels apart from the wardens presents peculiar difficulties, especially where the children are rather antisocial. With normal children the assistants can be young people who are learning the job, practising taking responsibility and acting on their own initiative, with a view to becoming wardens themselves at a later date. Where the children are antisocial, however, the management has to be strong, and cannot avoid being dictatorial, so that assistants have to be constantly carrying out orders from the warden when they would prefer to be working on their own initiative. They therefore become easily bored, or else they like being told what to do, in which case they are not much good. These problems are inherent in the work.

2

If it is recognised how intimately a child's sense of security is bound up with his relationship to his parents, it becomes obvious that no other people can give him so much. Every child has the right to his own good home in which to grow, and it is nothing but a misfortune that deprives him of it.

In our hostel work, therefore, we recognise that we cannot give to the children anything so good as their own good home would have been. We can only offer a substitute home.

Each hostel tries to reproduce as nearly as possible a home environment for each child in it. This means first of all the provision of positive things: a building, food, clothing, human love and understanding; a timetable, schooling; apparatus and ideas leading to rich play and constructive work. The hostel also provides substitute parents and other human relationships. And then, these things being provided, each child, according to the degree of his distrust, and according to the degree of his hopelessness about the loss of his own home (and sometimes his recognition of the inadequacies of that home while it lasted), is all the time testing the hostel staff as he would test his own parents. Sometimes he does this directly, but most of the time he is content to let another child do the testing for him. An important thing about this testing is that it is not something that can be achieved and done with. Always somebody has to be a nuisance. Often one of the staff will say: 'We'd be all right if it weren't for Tommy . . .', but in point of fact the others can only afford to be 'all right' because Tommy is being a nuisance, and is proving to them that the home can stand up to Tommy's testing, and could therefore presumably stand up to their own.

The usual response of a child who is placed in a good hostel can be described as having three phases. For the first short phase the child is remarkably 'normal' (it will be a long time before he is so normal again); he has new hope, he scarcely sees people as they are, and the staff and the other children have not yet had any reason to begin to disillusion him. Almost every child goes through a short period of good behaviour when he first comes to a hostel. It is a dangerous stage, because what he sees and responds to in the warden and his staff is his ideal of what a good father and mother would be like. Grown-ups are inclined to think, 'This child sees we are nice, and easily trusts us.' But he does not see they are nice; he does not see *them* at all; he just imagines they are nice. It is a symptom of illness to believe that anything can be 100 per cent good, and the child starts off with an ideal which is destined to be shattered.

The child sooner or later enters into the second phase, the breaking down of his ideal. He sets about this first by testing the building and the people physically. He wants to know what damage he can do, and how much he can do with impunity. Then if he finds that he can be physically managed, that is, that the place and the people in it have nothing to fear from him physically, he starts to test by subtlety, putting one member of the staff against another, trying to make people quarrel, trying to make people give each other away, and doing all he can to get favoured himself. When a hostel is being managed unsatisfactorily it is this second phase which becomes almost a constant feature.

If the hostel withstands these tests the child enters on the third phase, settles down with a sigh of relief, and joins in the life of the group as an ordinary member. It should be borne in mind that his first real contacts with the other children will probably be in the shape of a fight or some kind of attack, and we have noticed that often the first child to be attacked by a new child will later become that child's first friend.

In short, the hostels provide positive good things, and give opportunities for their value and reality to be tested continuously by the children. Sentimentality has no place in the management of children, and no ultimate good can come from offering children artificial conditions of indulgence; by carefully administered justice they must gradually be brought up against the consequences of their own destructive actions. Each child will be able to stand this in so far as he has been able to get some positive good out of hostel life, that is, in so far as he has found people who are truly reliable, and has begun to build up belief in them and in himself.

It must be remembered that the preservation of law and order is necessary to the children, and will be a relief to them, for it means that the hostel life and the good things for which the hostel stands will be preserved in spite of all that they can do.

The immense strain of the twenty-four-hour care of these children is not easily recognised in high quarters, and in fact any one who is only visiting a hostel, and who is not emotionally involved, can easily forget this fact. It might be asked why the wardens should let themselves get emotionally involved. The answer is that these children, who are seeking a primary home experience, do not get anywhere unless someone does, in fact, get emotionally involved with them. To get under someone's skin is the first thing these children do, when they begin to get hope. The experience subsequent to this state forms the essence of hostel therapeutics.

It follows, therefore, that hostels must be small. Moreover, wardens must not be burdened with one more child than they can emotionally stand at any given moment: for if one too many is put in a warden's care he is forced to protect himself, by ousting from 'under his skin' someone who is not ready for this. There is a limit to the number of people that a human being can be seriously concerned with at one time, and if this fact is ignored the warden is forced to do superficial and useless work, and to substitute dictatorial management for the healthy mixture of love and strength which he would prefer to show. Alternatively, and this is common, he breaks down, and the work he has done is undone. For every change of wardens produces casualties among the children, and interrupts the natural therapeutics of hostel work.

9 Children's hostels in war and peace

(A contribution to the symposium on 'Lessons for Child Psychiatry' given at a meeting of the Medical Section of the British Psychological Society on 27 February, 1946. Revised and published in 1948.)

Evacuation produced its own problems and wartime its own solutions to problems. Can we make use, in peace, of the results of what was so painfully experienced in time of acute stress and awareness of common danger?

Probably very little that was new in psychological theory came out of the evacuation experience, but there is little doubt that because of it things became known to very large numbers of people who would otherwise have remained ignorant. Especially did the general public become aware of the fact of antisocial behaviour, from bed-wetting to train-wrecking.

It has been truly said that the fact of antisocial behaviour is in itself a stabilising factor in society, it is (in one way of speaking) a return of the repressed, a reminder of individual spontaneity or impulsiveness, and of society's denial of the unconscious to which instinct is relegated.

For my part, I was fortunate in being employed by a county council (from 1939 to 1946) in connection with a group of five hostels for children who were difficult to billet. In the course of this work, which involved a visit each week to the county, I had detailed knowledge of 285 children, most of whom were observed over a period of years. Our job was to cope with the immediate problem and we succeeded or failed in so far as we did or did not relieve those in charge of the local evacuation arrangements of difficulties which threatened the success of their work. Now the war is over, there is still some value to be got out of the experience we went through, especially out of this fact of the public's new awareness of antisocial tendencies as psychological phenomena.

Of course, we must avoid seeming to suggest that hostels (or boarding-schools for maladjusted children, as they are officially called now) are a panacea for emotional disturbance of children. We tend to think of hostel management simply because the alternative is merely to do nothing at all through the shortage of psychotherapists. But this tendency has to be checked. With this proviso it can be said that there are children who urgently need to be cared for in some kind of home. In my clinic at the Paddington Green Children's Hospital (a medical out-patient department) there is a proportion of cases absolutely needing hostel management.

There are two broad categories of such children in peacetime: children whose homes do not exist or whose parents cannot form a stable background in which a child can develop, and children with an existing home which, nevertheless, contains a mentally ill parent. Such children appear in our peacetime clinics, and we find they need just what the children who were difficult to billet needed. Their home environment has failed them. Let us say that what these children need is *environmental stability*, *personal* management, and *continuity* of management. We assume an ordinary standard of physical care.

To ensure personal management the staffing of a hostel must be adequate, and the wardens must be able to stand the emotional strain that belongs to the proper care of any child, but especially to the care of children whose own homes have failed to bear such strain. Because of this the wardens need constant support from psychiatrist and psychiatric social worker.[1] The children (unself-consciously) look to the hostel, or failing that to society in a wider sense, to provide the framework for their lives that their own homes have failed to give them. Inadequate staffing not only makes personal management impossible, but also it leads to ill-health and breakdowns in the staff, and therefore interferes with continuity of personal relationship, which is essential in this work.

A psychiatrist who is in charge of a clinic from which cases are

[1] It would seem to be the psychiatrist's job to be to some extent responsible for the staffing because the mental and physical state of the staff is the main thing in the therapy. A hostel whose staff is appointed and managed by one authority and whose children are under the care of another is unlikely to be successful.

referred to hostels should be responsible for a hostel himself, so that he may keep in touch with the special problems involved in such work. The same is true of magistrates at juvenile courts, who would do well to sit on hostel committees.

Psychotherapy. In dealing with antisocial children in clinics it is useless just to recommend psychotherapy. The first essential is to get each child properly placed, and proper placing in itself works as a therapy in a fair proportion of cases, given time. Psychotherapy can be added. It is essential to get the therapy arranged tactfully. If a psychotherapist is available, and if the hostel wardens actually want to help with regard to a child, then individual psychotherapy can be added. But there is a complication which cannot be ignored; in the good care of a child of this type the child has to become almost a part of the warden, and if someone else is giving treatment the child is apt to lose something vital in his relation to the warden (or some member of the staff), and the psychotherapist cannot easily make up for this in spite of the fact that he can give deeper understanding. Wardens, if they are good at this special type of job, must tend to dislike psychotherapy of the children in their care. In the same way good parents hate their children to be undergoing analysis, even when they seek it and co-operate fully.

The psychiatric social worker and myself, in this scheme, kept in intimate contact with the wardens both in regard to their personal problems, and to the children and the problems of their management as they arose. This contrasts with ordinary clinic work in which the psychiatrist can do best in a direct personal relation to each child patient, and to the parents.

Provision of hostels. We must not be surprised to find ministries issuing edicts in favour of hostels, and also to meet children in need of hostels, and yet to find nothing happening, even to find hostels everywhere closing down. The contact between the supply and the need is only to be provided by men and women who are able and willing to live an experience with the children, willing to let a group steal a few years of their lives. Those of us who are clinically involved with these children must all the time play a part in bringing together the three things – official policy, wardens, and children – and must not expect anything good really to happen apart from our own personal voluntary deliberate efforts. Even in State Medicine the ideas and the clinical contacts belong to the clinician, without whom the best scheme is void.

Placing. The obvious method to be adopted by a large body (such as the London County Council, or a ministry) is to work the distribution of cases from a central bureau which keeps in touch with the various groups of hostels. If I have a child in my clinic needing a hostel (and it is always urgent), I am to send a report including Intelligence Quotient and school report to the central bureau, from which each case is to be distributed according to routine. But I do not play the game, nor do the parents, except when the child is so awful that the only need is to be rid of him immediately. In this mass-production arrangement something personal is lacking. The fact is that if a child comes under my care I cannot just put his or her name on a list somewhere. Doctors and parents must be allowed to maintain interest in the placing of their children; they must actually find out that what is provided is good.

There must be some personal link between clinic and hostel; someone must know someone. If no one knows any one then suspicion develops, because *in the imagination* there are bad parents, bad doctors, bad wardens, bad hostels, even bad ministries. And by bad I mean malicious. If a doctor or a hostel warden is not known as good, he is easily felt to be malevolent.

It will be apparent that our convalescent homes are unsuitable for these children, usually physically healthy, who need long-term management by specially chosen wardens supported by the psychiatric social worker and psychiatrist. Moreover, hospital-trained nurses seem to be rendered unsuitable for this work by their professional training; and many paediatricians turn a blind eye to psychology.

Prevention of delinquency. This work is prophylactic work for the Home Office, whose main job it is to implement the law. For some reason or other I have met opposition to this idea from doctors who work for the Home Office. But hostels for evacuees all over the country succeeded in preventing many children from reaching the courts, thereby saving immense sums of money as well as producing citizens instead of habitual offenders; and from our point of view as doctors, the important thing is that the children have been under the Ministry of Health, that is, they have been recognised as ill. One can only hope that the Ministry of Education, which is now taking over [written in 1945] will do as well during peacetime as the Ministry of Health did during the war, in this prophylactic work for the Home Office.

Main thesis. It happened that by my two appointments I was in touch with the London need for hostels at the same time as I was involved in the provision of hostels in an evacuation area. As physician to a London children's hospital, I was struck by the way in which this wartime provision solved the peacetime problem of management of the early antisocial case.

In sixteen instances I was able to draft London out-patient children to the hostels which I was visiting as psychiatrist. It came about by the chance that I held the two appointments, and it seemed to me to be a good arrangement, one that could be adapted to peace conditions. Because of my position I could be the link between the child, the parents or relatives, and the hostel wardens, and also between the child's past, present, and future.

The value of this work is not to be assessed only by the degree of relief of the psychiatric illness of each child. The value lies also in the provision of a place where the physician could care for these children who, without such provision, must degenerate at hospital or at home, causing great distress to adults, and badly affecting other children.

It is a sad reflection that many of the wartime hostels have closed down, and now there is no serious attempt to provide the hostel accommodation urgently needed for the early antisocial case. As for mad children, for them there is practically no provision. Officially, they do not exist.

Part II
The nature and origins of the
antisocial tendency

Editors' introduction

The order of the papers in Part II has been dictated by the need to bring together in an understandable and readable way the various facets of the whole statement about the antisocial tendency. Because destructiveness is so often a part of delinquent behaviour the section begins with two papers about the roots of aggression written for parents and others in charge of young children. The first, written in 1939, is a chapter in *The Child and the Family*, now out of print; the second, written in 1964, replaced it in *The Child, the Family and the Outside World* (Penguin Books). In both these papers aggression at root is seen as something inborn, co-existing with love. The first paper owes much to Melanie Klein, who pointed out (developing the ideas of Freud) that it is the elaboration of the destructive urge in the inner world of the child that eventually turns into the wish to repair, to construct, to take responsibility. The second paper gives a more original account: aggressiveness at the beginning of life is equated with bodily movement and with the establishment of what is and what is not the self. Here emphasis is placed on playing and the use of symbols as a way of containing inner destructiveness – an idea which is foreshadowed in the talk in Part I entitled 'Home Again'. Winnicott came to see it as characteristic of the antisocial child that he has no area in the personality for playing: this is replaced by acting out. These and other aspects of destructiveness are discussed from different points of view in the hitherto unpublished paper 'Aggression, Guilt and Reparation' (1960) in Part II, and in 'Do Progressive Schools Give Too Much Freedom to the Child?' (1965) in Part III.

The second chapter in this section is Winnicott's fullest statement, written in 1963, about the capacity in every individual to develop a sense of concern – of personal responsibility for the destructiveness that is in his or her own nature. This is the same theme that was touched on in the first paper and is essentially an adaptation of Klein's concept of the 'depressive position' worked out in Winnicott's own way, one of the main differences being Winnicott's greater emphasis on the importance of the human environment (particularly the mother) in meeting and nourishing the innate tendency in the child towards concern. This is especially relevant in the present context because Winnicott believed that it is at the time when the capacity for concern is developing – roughly from 6 months to 2 years of age – that deprivation or loss can have particularly devastating consequences: the beginnings of the process of socialization arising from the child's innate tendencies can be lost or dammed up.

The next paper, 'Absence of a Sense of Guilt' (1966), links the idea of this damming-up of the capacity for concern directly with the antisocial tendency. It also reminds us that social morality is a compromise; and here Winnicott gives his view that the earliest and fiercest morality lies in not betraying the self. 'The Psychology of Separation', written in 1958 for social workers, is also bound up with these ideas. It makes use of Freud's statement about mourning and shows how this depends on the ability to tolerate hatred of a person who has been loved and lost. Neither of these two papers has been published before.

The chapter entitled 'The Antisocial Tendency' (1956) is the centre-piece of the section, being Winnicott's most definitive statement on the subject. It describes what he saw as the two main trends in antisocial behaviour, exemplified by stealing and lying on the one hand and destructive acts on the other; and it traces their origins in the lives of infants and small children. It contains the idea of delinquency as a sign of hope. 'Some Psychological Aspects of Juvenile Delinquency', a talk given to magistrates some ten years earlier, is included here (though in a way it belongs with the wartime papers) because it covers in simpler language much of what is stated in 'The Antisocial Tendency', and also because it puts rather more emphasis on the destructive trend in delinquency – the seeking of a secure framework within which impulse and spontaneity are safe. This talk represents a point at which many of the ideas that Winnicott used in his later work were coming clearly into focus.

The last two chapters in Part II, 'Struggling Through the

Doldrums' (1961) and 'Youth Will Not Sleep' (1964) discuss the
association between adolescence and antisocial behaviour. The
contemporary climate is explored, and reasons are given, using
the theory of emotional development, for the characteristic
behaviour of the adolescent and for his mistrust of compromise.
Antisocial behaviour is here seen as a challenge to be met firmly
by the mature in society, who must contain it; but the only 'cure'
for adolescence is held to be the passage of time. It is probably true
to say that no writer on psychology has made such a positive
approach to the problems of adolescence as Winnicott.

10 Aggression and its roots

AGGRESSION
(Written for teachers, c. 1939)

Love and hate form the two chief elements out of which human affairs are built. Both love and hate involve aggression. Aggression, on the other hand, may be a symptom of fear.

It would be a big business to examine all the issues of this preliminary statement, but there are certain relatively simple things to be said about aggression, and these can be brought within the scope of this paper.

I start with an assumption, one which I am aware is not considered by every one to be justified, that whatever good and evil is to be found in the world of human relationships is to be found in the heart of the individual human being. I carry the assumption further, and say that in the infant there is love and hate of full human intensity.

If one thinks in terms of what the infant is organised to withstand, one can easily arrive at the conclusion that love and hate are not experienced more violently by the adult than by the little child.

If all this is accepted, it should follow that we have only to look at the adult human being or at the little child or at the infant, to see the love and hate that are there; but if the problem were as simple as that, there would be no problem. Of all human tendencies aggression, in particular, is hidden, disguised, side-tracked, ascribed to outside agencies, and when it appears it is always a difficult task to trace it to its origins.

Teachers are aware of their pupils' aggressive urges, whether latent or manifest, and every now and again they are forced to deal with aggressive outbreaks or with a child who is aggressive. As I write this I overhear the words, 'She must be suffering from superfluous energy that is not directed into the right channels.' (I write this while sitting at ease on a college lawn where teachers are in conference, and some of the teachers' Sunday afternoon conversation drifts my way.)

Here is awareness that instinctual energy that is pent up is a potential danger to the individual and to the community, but when it comes to applying such a truth complications arise which show that there is a lot to be learned about the origins of aggressiveness.

Again the teachers' small talk comes my way, '. . . and do you know what she did last term? She brought me a bunch of violets, so that I was nearly deceived, but I knew she had stolen them from the garden next door! "Render unto Caesar . . ." I said. Why she steals money and gives sweets to the other children . . .!'

Here, of course, is no simple aggression. The child wants to feel loving, but is hopeless about being able to do so. She just might feel loving for a moment if the teacher or the children could be deceived, but to be worthy of love she must get something from somewhere outside herself.

To understand such a girl's difficulties we have to understand her unconscious fantasies. It is here that we may be sure we can find the aggression that causes her feeling of hopelessness, and therefore that indirectly causes her antisocial attitude. For the aggressive behaviour of children that comes to the attention of a teacher is never a matter solely of emergence of primitive aggressive instincts. No useful theory of childhood aggressiveness can be built on such a false premise.

Before examining fantasy we will search for primary aggression showing in external relationships. How can we get near to this?

We must of course be prepared to find we can never see naked the hate that nevertheless we know exists in the human bosom. Even the little child who wants you to know he likes knocking over bricks only lets you know this because there exists at the moment a general atmosphere of building a tower with the bricks, within which he can be destructive without feeling hopeless.

A rather timid boy of 4 years has attacks of unreasonableness. He shouts at his nurse or mother or father, 'I'll b-burn your h-house d-down! I'll t-tear your insides out! You!'

These attacks are regarded by those who are unfamiliar with them as highly aggressive, and originally they were so. *Magically* they destroy. But in course of time the little boy has come to recognise that the magic fails, and he has transformed the aggressive attack into orgies in which he enjoys invective with his mouth. His mouth-work over the consonants is terrific. No actual violence is done.

But he does actually wound his parents when he fails to be able to enjoy the presents which they give him. And aggression is effectual when he is taken for a picnic for instance, for owing to his exasperating behaviour every one comes home exhausted. To tire out one's parents is something that the smallest child can do. At first he tires them out without knowing it; then he expects them to like to be tired out by himself; finally he tires them out when he is angry with them.

A little boy of 2½ years is brought to my Clinic because, although he is otherwise a model child, he 'suddenly ups and bites people, even drawing blood'. At times he pulls handfuls of hair out of the heads of those who are caring for him, or he throws crockery on the floor. The spasm over, he is sad about what he has done.

It happens that he only hurts those of whom he is very fond. Chiefly he hurts his mother's mother who is an invalid, and whom he usually cares for just as if he were a grown-up, putting her chair in place, and generally attending to her comfort.

Here is something rather like primary aggression, for the boy is constantly stimulated by both his mother and grandmother, and they feel (quite rightly, to my mind) that he bites 'only when he is excited and simply doesn't know what to do about it'. Just such a glimpse of primary aggression at this age is not very common. The remorse that follows the attacks more usually (by the time a child is this boy's age) takes the form of protecting effectually the people from actual harm. On analysis this boy's attacks would certainly be found to have something more in them than primary aggression.

Encouraged by partial success, let us go to the tiny infant. If an infant should go all out to hurt, not much real harm can be done. Surely the infant can show us naked aggression?

In fact, this is not clearly understood. It is well known that infants do bite their mothers' breasts, even producing blood. They can cause cracked nipples with their gums, and once teeth are present they have the power to do a lot of damage. One mother

I know said, 'When the baby was brought to me she went for my breast in a savage way, tore at the nipples with her gums, and in a few moments blood was flowing. I felt torn to pieces and terrified. It took me a long time to recover from the hate roused in me against the little beast, and I think this was a big reason why she never developed real confidence about good food.'

Here is a mother's account of facts revealing her fantasy as well as what may have happened. Whatever this baby really did, it is certain that the majority of infants do not destroy the breasts that are offered them, though we have good evidence that they want to, and even that they believe they do destroy them by feeding from them.

The usual story is that in the course of two or three hundred feeds they bite less than a dozen times. And they bite chiefly when they are excited, and not chiefly when frustrated!

An infant I know, who was born with a lower incisor already cut, and so could have torn the nipple badly, actually suffered partial starvation himself through protecting the breast from damage. Instead of biting the breast the baby chewed on the inside of his lower lip, causing a sore.

It seems that as soon as we admit that the infant can, and has the urge to, hurt, we must admit the existence of an inhibition of aggressive urges making for protection of what is loved and is therefore in danger. Already, soon after birth, infants are unalike in the degree to which they show or hide direct expression of feelings, and it is of some comfort to mothers of angry, screaming babies that the other mother's nice docile infant who sleeps when not fed, and feeds when not asleep, is not necessarily laying down any better foundations for mental health than her own child is doing. It is evidently of value to the developing infant that he has frequently experienced rage at an age when he need not feel remorse. To be angry for the first time at eighteen months must be truly terrifying for the child.

If it is true, then, that the infant has a vast capacity for destruction it is also true that he has a vast capacity for protecting what he loves from his own destructiveness, and the main destruction must always exist in his fantasy. And the important thing to note about this instinctual aggressiveness is that although it soon becomes something that can be mobilised in the service of hate, it is originally a part of appetite, or of some other form of instinctual love. It is something that increases during excitement, and the exercise of it is highly pleasurable.

Perhaps the word *greed* conveys more easily than any other the idea of original fusion of love and aggression, though the love here is confined to mouth-love.

So far I think we have described three things. Firstly there is a theoretical greed or primary appetite-love, which can be cruel, hurting, dangerous, but which is so by chance. The infant's aim is gratification, peace of mind and body. Gratification brings peace, but the infant perceives that to become gratified he endangers what he loves. Normally he compromises, and allows himself enough gratification while not allowing himself to be too dangerous. But to some extent he frustrates himself; so he must hate some part of himself, unless he can find someone outside himself to frustrate him and to bear being hated.

Secondly there comes a separation of what may hurt from what is less likely to hurt. Biting, for instance, can be enjoyed separately from loving people, through the biting of objects that cannot feel. In this way the aggressive elements of appetite can be isolated and saved up for use when the child is angry, and eventually mobilised to combat external reality perceived as bad.

Our search for naked aggression through study of the infant has partially failed, and we must try to profit from our failure. I have already indicated the clue to the reason for our failure, by mentioning the word fantasy.

The truth is that by giving a most minute description of the behaviour of an infant or a child we leave out at least half, for richness of personality is largely a product of the world of inner relationships which the child is all the time building up through taking in and giving out psychically, something which goes on all the while and is parallel to the physical taking in and giving out which is easily witnessed.

The main part of this inner reality, a world felt to be inside the body or within the personality, is unconscious, except in so far as it can be isolated by the individual from the millions of instinctual expressions that have gone to make up its quality.

We see now that here is a field play of destructive forces which we have not explored, one inside the child's personality, and here indeed we can find (in the course of psychoanalysis, for instance) the good and bad forces at their strongest.

To be able to tolerate all that one may find in one's inner reality is one of the great human difficulties, and an important human aim is to bring into harmonious relationship one's personal inner and outer realities.

Without attempting to go deeply into the origin of the forces that contend for mastery within the personality, I can point out that when the cruel or destructive forces there threaten to dominate over the loving, the individual has to do something to save himself, and one thing he does is to turn himself inside out, to dramatise the inner world outside, to act the destructive role himself and to bring about control by external authority. Control can be established in this way, in the dramatised fantasy, without serious damping down of instincts, whereas the alternative, control within, would need to be generally applied, and would result in a state of affairs known clinically as depression.

When there is hope in regard to the inside things, instinctual life is active, and the individual can enjoy using instinctual urges, including aggressive ones, in making good in real life what has been hurt in fantasy. This forms the basis for both play and work. It can be seen that in applying the theory one is limited in the amount one can help a child on the road to sublimation by the state of the child's inner world. If destruction there is excessive and unmanageable, very little reparation is possible and we can do nothing to help. All that the child can do is either to deny ownership of bad fantasies or to dramatise them.

Aggressiveness, which presents a serious problem of management to the teacher, is nearly always this dramatisation of inner reality which is too bad to be tolerated as such. Often it implies a breakdown of masturbation or of sensuous exploitation which, when successful, provides a link between outer and inner reality, between bodily senses and fantasy (though the fantasy is mainly unconscious fantasy). It has been pointed out that there is a relation between the giving up of masturbation and onset of antisocial behaviour (recently mentioned by Anna Freud in an unpublished lecture) and the cause of this relationship is to be found in the attempt of the child to bring an inner reality that is too terrible to be acknowledged into relation with external reality. Masturbation and dramatisation provide alternative methods, but each must fail in its object, because the only true link is the relation of inner reality to the original instinctual experiences that built it up. This relationship can only be traced by psychoanalytic treatment, and as the fantasy is too terrible to be accepted and tolerated it cannot be used in sublimation.

Normal individuals are always doing what abnormal ones can only do by analytic treatment, that is, altering their inner selves by new experiences of intake and output. It is a constant problem of children and adults to find safe ways of disposing of badness. Much is dramatised and dealt with (falsely) through care over disposal of physical elements that come from the body. Another method is by means of games or work which involve distinctive action which can be enjoyed, with consequent lifting of the sense of frustration and grievance: a boy boxing or kicking a football feels better for what he is doing, partly because he has enjoyed hitting and kicking, and partly because he unconsciously feels (falsely) that he has driven badness out of his fists and feet.

A girl who longs for a baby to some extent longs for the reassurance that she has taken in something good, has retained it, and has something good developing inside her. This is a reassurance she needs (though it is a false one) because of her unconscious feeling that she may be empty, or full of bad things. It is her aggression that gives her these ideas. She also, of course, seeks the peace she feels she may get if instinctually gratified, which means she fears the aggressive elements of her appetite which threaten to dominate her if she is frustrated during excitement. Masturbation can help in the latter need, but not in the former.

Following this, it can be seen that environmental hate or frustration arouses manageable or unmanageable reactions in the individual according to the amount of tension that already exists in the individual's personal unconscious fantasy.

Another important method for dealing with aggression in the inner reality is the masochistic one by which the individual finds suffering, and by one stroke expresses aggression, gets punished and so relieved of guilt feelings, and enjoys sexual excitement and gratification. This is outside the present subject.

Secondly there is the management of fear-driven aggression, the dramatised version of a too-awful inner world. The object of this aggression is to seek out control, and to compel it to function. It is the adult's job to prevent this aggression from becoming out of hand by provision of confident authority, within the bounds of which some degree of badness can be dramatised and enjoyed without danger. The gradual withdrawal of this authority is an important part of the management of adolescents, and adolescent boys and girls can be grouped according to their capacity to stand withdrawal of imposed authority.

It is the task of parents and teachers to see that children never meet so weak an authority that they run amok, or that they must, from fear, take over the authority themselves. Anxiety-driven assumption of authority is dictatorship, and those who have made the experiment of letting children control their own destinies know that the calm adult is less cruel as a manager than a child quickly becomes when he is responsible for too much.

Thirdly (and here sex makes a difference), there is the management of mature aggressiveness, that which is clearly seen in adolescent boys and which to a large extent motivates adolescent competition in games and work. Potency involves toleration of the idea of killing a rival (which leads to the problem of the value of the idea of war, an unpopular subject).

Mature aggressiveness is not something to be cured; it is something to be noted and allowed for. If it is unmanageable, we jump aside, and the law takes over. The law is learning to respect adolescent aggression, and the country counts on it in wartime.

Finally, all aggression that is not denied, and for which personal responsibility can be accepted, is available to give strength to the work of reparation and restitution. At the back of all play, work, and art, is unconscious remorse about harm done in unconscious fantasy, and an unconscious desire to start putting things right.

Sentimentality contains an unconscious denial of the destructiveness underlying construction. It is withering to the developing child, and eventually it can make him need to show in direct form destructiveness which, in a less sentimental milieu, he could have conveyed indirectly by showing a desire to construct.

It is partly false to state that we 'should provide opportunity for creative expression if we are to counter children's destructive urges'. What is needed is an unsentimental attitude towards *all* productions, which means the appreciation not so much of talent as of the struggle behind all achievement, however small. For, apart from sensual love, no human manifestation of love is felt to be valuable that does not imply aggression acknowledged and harnessed.

An aim in personality-building is to become able to tap more and more of the instinctual. This involves becoming more and more able to acknowledge one's own cruelty and greed, which can then, and only then, be harnessed to sublimated activity.

Only if we know the child wants to knock the tower of bricks down is it a valuable thing for him if we see that he can built it up.

ROOTS OF AGGRESSION
(Written for *The Child, the Family and the Outside World*, 1964)

The reader will have gathered from various odd references scattered throughout this book that I know that babies and children scream and bite and kick and pull their mothers' hair, and have impulses that are aggressive or destructive, or unpleasant one way or another.

The care of babies and children is complicated by destructive episodes that may need management and certainly need understanding. It would help in the understanding of these day to day events if I could make a theoretical statement on the roots of aggression. How can I do justice to this vast and difficult subject, however, while at the same time remembering that many of my readers are not studying psychology but are engaged in child or infant care of a practical kind?

Put in a nutshell, aggression has two meanings. By one meaning it is directly or indirectly a reaction to frustration. By the other meaning it is one of the two main sources of an individual's energy. Immensely complex problems arise out of further consideration of this simple statement, and here I can only begin to elaborate the main theme.

It will be agreed that we cannot just talk about aggressiveness as it shows itself in the life of the child. The subject is wider than that; and in any case we are always dealing with a developing child, and it is the growth of one thing out of another that concerns us most deeply.

Sometimes aggression shows itself plainly, and expends itself, or needs someone to meet it and to do something to prevent damage from being done. Just as often aggressive impulses do not show openly, but they appear in the form of some kind of opposite. It will perhaps be a good idea for me to look at some of the various kinds of opposite of aggression.

But first I must make a general observation. It is wise to assume that fundamentally all individuals are essentially alike, and this in spite of the hereditary factors which make us what we are and make us individually distinct. I mean, there are some features in human nature *that can be found in all infants*, and in all children, and in all people of whatever age, and a comprehensive statement of the development of the human personality from earliest infancy to adult independence would be applicable to all human beings whatever their sex, race, colour of skin, creed, or social setting. Appearances may vary, but there are common denominators in human affairs. One infant may tend to be aggressive and another may seem to show hardly any aggressiveness from the beginning; yet each has the same problem. It is simply that the two children are dealing with their load of aggressive impulses in different ways.

If we look and try to see the start of aggression in an individual what we meet is the fact of infantile movement. This even starts before birth, not only in the twistings of the unborn baby, but also in the more sudden movements of limbs that make the mother say she feels a quickening. A part of the infant moves and by moving meets something. An observer could perhaps call this a hit or a kick, but the substance of hitting or kicking is missing because the infant (unborn or newly born) has not yet become a person who could have a clear reason for an action.

So in every infant there is this tendency to move and to get some kind of muscle pleasure in movement, and to gain from the experience of moving and meeting something. Following this one feature through we could describe the development of an infant by noting a progression from simple movement to actions that express anger, or to states that denote hate and control of hate. We could go on to describe the way that chance hitting may become hurting that is meant to hurt, and along with this we may find a protection of the object that is both loved and hated. Furthermore, we could trace the organization of destructive ideas and impulses in an individual child into a pattern of behaviour; and in healthy development all this can show as the way that conscious and unconscious destructive ideas, and reactions to such ideas, appear in the child's dreaming and playing, and also in aggression that is directed against that which is accepted in the child's immediate environment as worthy of destruction.

We can see that these early infantile hittings lead to a discovery of the world that is not the infant's self, and to the beginnings of a relationship to external objects. What will quite soon be aggressive behaviour is therefore at the start a simple impulse that leads to a movement and to the beginnings of exploration. Aggression is always linked in this way with the establishment of a clear distinction between what is the self and what is not the self.

Having made it clear, I hope, that all human individuals are alike in spite of the fact that each is essentially distinct, I can now refer to some of the many opposites of aggression.

For one example, there is the contrast between the bold and the timid child. In the one the tendency is to obtain the relief that belongs to open expression of aggression and hostility, and in the other there is the tendency to find this aggression not in the self but elsewhere, and to be scared of it, or to be apprehensive in expectation of its coming at the child from the external world. The first child is lucky because he finds out that expressed hostility is limited and expendable, whereas the second child never reaches satisfactory end-points, but goes on expecting trouble. And in some cases trouble really is there.

Some children definitely tend to see their own controlled (repressed) aggressive impulses in the aggression of others. This can develop in an unhealthy way, since the supply of persecution may run short, and have to be made up by delusions. So we find a child always expecting persecution and perhaps becoming aggressive in self-defence against imagined attack. This is an illness, but the pattern can be found as a phase in the development of almost any child.

In looking at another kind of opposite we may contrast the child who is easily aggressive with one that holds the aggression 'inside', and so becomes tense, over-controlled, and serious. There naturally follows a degree of inhibition of all impulses, and so of creativity, for creativity is bound up with the irresponsibility of infancy and childhood and with free-hearted living. Nevertheless, in the case of this latter alternative, although the child loses something in terms of inner freedom it can be said that there is a gain in that self-control has begun to develop, along with some consideration for others, and a protection of the world from what would otherwise be the child's ruthlessness. For in health there develops in each child a capacity to stand in other people's shoes, and to become identified with external objects and persons.

One of the awkward things about excessive self-control is that in a nice child, one who would not hurt a fly, there may come about a periodical break-through of aggressive feelings and behaviour, a temper tantrum, for example, or a vicious action, and this has no positive value for anyone, least of all for the child, who afterwards may not even remember what has happened. All that parents can do here is to find some way of getting through such an awkward episode, and to hope that with the child's growth a more meaningful expression of aggression may evolve.

In another more mature alternative to aggressive behaviour the child dreams. In dreaming, destruction and killing are experienced in fantasy, and this dreaming is associated with any degree of excitement in the body, and is a real experience and not just an intellectual exercise. The child who can manage dreams is becoming ready for all kinds of playing, either alone or with other children. If the dream contains too much destruction or involves too severe a threat to sacred objects, or if chaos supervenes, then the child wakes screaming. Here the mother plays her part by being available and by helping the child to wake from the nightmare so that external reality may play its reassuring part once more. This process of waking may take the child the best part of half an hour. The nightmare itself may be a strangely satisfactory experience for the child.

Here I must make a clear distinction between dreaming and day-dreaming. The stringing together of fantasies during waking life is not what I am referring to. The essential thing about dreaming as opposed to day-dreaming is that the dreamer is asleep, and can be awakened. The dream may be forgotten, but it has been dreamed, and this is significant. (There is also the true dream that spills over into the child's waking life, but that is another story.)

I have spoken of playing, which draws on fantasy and on the total reservoir of what might be dreamed, and of the deeper and even the deepest layers of the unconscious. It will readily be seen what an important part is played in healthy development by the child's acceptance of symbols. One thing 'stands for' another, and the consequence is that there is a great relief from the crude and awkward conflicts that belong to stark truth.

It is awkward when a child loves mother tenderly and also

wants to eat her; or when a child loves and hates father at one and the same time, and cannot displace either the hate or the love on to an uncle; or when a child wants to be rid of a new baby and cannot satisfactorily express the feeling by losing a toy. There are some children who are like that and they just suffer.

Ordinarily, however, acceptance of symbols starts early. The acceptance of symbols gives elbow room to the child in his or her living experience. For instance, when infants adopt some special object for cuddling very early on, this stands both for them and for the mother. It is then a symbol of union, like the thumb of a thumb-sucker, and this symbol may itself be attacked, as well as valued beyond all later possessions.

Play, based as it is on the acceptance of symbols, has infinite possibility in it. It enables the child to experience whatever is to be found in his or her personal *inner psychic reality*, which is the basis of the growing sense of identity. There will be aggression there as well as love.

In the maturing individual child there appears another alternative to destruction, and a very important one. This is *construction*. I have tried to describe something of the complex way in which, under favourable environmental conditions, a constructive urge relates to the growing child's personal acceptance of responsibility for the destructive side of his or her nature. It is a most important sign of health in a child when constructive play appears and is maintained. This is something that cannot be implanted, any more than trust can be implanted. It appears in the course of time as a result of the totality of the child's living experiences in the surroundings provided by the parents or those acting as parents.

This relationship between aggression and construction can be tested if we withdraw from a child (or from an adult for that matter) the opportunity to do something for those who are near and dear, or the chance to 'contribute-in', the chance to participate in the satisfaction of family needs. By 'contribute-in' I mean doing things for pleasure, or to be like someone, but at the same time finding that this is what is needed for the happiness of mother, or for the running of the home. It is like 'finding one's niche'. A child participates by pretending to nurse the baby or to make a bed or to use the Hoover or to make pastry, a condition of satisfying participation being that this pretence is taken seriously by someone. If it is laughed at, then it becomes mere mimicry, and the child experiences a sense of physical impotence and uselessness. At this point there may easily be an outbreak in the child of frank aggression or destructiveness.

Apart from experiments, such a state of affairs may come about in the ordinary course of events because no one understands that a child needs to give even more than to receive.

It will be seen that the activity of a healthy infant is characterized by natural movements and a tendency to knock up against things, and that the infant gradually comes to employ these, along with screaming and spitting and the passing of urine and faeces, in the service of anger, hate, revenge. The child comes to love and hate simultaneously, and to accept the contradiction. One of the most important examples of the joining up of aggression and loving comes with the urge to bite, which makes sense from about five months onwards. Eventually this becomes incorporated into the enjoyment that goes with the eating of all kinds of food. Originally, however, it is the good object, the mother's body, that is exciting to bite, and that produces ideas of biting. Thus food comes to be accepted as a symbol of the mother's body, or of the body of the father or any other loved person.

It is all very complicated, and plenty of time is needed for a baby and a child to master aggressive ideas and excitements and to be able to control them without losing the ability to be aggressive at appropriate moments, whether in hating or in loving.

Oscar Wilde said: 'Each man kills the thing he loves.' It is brought to our notice every day that along with loving we must expect hurting. In child care we see that children tend to love the thing they hurt. Hurting is very much a part of child life, and the question is: how will your child find a way of harnessing these aggressive forces to the task of living, loving, playing, and (eventually) working?

And this is not all. There is still the question: where is the point of origin of aggression? We have seen that in the development of the newborn infant there are the first natural movements and there is screaming, and that these may be pleasurable but they do not add up to a clearly aggressive meaning because the infant is not yet properly organized as a person. We want to know, however, how it comes about, perhaps quite early, that an infant destroys the world. This is of vital importance because it is the residue of this infantile 'unfused' destruction that may actually destroy the world we live in and love. In infantile magic the world can be annihilated by a closing of the eyes and recreated by a new looking and a new phase of needing. Poisons and explosive weapons give to infantile magic a reality that is the very opposite of magical.

The vast majority of infants receive good enough care in the earliest stages so that some degree of integration is achieved in the personality, and the danger of a massive break-through of entirely senseless destructiveness is rendered unlikely. By way of prevention, the most important thing is for us to recognize the part the parents play in facilitating each infant's maturational processes in the course of family life; and especially we can learn to evaluate the part the mother plays at the very beginning, when the infant's relationship to the mother changes over from a purely physical one to one in which the infant meets the mother's attitude, and when the purely physical is beginning to be enriched and complicated by emotional factors.

But the question remains: do we know about the origin of this force that is inherent in human beings and that underlies destructive activity or its equivalent in suffering under self-control? Behind it all is *magical destruction*. This is normal to infants in the very early stages of their development, and goes side by side with magical creation. Primitive or magical destruction of all objects belongs to the fact that (for the infant) objects change from being part of 'me' to being 'not me', from being subjective phenomena to being perceived objectively. Ordinarily such a change takes place by subtle gradations that follow the gradual changes in the developing infant, but with defective maternal provision these same changes occur suddenly, and in ways that the infant cannot predict.

By taking each infant through this vital stage in early development in a sensitive way the mother gives time for her infant to acquire all sorts of ways of dealing with the shock of recognizing the existence of a world that is outside his or her magical control. If time is allowed for maturational processes, then the infant becomes able to be destructive and becomes able to hate and to kick and to scream instead of magically annihilating that world. In this way *actual aggression is seen to be an achievement*. As compared with magical destruction, aggressive ideas and behaviour take on a positive value, and hate becomes a sign of civilization, when we keep in mind the whole process of the emotional development of the individual, and especially the earliest stages.

Elsewhere I have tried to give an account of just these subtle stages by which, when there is good enough mothering and good enough parentage, the majority of infants do achieve health and a capacity to leave magical control and destruction aside, and to enjoy the aggression that is in them alongside the gratifications, and alongside all the tender relationships and the inner personal riches that go to make up the life of childhood.

11 *The development of the capacity for concern*

(A paper presented to the Topeka Psychoanalytic Society, 12 October, 1962. First published in 1963.)

The origin of the capacity to be concerned presents a complex problem. Concern is an important feature in social life. Psychoanalysts usually seek origins in the emotional development of the individual. We want to know the aetiology of concern, and the place where concern appears in the child's development. We also are interested in the failure of the establishment of an individual's capacity for concern, and in the loss of concern that has to some extent been established.

The word 'concern' is used to cover in a positive way a phenomenon that is covered in a negative way by the word 'guilt'. A sense of guilt is anxiety linked with the concept of ambivalence, and implies a degree of integration in the individual ego that allows for the retention of good object-imago along with the idea of a destruction of it. Concern implies further integration, and further growth, and relates in a positive way to the individual's sense of responsibility, especially in respect of relationships into which the instinctual drives have entered.

Concern refers to the fact that the individual *cares*, or *minds*, and both feels and accepts responsibility. At the genital level in the statement of the theory of development, concern could be said to be the basis of the family, where both partners in intercourse – beyond their pleasure – take responsibility for the result. But in the total imaginative life of the individual, the subject of concern raises even wider issues, and a capacity for concern is at the back of all constructive play and work. It belongs to normal, healthy living, and deserves the attention of the psychoanalyst.

There is much reason to believe that concern – with its positive sense – emerges in the earlier emotional development of the child at a period before the period of the classical Oedipus complex, which involves a relationship between three persons, each felt to be a whole person by the child. But there is no need to be precise about timing, and indeed most of the processes that start up in early infancy are never fully established, and continue to be strengthened by the growth that continues in later childhood, and indeed in adult life, even in old age.

It is usual to describe the origin of the capacity for concern in terms of the infant-mother relationship, when already the infant is an established unit, and when the infant feels the mother, or mother-figure, to be a whole person. It is a development belonging essentially to the period of a two-body relationship.

In any statement of child-development, certain principles are taken for granted. Here I wish to say that the maturation processes form the basis of infant- and child-development, in psychology as in anatomy and physiology. Nevertheless, in emotional development it is clear that certain external conditions are necessary if maturation potentials are to become actual. That is, development depends on a good-enough environment, and the earlier we go back in our study of the baby, the more true it is that without good-enough mothering the early stages of development cannot take place.

A great deal has happened in the development of the baby before we begin to be able to refer to concern. The capacity to be concerned is a matter of health, a capacity which, once established, presupposes a complex ego-organization which cannot be thought of in any way but as an achievement, both an achievement of infant- and child-care and an achievement in terms of the internal growth-processes in the baby and child. I shall take for granted a good-enough environment in the early stages, in order to simplify the matter that I wish to examine. What I have to say, then, follows on complex maturational processes dependent for their becoming realized on good-enough infant- and child-care.

Of the many stages that have been described by Freud and the psycho-analysts who have followed him, I must single out one stage which has to involve the use of the word 'fusion'. This is the achievement of emotional development in which the baby experiences erotic and aggressive drives toward the same object at the same time. On the erotic side there is both satisfaction-seeking and object-seeking, and on the aggressive side, there is a complex of anger employing muscle erotism, and of hate, which involves the retention of a good object-imago for comparison. Also in the whole aggressive-destructive impulse is contained a primitive type of object relationship in which love involves destruction. Some of this is necessarily obscure, and I do not need to know all about the origin of aggression in order to follow my argument, because I am taking it for granted that the baby has become able to combine erotic and aggressive experience, and in relation to one object. Ambivalence has been reached.

By the time that this becomes a fact in the development of a child, the infant has become able to experience ambivalence in fantasy, as well as in body-function of which the fantasy is originally an elaboration. Also, the infant is beginning to relate himself to objects that are less and less subjective phenomena, and more and more objectively perceived 'not-me' elements. He has begun to establish a self, a unit that is both physically contained in the body's skin and that is psychologically integrated. The mother has now become—in the child's mind—a coherent image, and the term 'whole object' now becomes applicable. This state of affairs, precarious at first, could be nicknamed the 'humpty-dumpty stage', the wall on which Humpty Dumpty is precariously perched being the mother who has ceased to offer her lap.

This development implies an ego that begins to be independent of the mother's auxiliary ego, and there can now be said to be an inside to the baby, and therefore an outside. The body-scheme has come into being and quickly develops complexity. From now on, the infant lives a psychosomatic life. The inner psychic reality which Freud taught us to respect now becomes a real thing to the infant, who now feels that personal richness resides within the self. This personal richness develops out of the simultaneous love-hate experience which implies the achievement of ambivalence, the enrichment and refinement of which leads to the emergence of concern.

It is helpful to postulate the existence for the immature child of two mothers—shall I call them the object-mother and the environment-mother? I have no wish to invent names that become stuck and eventually develop a rigidity and an obstructive quality, but it seems possible to use these words 'object-mother' and 'environment-mother' in this context to describe the vast difference that there is for the infant between two aspects of infant-care, the mother as object, or owner of the part-object that may satisfy the infant's urgent needs, and the mother as the person who wards off the unpredictable and who actively provides care in handling and in general management. What the infant does at the height of id-tension and the use thus made of the object seems to me very different from the use the infant makes of the mother as part of the total environment.[1]

In this language it is the environment-mother who receives all that can be called affection and sensuous co-existence; it is the object-mother who becomes the target for excited experience backed by crude instinct-tension. It is my thesis that concern turns up in the baby's life as a highly sophisticated experience in the coming-together in the infant's mind of the object-mother and the environment-mother. The environmental provision continues to be vitally important here, though the infant is beginning to be able to have that inner stability that belongs to the development of independence.

In favourable circumstances, when the baby has reached the necessary stage in personal development, there comes about a new fusion. For one thing, there is the full experience of, and fantasy of, object-relating based on instinct, the object being used without regard for consequences, used ruthlessly (if we use the term as a description of our view of what is going on). And alongside this is the more quiet relationship of the baby to the environment-mother. These two things come together. The result is complex, and it is this that I especially wish to describe.

The favourable circumstances necessary at this stage are these: that the mother should continue to be alive and available, available physically and available in the sense of not being pre-occupied with something else. The object-mother has to be found to survive the instinct-driven episodes, which have now acquired the full force of fantasies of oral sadism and other results of fusion. Also, the environment-mother has a special function, which is to continue to be herself, to be empathic towards her infant, to be there to receive the spontaneous gesture, and to be pleased.

[1] This is a theme that has recently been developed in a book by Harold Searles: *The Non-Human Environment in Normal Development and in Schizophrenia*. New York: International Universities Press, 1960.

The fantasy that goes with full-blooded id-drives contains attack and destruction. It is not only that the baby imagines that he eats the object, but also that the baby wants to take possession of the contents of the object. If the object is not destroyed, it is because of its own survival capacity, not because of the baby's protection of the object. This is one side of the picture.

The other side of the picture has to do with the baby's relation to the environment-mother, and from this angle there may come so great a protection of the mother that the child becomes inhibited or turns away. Here is a positive element in the infant's experience of weaning and one reason why some infants wean themselves.

In favourable circumstances there builds up a technique for the solution of this complex form of ambivalence. The infant experiences anxiety, because if he consumes the mother he will lose her, but this anxiety becomes modified by the fact that the baby has a contribution to make to the environment-mother. There is a growing confidence that there will be opportunity for contributing-in, for giving to the environment-mother, a confidence which makes the infant able to hold the anxiety. The anxiety held in this way becomes altered in quality and becomes a sense of guilt.

Instinct-drives lead to ruthless usage of objects, and then to a guilt-sense which is held, and is allayed by the contribution to the environment-mother that the infant can make in the course of a few hours. Also, the opportunity for giving and for making reparation that the environment-mother offers by her reliable presence, enables the baby to become more and more bold in the experiencing of id-drives; in other words, frees the baby's instinctual life. In this way, the guilt is not felt, but it lies dormant, or potential, and appears (as sadness or a depressed mood) only if opportunity for reparation fails to turn up.

When confidence in this benign cycle and in the expectation of opportunity is established, the sense of guilt in relation to the id-drives becomes further modified, and we then need a more positive term, such as 'concern'. The infant is now becoming able to be concerned, to take responsibility for his own instinctual impulses and the functions that belong to them. This provides one of the fundamental constructive elements of play and work. But in the developmental process, it was the opportunity to contribute that enabled concern to be within the child's capacity.

A feature that may be noted, especially in respect of the concept of anxiety that is 'held', is that integration *in time* has become added to the more static integration of the earlier stages. Time is kept going by the mother, and this is one aspect of her auxiliary ego-functioning; but the infant comes to have a personal time-sense, one that lasts at first only over a short span. This is the same as the infant's capacity to keep alive the imago of the mother in the inner world which also contains the fragmentary benign and persecutory elements that arise out of the instinctual experiences. The length of the time-span over which a child can keep the imago alive in inner psychic reality depends partly on maturational processes and partly on the state of the inner defence organization.

I have sketched some aspects of the origins of concern in the early stages in which the mother's continued presence has a specific value for the infant, that is, if the instinctual life is to have freedom of expression. But this balance has to be achieved over and over again. Take the obvious case of the management of adolescence, or the equally obvious case of the psychiatric patient, for whom occupational therapy is often a start on the road towards a constructive relation to society. Or consider a doctor, and his needs. Deprive him of his work, and where is he? He needs his patients, and the opportunity to use his skills, as others do.

I shall not develop at length the theme of lack of development of concern, or of loss of this capacity for concern that has been almost, but not quite, established. Briefly, failure of the object-mother to survive or of the environment-mother to provide reliable opportunity for reparation leads to a loss of the capacity for concern, and to its replacement by crude anxieties and by crude defences, such as splitting, or disintegration. We often discuss separation-anxiety, but here I am trying to describe what happens between mothers and their babies and between parents and their children when there is *no* separation, and when external continuity of child-care is *not* broken. I am trying to account for things that happen when separation is avoided.

12 *The absence of a sense of guilt*

(A talk prepared for the Devon and Exeter Association for Mental Health, 10 December, 1966)

There is no need for me to describe the conventional idea of right and wrong. In an environment (mother, family, home, cultural group, school, etc.) this is good, that is not good. Children fit in their own ideas so as to comply, or else they rebel and hold the opposite view in some or other respect. Gradually this state of affairs is altered because complexity makes nonsense of it or else the child becomes mature in respect of having established a sense of self, and a right to have a personal view of everything. The mature child still likes or needs to be able to check up against the accepted code, even if only to know how things stand as between him or her and the community. This is a permanent feature, characteristic even of mature adults.

The question arises early in this sort of discussion – how far is the moral code taught and how far is it innate? In practical language, do you wait for your child to use a pot, or do you fight incontinence from the word go? The answer to this sort of question needs to involve the enquirer in a study of the very subtle interplay, in the developing child's life, of the inherited or personal developmental tendency, or the maturational process, and of the facilitating environment represented by human beings who adapt to the child's needs, and who in a human way fail to adapt.

In making such a study we soon come across the existence of two schools of thought. At the extremes they are very different, irreconcilable in fact:

(a) We cannot risk it. How do we know there are innate factors in the developing child tending towards the arrival in the child of a sense of right and wrong? The risk is too great. We must plant a moral code in the virgin soil, and do so before the individual child is old enough to resist what we do. Then, with luck, the morality we have adopted as 'revealed' will appear in all those who are not endowed with too much of something which could be called original sin.

At the other extreme there is this point of view:

(b) The only morality that counts is what comes from the individual. After all, the 'revealed' morality of the other extreme group was built up over the centuries, or millennia, by thousands of generations of individuals, helped on by a few prophets. It is better to wait and wait, till by natural processes each child comes to have a sense of right and wrong that is personal. It is not behaviour that matters but the feelings of right and wrong that a child may have apart from compliance.

There is no need for us to try to bring together the protagonists of these two extreme points of view. Better if we try to keep them separated so that they do not meet and fight. They can never come to terms with each other.

I like to think that there is a way of life that starts from the assumption that morality that is linked with compliance has little ultimate value, and that it is the individual child's own sense of right and wrong that we hope to find developing along with everything else that develops because of the inherited processes leading towards all kinds of growth, and starting from this assumption recognizes the difficulties and sets out to study these and to learn how to meet these difficulties both in theory and in practice.

In banal practical terms, a mother may find that two of her infants become naturally dry – how convenient! The third, however, just goes on and on wetting and messing, and causing her backache. When she thinks about her third child she may find herself thinking twice about innate morality, and wondering how to switch over to demanding compliance without destroying the third child's soul.

In this third way of looking at things we need to take into full consideration the following facts:

(1) The absolute dependence of the infant at the start, this quickly becoming near-absolute, then relative – the tendency being towards independence. It will be seen that here is a very

heavy leaning on the capacity of the mothers (parents, etc.) who cannot ever be better than human (perfection has no meaning), who must have differing attitudes to the various children, and who are themselves changing all the time because of their own growth, their own emotional experiences, their own private lives that they are living or temporarily setting aside for the sake of this one baby.

(2) Each child is different from the one before and the one after in the sense that what is inherited is personal. Even identical twins are not identical in inherited tendencies, though perhaps similar. In this way experiences in the narrow field of the infant-mother relationship are specific, not general, and this without any notice being taken of the abnormalities.

(3) There are abnormalities in varying degree – circumstances favour the early experiences in one case, and in another there occur impingements that produce crude reactions. Perhaps our mother with just the first two babies made no significant technical slips, but with the third failed (she slipped and nearly broke her wrist, and had to attend to this before she answered her baby's subtle communication indicating a need which she would naturally meet if not for the moment concerned with her own troubles – quite beyond the ken of the baby). She and the third baby may have settled down into a pattern of technique which if verbalized would be, 'OK, I can trust you as I did earlier on, provided I claim your acceptance of my right to postpone compliance in regard to cleanliness'. Mothers and parents are all the time doing successful psychotherapy in respect of their inevitable failures of techniques and the effects of these failures on the line of life of each infant. We who are looking on are apt to say 'you are "spoiling" your child, you know'. In this way we offer reproof just as the public reproves the psychotherapist who allows a measure of freedom to a child in the therapy hour, or we even reprove those who try to understand antisocial behaviour when, surely, we ought to be stamping on it.

If we look at fairly normal examples of children growing up in the setting of fairly reliable human relationships we can profitably study the way in which a sense of right and wrong develops in each child. The subject is immensely complex, but we are no longer at sea. Or we already know our lighthouses.

Just as Freud pointed out the value of the concept of the superego, as an area in the mind, much influenced by introjected parent figures, so Melanie Klein developed the concept of early superego formations that appear even in the infant mind, and that are relatively independent of the introjections of parents. Naturally there cannot be independence of parental *attitudes*; this can be verified every time you see a baby reaching out for some object, and checking the impulse in order to first assess the mother's attitude. This may be mad (she thinks that everything that is green may contain arsenic) or sane (the saucepan contains boiling water). For a time, till the baby starts to become a scientist, it all has to be quite bewildering. Happy is the baby whose mother is at any rate consistent.

I have tried to give a résumé of Melanie Klein's concept of the Depressive Position[1] (which is important in this context though badly named) and I cannot go over this ground again here. But I would say that as a baby or small child becomes at times a whole thing, a unit, an integrate, someone who could say 'I am' (if words were available) so there comes about a state of affairs by which there is a sense of personal responsibility, and when in relationships the child has impulses and ideas that are destructive (such as, I love you, I eat you) then there is a clear and natural beginning of a personal sense of guilt. As Freud said somewhere, the sense of guilt enables the individual to *be* wicked. In the pattern the child has the impulse, perhaps bites (or eats a biscuit) and has the idea of eating the object (let us say mother's breast) and then feels guilty. Oh dear how awful I am! Out of this comes the urge to be constructive.

If the child's sense of guilt is absent in the pattern, then the child does not get so far as allowing the impulse. Fear is there instead, and the child is inhibited in respect of the whole of the feeling that naturally builds round this impulse.

I come here to the absence of a sense of guilt. Working backwards from what Melanie Klein called the Depressive Position, which is an achievement of healthy development, I come to the

---

[1] D. W. Winnicott, 'The Depressive Position in Normal Emotional Development' (1954–55) in *Through Paediatrics to Psycho-Analysis*. London: Hogarth Press, 1975.
See also 'The Development of the Capacity for Concern' (Chapter 11 of this volume) which contains Winnicott's development of Klein's concept. Eds.

baby whose experience has not enabled such a state of affairs to come about.

(1) The unreliability of the mother figure makes constructive effort futile, so that guilt sense becomes intolerable, and the child is driven back on inhibition, or loss of the impulse which is in fact part of primitive loving.

(2) Worse, the early experiences have not enabled the innate process towards integration to have effect, so that there is no unit and no total responsibility felt for anything. Impulses and ideas arise and affect behaviour, but it can never be said: this baby had the impulse to eat the breast (keeping artificially to this limited field for illustrative purposes).

It is difficult for me to know how to dig more deeply into my subject here and now, in the limited time available. I would like to draw your attention to the special case of the child affected by the anti-social tendency, perhaps in process of becoming a delinquent. It is here especially that we get told: this boy or girl has no moral sense – no clinical sense of guilt. But we refute this idea because we do not find it to be true when we have a chance to make a psychiatric investigation of the child, especially at the stage before secondary gains have taken hold. There is this stage before the arrival of secondary gains, when the child needs help and feels mad because of being compelled from within to steal, to destroy.

In fact, the pattern is that

(a) things went well enough for the child;
(b) something disturbed this;
(c) the child was taxed beyond capacity (ego defences broke down);
(d) the child reorganized on the basis of a new pattern of ego defence, inferior in quality;
(e) the child begins to become hopeful again and organizes antisocial acts in hope, hope of compelling society to go back with him or her to the position where things went wrong, and to acknowledge the fact;
(f) if this is done (either by a period of spoiling or directly in a psychiatric interview) then the child can reach back to the period before the moment of deprivation and rediscover the

good object and the good human controlling environment which by existing originally enabled him or her to experience impulses, including destructive ones.

It will be seen that (f), the last of these stages, is difficult to do. But the principle must first be understood and accepted. And in fact any parent with several children knows how over and over again this mending by the employment of special and temporary adaptive techniques does actually take place and is successful.

However difficult we find the application of these ideas we do need to abandon absolutely the theory that children can be born innately amoral. This means nothing in terms of the study of the individual developing along the lines of the inherited matura- tional processes all the time intertwined with the operation of the facilitating environment.

And now finally let me introduce you to some of the things that our schizoid patients teach us, or require us to know. These patients are in some ways more moral than we are, but they are of course terribly uncomfortable. They perhaps prefer to remain uncomfortable and not to be 'cured'. Sanity spells compromise. That is what they feel to be wicked. Extra-marital intercourse is of no consequence to them as compared with betrayal of the self. And it is true (I think I could show you) that sane people relate to the world by what I call cheating. Or rather, if there is a sanity that is ethically respectable it arrived very early in the infancy of the individual when cheating was of no consequence. (The baby creates the object that it relates to, but the object was there already, so in another sense the baby found the object and then created it.) But this is not good enough. Each child must be enabled to create the world (the mother's adaptive technique enables this to feel to be a fact) else the world is to have no meaning. Each baby must have enough experience of omnipotence if he or she is to become able to give over omnipotence to external reality or to a God- principle.)

So the only real eating has as its basis *not* eating. It is out of not being creative, out of being isolated, that the creation of objects and of the world comes to have meaning. There is no enjoyment of company except as a development from essential isolation, the isolation that reappears as the individual dies.

Some must spend all their lives not being, in a desperate effort to find a basis for being. For schizoid persons (I feel humble in their presence although I spend much time and energy trying to cure them because they are so uncomfortable) wicked means anything false, like being alive because of compliance. I could illustrate this idea, but perhaps I had better leave things just stated like this. If anyone can glean something from this untidy harvest may the gleanings be of value. In the end you see I come down to the concept of a sense of guilt that is so fundamental to human nature that babies die of it, or if they cannot die they organize a compliant or false self which betrays the true self in so far as it seems to succeed in terms of what the onlookers believe to have value.

Compared with these powerful forces (which appear in life and in the arts and in terms of *integrity*) the *mores* of local society are mere distractions. Your adolescent children, some of them patients, are more concerned with not betraying themselves than with whether they smoke or not, or whether they do or do not sleep around. It can be seen that for them (as with small children, though it is more obscure here) the false solution is OUT.

It's awkward, but most disturbingly true. For a quiet life, I recommend either no children at all (you've got yourselves to cope with, and that could be enough) or else plunging right in at the beginning when what you do may (with luck) have the effect of getting these individuals past the cheating bit before they have become old enough to meet the reality principle, and the fact that omnipotence is subjective. Not only is omnipotence subjective, but as a subjective phenomenon it is an actual experience – that is to say, at the beginning, when all goes well enough.

13 Some psychological aspects of juvenile delinquency

(An address to magistrates, 1946)

I find I want to give a simple and yet not untrue description of one aspect of delinquency, a description that links delinquency with deprivation of home life. This could prove helpful to those who wish to understand the roots of the delinquent's problem.

First I invite consideration of the word unconscious. This talk is addressed to magistrates, who are, by training, accustomed to weighing up evidence, to thinking things out as well as feeling things. Now Freud contributed something really useful here. He showed that if we substitute thinking-out for feeling we cannot leave out the unconscious without making gross errors; in fact not without making fools of ourselves. The unconscious may be a nuisance for those who like everything tidy and simple, but it definitely cannot be left out of account by planners and thinkers.

Man the feeler, man the intuitive, far from leaving the unconscious out of account, has always been swayed by his unconscious. But man the thinker has not yet realised that he can both think and also at the same time include the unconscious in his thinking. Thinking people, having tried logic and having found it shallow, have started on a reaction towards unreason, which is a dangerous tendency indeed. The strange thing is to what a degree front-rank thinkers, even scientists, have failed to make use of this particular scientific advance. Do we not see economists leaving out of account unconscious greed, politicians ignoring repressed hate, doctors unable to recognise the depression and hypochondria that underlie such illnesses as rheumatism and that impair the industrial machine? We even have magistrates who fail to see that thieves are unconsciously looking for something more important than bicycles and fountain pens.

Every magistrate is fully aware of the fact that thieves have unconscious motives. First, however, I want to state and emphasise quite a different application of the same principle. I want to ask for consideration of the unconscious in its relation to the job of being a magistrate, this job being the implementing of the law.

It is because I am so anxious to see psychological methods used in the investigation of court cases, and in the management of antisocial children, that I want to make an attack on one of the biggest threats to an advance in that direction; this threat comes from the adoption of a sentimental attitude towards crime. If advances seem to come but are based on sentimentality, they are valueless; reaction must surely set in, and the advances had better never have been made. In sentimentality there is repressed or unconscious hate, and this repression is unhealthy. Sooner or later the hate turns up.

Crime produces public revenge feelings. Public revenge would add up to a dangerous thing were it not for the law and those who implement it. First and foremost in court work, the magistrate gives expression to public revenge feelings, and only by so doing can the foundation be laid for a humane treatment of the offender.

I find that there can be very strong resentment over this idea. Many people, if asked, may claim that they do not want to punish criminals, that they would rather see them treated. But my suggestion, one based on very definite premises, is that no offence can be committed without an addition being made to the general pool of unconscious public revenge feelings. It is one function of the law to protect the criminal against this same unconscious, and therefore blind, revenge. Society feels frustrated, but it allows the offender to be dealt with in the courts, after the passage of time and the cooling of passion; some satisfaction follows when justice is done. There is a real danger lest those who want to see offenders treated as ill people (as they are indeed) will be thwarted just as they are seeming to succeed, through not taking into account the unconscious revenge potential. There would be danger in the adoption of a purely therapeutic aim on the magisterial bench.

This having been said, I can go on to what interests me so very much more, the understanding of crime as a psychological illness. It is a huge and complex subject, but I will try to say something simple about antisocial children, and the relation of delinquency to deprivation of home life.

You know that in investigation of the several pupils in an

approved school diagnosis may range from normal (or healthy) to schizophrenic. However, something binds together all delinquents. What is it?

In an ordinary family, a man and woman, husband and wife, take joint responsibility for their children. Babies are born, mother (supported by father) brings each child along, studying the personality of each, coping with each one's personal problem as it affects society in its smallest unit, the family and the home.

What is the normal child like? Does he just eat and grow and smile sweetly? No, that is not what he is like. A normal child, if he has confidence in father and mother, pulls out all the stops. In the course of time he tries out his power to disrupt, to destroy, to frighten, to wear down, to waste, to wangle, and to appropriate. Everything that takes people to the courts (or to the asylums, for that matter) has its normal equivalent in infancy and early childhood, in the relation of the child to his own home. If the home can stand up to all the child can do to disrupt it, he settles down to play; but business first, the tests must be made, and especially so if there is some doubt as to the stability of the parental set-up and the home (by which I mean so much more than house). At first the child needs to be conscious of a framework if he is to feel free, and if he is to be able to play, to draw his own pictures, to be an irresponsible child.

Why should this be? The fact is that the early stages of emotional development are full of potential conflict and disruption. The relation to external reality is not yet firmly rooted; the personality is not yet well integrated; primitive love has a destructive aim, and the small child has not yet learned to tolerate and cope with instincts. He can come to manage these things, and more, if his surroundings are stable and personal. At the start he absolutely needs to live in a circle of love and strength (with consequent tolerance) if he is not to be too fearful of his own thoughts and of his imaginings to make progress in his emotional development.

Now what happens if the home fails a child before he has got the idea of a framework as part of his own nature? The popular idea is that, finding himself 'free' he proceeds to enjoy himself. This is far from the truth. Finding the framework of his life broken, he no longer feels free. He becomes anxious, and if he has hope he proceeds to look for a framework elsewhere than at home. The child whose home fails to give a feeling of security looks outside his home for the four walls; he still has hope, and he looks to grandparents, uncles and aunts, friends of the family, school. He seeks an external stability without which he may go mad. Provided at the proper time, this stability might have grown into the child like the bones in his body, so that gradually in the course of the first months and years of his life he would have passed on to independence from dependence and a need to be managed. Often a child gets from relations and school what he missed in his own actual home.

The antisocial child is merely looking a little farther afield, looking to society instead of to his own family or school to provide the stability he needs if he is to pass through the early and quite essential stages of his emotional growth.

I put it this way. When a child steals sugar he is looking for the good mother, his own, from whom he has a right to take what sweetness is there. In fact this sweetness is his, for he invented her and her sweetness out of his own capacity to love, out of his own primary creativity, whatever that is. He is also looking for his father, one might say, who will protect mother from his attacks on her, attacks made in the exercise of primitive love. When a child steals outside his own home he is still looking for his mother, but he is seeking with more sense of frustration, and increasingly needing to find at the same time the paternal authority that can and will put a limit to the actual effect of his impulsive behaviour, and to the acting out of the ideas that come to him when he is in a state of excitement. In full-blown delinquency it is difficult for us as observers, because what meets us is the child's acute need for the strict father, who will protect mother when she is found. The strict father that the child evokes may also be loving, but he must first be strict and strong. Only when the strict and strong father figure is in evidence can the child regain his primitive love impulses, his sense of guilt, and his wish to mend. Unless he gets into trouble, the delinquent can only become progressively more and more inhibited in love, and consequently more and more depressed and depersonalised, and eventually unable to feel the reality of things at all, except the reality of violence.

Delinquency indicates that some hope remains. You will see that it is not *necessarily* an illness of the child when he behaves antisocially, and antisocial behaviour is at times no more than an S.O.S. for control by strong, loving, confident people. Most delinquents are to some extent ill, however, and the word illness becomes appropriate through the fact that in many cases the sense of security did not come into the child's life early enough to be incorporated into his beliefs. While under strong management, an antisocial child may seem to be all right; but give him freedom and he soon feels the threat of madness. So he offends against society (without knowing what he is doing) in order to re-establish control from outside.

The normal child, helped in the initial stages by his own home, grows a capacity to control himself. He develops what is some-times called an 'internal environment', with a tendency to find good surroundings. The antisocial, ill child, not having had the chance to grow a good 'internal environment', absolutely needs control from without if he is to be happy at all, and if he is to be able to play or work. In between these two extremes of normal and antisocial ill children are children who can still achieve a belief in stability if a continuous experience of control by loving persons can be given them over a period of years. A child of 6 or 7 stands a much better chance of getting help in this way than one of 10 or 11.

In the war many of us had experience of just this belated pro-vision of a stable environment for children deprived of home life, in the hostels for evacuated children, especially for those who were difficult to billet. These have been under the Ministry of Health. In the war years, children with antisocial tendencies were treated as ill. I am glad to say these hostels are not all closing down now, and they have been transferred to the care of the Ministry of Education. These hostels do prophylactic work for the Home Office. They can treat delinquency *as an illness* the more easily because most of the children have not yet come before the Juvenile Courts. Here, surely, is the place for the treatment of delinquency as an illness of the individual, and here, surely, is the place for research, and opportunity to gain experience. We all know the fine work done in some approved schools, but the fact that most of the children in them have been convicted in a court makes for difficulty.

In these hostels, sometimes called boarding-homes for mal-adjusted children, there is an opportunity for those who see anti-social behaviour as the S.O.S. of an ill child to play their part, and so to learn. Each hostel or group of hostels under the Ministry of Health in wartime had a committee of management, and in the group with which I was connected the lay committee really interested itself in, and took responsibility for, the details of the hostel work. Surely many magistrates could be elected to such committees, and so get into close contact with the actual management of children who have not yet come before the Juvenile Courts. It is not enough to visit approved schools or hostels, or to hear people talking. The only interesting way is to take some responsibility, even if indirectly, by intelligently supporting those who manage boys and girls who tend towards antisocial behaviour.

In such hostels for the so-called maladjusted one is free to work with a therapeutic aim, and this makes a lot of difference. Failures will eventually come to the courts, but successes become citizens.

Of course, the work done in these small and properly staffed hostels is done by the wardens. These wardens have to start as the right kind, but they need education and opportunities for discussing their work as they go along, and also they need someone in between them and that impersonal thing called a ministry. In the scheme I knew, this was the job of the psychiatric social worker and the psychiatrist. These in turn needed a committee which could grow with the scheme, and profit from experience. It is on this sort of committee that a magistrate could profitably serve.

Now to return to the theme of children deprived of home life. Apart from being neglected (in which case they reach the Juvenile Courts as delinquents) they can be dealt with in two ways. They can be given personal psychotherapy, or they can be provided with a strong stable environment with personal care and love, and gradually increasing doses of freedom. As a matter of fact, without this latter the former (personal psychotherapy) is not likely to succeed. And with the provision of a suitable home-substitute, psychotherapy may become unnecessary, which is fortunate because it is practically never available. It will be years before properly-trained psychoanalysts are available even in moderate numbers for giving the personal treatments that are so urgently needed in many cases.

Personal psychotherapy is directed towards enabling the child to complete his or her emotional development. This means many things, including establishing a good capacity for feeling the reality of real things, both external and internal, and establishing the integration of the individual personality. Full emotional development means this and more. After these primitive things, there follow the first feelings of concern and guilt, and the early impulses to make reparation. And in the family itself there are the first triangular situations, and all the complex interpersonal relationships that belong to life at home.

Further, if this all goes well, and if the child becomes able to manage himself and his relationship to grown-ups and to other children, he still has to begin dealing with complications, such as a mother who is depressed, a father with maniacal episodes, a brother with a cruel streak, a sister with fits. The more we think of these things the more we understand why infants and little children absolutely need the background of their own family, and if possible a stability of physical surroundings as well; and from such considerations we see that children deprived of home life must either be provided with something personal and stable when they are yet young enough to make use of it to some extent, or else they must force us later to provide stability in the shape of an approved school, or, in the last resort, four walls in the shape of a prison cell.

14 *The antisocial tendency*

(A paper read before the British Psycho-Analytical Society, 20 June, 1956)

The antisocial tendency provides psychoanalysis with some awkward problems, problems of a practical as well as a theoretical nature. Freud, through his introduction to Aichhorn's *Wayward Youth*, showed that psychoanalysis not only contributes to the understanding of delinquency, but it is also enriched by an understanding of the work of those who cope with delinquents.

I have chosen to discuss the antisocial tendency, not delinquency. The reason is that the organized antisocial defence is overloaded with secondary gain and social reactions which make it difficult for the investigator to get to its core. By contrast the antisocial tendency can be studied as it appears in the normal or near-normal child, where it is related to the difficulties that are inherent in emotional development.

I will start with two simple references to clinical material:

> For my first child analysis I chose a delinquent. This boy attended regularly for a year and the treatment stopped because of the disturbance that the boy caused in the clinic. I could say that the analysis was going well, and its cessation caused distress both to the boy and to myself in spite of the fact that on several occasions I got badly bitten on the buttocks. The boy got out on the roof and also he spilt so much water that the basement became flooded. He broke into my locked car and drove it away in bottom gear on the self-starter. The clinic ordered termination of the treatment for the sake of the other patients. He went to an approved school.
>
> I may say that he is now 35, and he has been able to earn his living in a job that caters for his restlessness. He is married, with several children. Nevertheless I am afraid to follow up his case for fear that I should become involved again with a

psychopath, and I prefer that society should continue to take the burden of his management.

It can easily be seen that the treatment for this boy should have been not psychoanalysis but placement. Psychoanalysis only made sense if added after placement. Since this time I have watched analysts of all kinds fail in the psychoanalysis of antisocial children.

By contrast, the following story brings out the fact that an antisocial tendency may sometimes be treated very easily if the treatment be adjunctive to specialized environmental care.

I was asked by a friend to discuss the case of her son, the eldest of a family of four. She could not bring John to me in an open way because of her husband who objects to psychology on religious grounds. All she could do was to have a talk with me about the boy's compulsion to steal, which was developing into something quite serious; he was stealing in a big way from shops as well as at home. It was not possible for practical reasons to arrange for anything else but for the mother and myself to have a quick meal together in a restaurant, in the course of which she told me about the troubles and asked me for advice. There was nothing for me to do unless I could do it then and there. I therefore explained the meaning of the stealing and suggested that she should find a good moment in her relationship with the boy and make an interpretation to him. It appeared that she and John had a good relationship with each other for a few moments each evening after he had gone to bed; usually at such a time he would discuss the stars and the moon. This moment could be used.

I said: 'Why not tell him that you know that when he steals he is not wanting the things that he steals but he is looking for something that he has a right to: that he is making a claim on his mother and father because he feels deprived of their love.' I told her to use language which he could understand. I may say that I knew enough of this family, in which both the parents are musicians, to see how it was that this boy had become to some extent a deprived child, although he has a good home.

Some time later I had a letter telling me that she had done what I suggested. She wrote: 'I told him that what he really wanted when he stole money and food and things was his mum;

and I must say I didn't really expect him to understand, but he did seem to. I asked him if he thought we didn't love him because he was so naughty sometimes, and he said right out that he didn't think we did, much. Poor little scrap! I felt so awful, I can't tell you. So I told him never, never to doubt it again and if he ever did feel doubtful to remind me to tell him again. But of course I shan't need reminding for a long time, it's been such a shock. One seems to need these shocks. So I'm being a lot more demonstrative to try and keep him from being doubtful any more. And up to now there's been absolutely no more stealing.'

The mother had had a talk with the form teacher and had explained to her that the boy was in need of love and appreciation, and had gained her co-operation although the boy gives a lot of trouble at school.

Now after eight months it is possible to report that there has been no return of stealing, and the relationship between the boy and his family has very much improved.

In considering this case it must be remembered that I had known the mother very well during her adolescence and to some extent had seen her through an antisocial phase of her own. She was the eldest in a large family. She had a very good home but very strong discipline was exerted by the father, especially at the time when she was a small child. What I did therefore had the effect of a double therapy, enabling this young woman to get insight into her own difficulties through the help that she was able to give to her son. When we are able to help parents to help their children we do in fact help them about themselves.

(In another paper I propose to give clinical examples illustrating the management of children with antisocial tendency; here I do no more than attempt a brief statement of the basis of my personal attitude to the clinical problem.)

Nature of antisocial tendency

The antisocial tendency *is not a diagnosis*. It does not compare directly with other diagnostic terms such as neurosis and psychosis. The antisocial tendency may be found in a normal individual, or in one that is neurotic or psychotic.

For the sake of simplicity I will refer only to children, but the antisocial tendency may be found at all ages. The various terms in use in Great Britain may be brought together in the following way:

A child becomes a *deprived child* when deprived of certain essential features of home life. Some degree of what might be called the 'deprived complex' becomes manifest. *Antisocial behaviour* will be manifest at home or in a wider sphere. On account of *the antisocial tendency* the child may eventually need to be *deemed maladjusted,* and to receive treatment in a *hostel for maladjusted children,* or may be brought before the courts as *beyond control.* The child, now *a delinquent,* may then become *a probationer* under a court order, or may be sent to *an approved school.* If the home ceases to function in an important respect the child may be taken over by the Children's Committee (under the Children Act, 1948) and be given *'care and protection'.* If possible a foster home will be found. Should these measures fail the young adult may be said to have become a *psychopath* and may be sent by the courts to a *Borstal* or to prison. There may be an established tendency to repeat crimes for which we use the term *recidivism.*

All this makes no comment on the individual's psychiatric diagnosis.

The antisocial tendency is characterized by an *element in it which compels the environment to be important.* The patient through unconscious drives compels someone to attend to management. It is the task of the therapist to become involved in this the patient's unconscious drive, and the work is done by the therapist in terms of management, tolerance, and understanding.

The antisocial tendency implies hope. Lack of hope is the basic feature of the deprived child who, of course, is not all the time being antisocial. In the period of hope the child manifests an antisocial tendency. This may be awkward for society, and for you if it is your bicycle that is stolen, but those who are not personally involved can see the hope that underlies the compulsion to steal. Perhaps one of the reasons why we tend to leave the therapy of the delinquent to others is that we dislike being stolen from?

The understanding that the antisocial act is an expression of hope is vital in the treatment of children who show the antisocial tendency. Over and over again one sees the moment of hope wasted, or withered, because of mismanagement or intolerance. This is another way of saying that the treatment of the antisocial tendency is not psychoanalysis but management, a going to meet and match the moment of hope.

There is a direct relationship between the antisocial tendency and deprivation. This has long been known by specialists in the field, but it is largely due to John Bowlby that there is now a widespread recognition of the relationship that exists between the antisocial tendency in individuals and emotional deprivation, typically in the period of late infancy and the early toddler stage, round about the age of one and two years.

When there is an antisocial tendency *there has been a true deprivation* (not a simple privation); that is to say, there has been a loss of something good that has been positive in the child's experience up to a certain date,[1] and that has been withdrawn; the withdrawal has extended over a period of time longer than that over which the child can keep the memory of the experience alive. The comprehensive statement of deprivation is one that includes both the early and the late, both the pinpoint trauma and the sustained traumatic condition and also both the near normal and the clearly abnormal.

Note

In a statement in my own language of Klein's depressive position, I have tried to make clear the intimate relationship that exists between Klein's concept and Bowlby's emphasis on deprivation. Bowlby's three stages of the clinical reaction of a child of two years who goes to hospital can be given a theoretical formulation in terms of the gradual loss of hope because of the death of the internal object or introjected version of the external object that is lost. What can be further discussed is the relative importance of death of the internal object through anger and contact of 'good objects' with hate products within the psyche, and ego maturity or immaturity in so far as this affects the capacity to keep alive a memory.

Bowlby needs Klein's intricate statement that is built round the

[1] This idea seems to be implied in Bowlby's *Maternal Care and Mental Health*, page 47, where he compares his observations with those of others and suggests that the different results are explained according to the age of a child at the time of deprivation.

understanding of melancholia, and that derives from Freud and Abraham,[2] but it is also true that psychoanalysis needs Bowlby's emphasis on deprivation, if psychoanalysis is ever to come to terms with this special subject of the antisocial tendency.

There are always two trends in the antisocial tendency although the accent is sometimes more on one than on the other. One trend is represented typically in stealing, and the other in destructiveness. By *one* trend the child is looking for something, somewhere, and failing to find it seeks it elsewhere, when hopeful. By the *other* the child is seeking that amount of environmental stability which will stand the strain resulting from impulsive behaviour. This is a search for an environmental provision that has been lost, a human attitude which, because it can be relied on, gives freedom to the individual to move and to act and to get excited.

It is particularly because of the second of these trends that the child provokes total environmental reactions, as if seeking an ever-widening frame, a circle which had as its first example the mother's arms or the mother's body. One can discern a series – the mother's body, the mother's arms, the parental relationship, the home, the family including cousins and near relations, the school, the locality with its police-stations, the country with its laws.

In examining the near-normal and (in terms of individual development) the early roots of the antisocial tendency I wish to keep in mind all the time these two trends: object-seeking and destruction.

Stealing

Stealing is at the centre of the antisocial tendency, with the associated lying.

The child who steals an object is not looking for *the object stolen but seeks the mother over whom he or she has rights.* These rights derive from the fact that (from the child's point of view) the mother was created by the child. The mother met the child's primary creativity, and so became the object that the child was ready to find. (The child could not have created the mother; also the mother's meaning for the child depends on the child's creativity.)

[2]See Chapter 15 in this volume. Eds.

Is it possible to join up the two trends, the stealing and the destruction, the object-seeking and that which provokes, the libidinal and the aggressive compulsions? I suggest that the union of the two trends is in the child and that it represents *a tendency towards self-cure*, cure of a de-fusion of instincts.

When there is at the time of the original deprivation some fusion of aggressive (or motility) roots with the libidinal the child claims the mother by a mixture of stealing and hurting and messing, according to the specific details of that child's emotional developmental state. When there is less fusion the child's object-seeking and aggression are more separated off from each other, and there is a greater degree of dissociation in the child. This leads to the proposition that *the nuisance value of the antisocial child is an essential feature*, and is also, at its best, *a favourable feature* indicating again a potentiality for recovery of lost fusion of the libidinal and motility drives.

In ordinary infant care the mother is constantly dealing with the nuisance value of her infant. For instance, a baby commonly passes water on the mother's lap while feeding at the breast. At a later date this appears as a momentary regression in sleep or at the moment of waking and bed-wetting results. Any exaggeration of the nuisance value of an infant may indicate the existence of a degree of deprivation and antisocial tendency.

The manifestation of the antisocial tendency includes stealing and lying, incontinence and the making of a mess generally. Although each symptom has its specific meaning and value, the common factor for my purpose in my attempt to describe the antisocial tendency is *the nuisance value of the symptoms*. This nuisance value is exploited by the child, and is not a chance affair. Much of the motivation is unconscious, but not necessarily all.

First signs of antisocial tendency

I suggest that the first signs of deprivation are so common that they pass for normal; take for example the imperious behaviour which most parents meet with a mixture of submission and reaction. *This is not infantile omnipotence*, which is a matter of psychic reality, not of behaviour.

A very common antisocial symptom is greediness, with the closely related inhibition of appetite. If we study greediness we shall find the deprived complex. In other words, if an infant is greedy there is some degree of deprivation and some compulsion towards seeking for a therapy in respect of this deprivation through the environment. The fact that the mother is herself willing to cater for the infant's greediness makes for therapeutic success in the vast majority of cases in which this compulsion can be observed. Greediness in an infant is not the same as greed. The word greed is used in the theoretical statement of the tremendous instinctual claims than an infant makes on the mother at the beginning, that is to say, at the time when the infant is only starting to allow the mother a separate existence, at the first acceptance of the Reality Principle.

In parenthesis, it is sometimes said that a mother must fail in her adaptation to her infant's needs. Is this not a mistaken idea based on a consideration of id needs and a neglect of the needs of the ego? A mother must fail in satisfying instinctual demands, but she may completely succeed in not 'letting the infant down', *in catering for ego needs*, until such a time as the infant may have an introjected ego-supportive mother, and may be old enough to maintain this introjection in spite of failures of ego support in the actual environment.

The (pre-ruth) primitive love impulse is not the same as ruthless greediness. In the process of the development of an infant the primitive love impulse and greediness are separated by the mother's adaptation. The mother necessarily fails to maintain a high degree of adaptation to id needs and to some extent therefore every infant may be deprived, but is able to get the mother to cure this sub-deprived state by her meeting the greediness and messiness, etc., these being symptoms of deprivation. The greediness is part of the infant's compulsion to seek for a cure from the mother who caused the deprivation. This greediness is anti-social; it is the precursor of stealing, and it can be met and cured by the mother's therapeutic adaptation, so easily mistaken for spoiling. It should be said, however, that whatever the mother does, this does not annul the fact that the mother first failed in her adaptation to her infant's ego needs. The mother is usually able to meet the compulsive claims of the infant, and so to do a successful *therapy* of the deprived complex which is near its point of origin. She gets near to a cure because she enables the infant's hate to be expressed while she, the therapist, is in fact the depriving mother.

It will be noted that whereas the infant is under no obligation to the mother in respect of her meeting the primitive love impulse, there is some feeling of obligation as the result of the mother's therapy, that is to say her willingness to meet the claims arising out of frustration, claims that begin to have a nuisance value. Therapy by the mother may cure, but this is not mother-love.

This way of looking at the mother's indulgence of her infant involves a more complex statement of mothering than is usually acceptable. Mother-love is often thought of in terms of this indulgence, which in fact is a *therapy in respect of a failure of mother-love*. It is a therapy, a second chance given to mothers who cannot always be expected to succeed in their initial most delicate task of primary love. If a mother does this therapy as a reaction formation arising out of her own complexes, then what she does is called spoiling. In so far as she is able to do it because she sees the necessity for the child's claims to be met, and for the child's compulsive greediness to be indulged, then it is a therapy that is usually successful. Not only the mother, but the father, and indeed the family, may be involved.

Clinically, there is an awkward borderline between the mother's therapy which is successful and that which is unsuccessful. Often we watch a mother spoiling an infant and yet this therapy will not be successful, the initial deprivation having been too severe for mending 'by first intention' (to borrow a term from the surgery of wounds).

Just as greediness may be a manifestation of the reaction to deprivation and of an antisocial tendency, so may messiness and wetting and compulsive destructiveness. All these manifestations are closely interrelated. In bed-wetting, which is so common a complaint, the accent is on regression at the moment of the dream, or on the antisocial compulsion to claim the right to wet on mother's body.

In a more complete study of stealing I would need to refer to the compulsion to go out and buy something, which is a common manifestation of the antisocial tendency that we meet in our psychoanalytic patients. It is possible to do a long and interesting analysis of a patient without affecting this sort of symptom, which belongs not to the patient's neurotic or psychotic defences but which does belong to the antisocial tendency, that which is a reaction to deprivation of a special kind and that took place at a special time. From this it will be clear that birthday presents and pocket money absorb some of the antisocial tendency that is to be normally expected.

In the same category as the shopping expedition we find, clinically, a 'going out', without aim, *truancy*, a centrifugal tendency that replaces the centripetal gesture which is implicit in thieving.

The original loss

There is one special point that I wish to make. At the basis of the antisocial tendency is a good early experience that has been lost. Surely, *it is an essential feature that the infant has reached to a capacity to perceive that the cause of the disaster lies in an environmental failure.* Correct knowledge that the cause of the depression or disintegration is an external one, and not an internal one, is responsible for the personality distortion and for the urge to seek for a cure by new environmental provision. The state of ego maturity enabling perception of this kind determines the development of an antisocial tendency instead of a psychotic illness. A great number of antisocial compulsions present and become successfully treated in the early stages by the parents. Antisocial children, however, are constantly pressing for this cure by environmental provision (unconsciously, or by unconscious motivation) but are unable to make use of it.

It would appear that the time of the original deprivation is during the period when in the infant or small child the ego is in process of achieving fusion of the libidinal and aggressive (or motility) id roots. In the hopeful moment the child:

Perceives a new setting that has some elements of reliability.
Experiences a drive that could be called object-seeking.
Recognizes the fact that ruthlessness is about to become a feature and so
Stirs up the immediate environment in an effort to make it alert to danger, and organized to tolerate nuisance.
If the situation holds, the environment must be tested and retested in its capacity to stand the aggression, to prevent or repair the destruction, to tolerate the nuisance, to recognize the

positive element in the antisocial tendency, to provide and preserve the object that is to be sought and found.

In a favourable case, when there is not too much madness or unconscious compulsion or paranoid organization, etc., the favourable conditions may in the course of time enable the child to find and love a person, instead of continuing the search through laying claims on substitute objects that had lost their symbolic value.

In the next stage the child needs to be able to experience despair in a relationship, instead of hope alone. Beyond this is the real possibility of a life for the child. When the wardens and staff of a hostel carry a child through all the processes *they have done a therapy that is surely comparable to analytic work.*

Commonly, parents do this complete job with one of their own children. But many parents who are well able to bring up normal children are not able to succeed with one of their children who happens to manifest an antisocial tendency.

In this statement I have deliberately omitted references to the relationship of the antisocial tendency to:

Acting out.
Masturbation.
Pathological super-ego, unconscious guilt.
Stages of libidinal development.
Repetition compulsion.
Regression to pre-concern.
Paranoid defence.
Sex-linkage in respect of symptomatology.

Treatment

Briefly, the treatment of the antisocial tendency is not psycho-analysis. It is the provision of child care which can be redis-covered by the child, and into which the child can experiment again with the id impulses, and which can be tested. It is the stability of the new environmental provision which gives the therapeutics. Id impulses must be experienced, if they are to make sense, in a framework of ego relatedness, and when the patient is a deprived child ego relatedness must derive support from the therapist's side of the relationship. According to the theory put forward in this paper it is the environment that must give new opportunity for ego relatedness since the child has perceived that it was an environmental failure in ego support that originally led to the antisocial tendency.

If the child is in analysis, the analyst must either allow the weight of the transference to develop outside the analysis, or else must expect the antisocial tendency to develop full strength in the analytic situation, and must be prepared to bear the brunt.

15   The psychology of separation

(Written for social workers in March, 1958)

A great deal has been written recently on the subject of separation and its effects. The effects can be stated in terms of clinical findings, and there is now considerable agreement as to what may be expected when there is a separation of the infant or small child from the parent figure over a period of time which is too long. It is established that there is a relationship between the antisocial tendency and deprivation.

In what follows an attempt will be made to study the psychology of reaction to loss, using the great enrichment of our understanding which dates from Freud's 'Mourning and Melancholia', which in itself was influenced by Karl Abraham's ideas.

There are certain words which need to be related to each other if there is to be a full understanding of the psychology of separation anxiety. It is important to attempt to relate reaction to loss with weaning, with grief, with mourning, and with depression

The first principle which those who are working with deprived children need as a theoretical basis for their work is that illness results not from loss itself but from the occurrence of loss at a stage in the child's or infant's emotional development when a mature reaction to loss cannot take place. The immature ego cannot mourn. It is necessary therefore to base whatever has to be said about deprivation and separation anxiety on an understanding of the psychology of mourning.

Psychology of mourning

Mourning in itself indicates maturity in the individual. The mechanism of mourning is complex and includes the following: an individual subjected to loss of an object introjects the object and the object is subjected to hate within the ego. Clinically there is a variable deadness of the introjected object according to whether at one particular moment this object is more hated or more loved. In the course of mourning the individual may be temporarily happy. It is as if the object has come alive because it has come alive within the individual, but there is more hate due and sooner or later depression returns, sometimes without obvious cause and sometimes on account of chance events or anniversaries which recall the relationship with the object and re-emphasize the failure of the object due to its having disappeared. In the course of time in health the internalized object begins to be free from hate which at first is so powerful. In time the individual recovers the capacity for happiness in spite of loss of the object and because of its having come alive again within the ego of the individual.

It is not possible for so complex a process to be followed by an infant who has not reached a certain stage of maturity ; also even for the individual who has reached that stage certain conditions are necessary for the working-through of the mourning process. The environment must remain supportive over a period of time while the working-through takes place and also the individual must be free from the sort of attitude which makes sadness impossible. Also individuals who have reached a capacity for mourning can be hindered from a working-through of the processes by a starvation of intellectual understanding, as for instance when in a child's life there is a conspiracy of silence about a death. In such a case simple information in regard to fact can sometimes make a child able to go through the process of mourning, the alternative being confusion. This is the same subject as that of the giving of information about adoption.

It has usefully been pointed out that some of the hate of the lost object may be conscious, but it must be expected that there is more than is available. No doubt it is again a sign of health when this hate is to some extent conscious and the ambivalence towards the lost object is to some extent conscious.

On the basis of this brief statement of the psychology of mourning it is possible to look at the whole subject of deprivation and to see that what the social worker is dealing with is the effect of loss which is occurring or which has occurred and which is beyond the capacity of the immature ego of the individual to deal with in a mature way, that is to say, by the mourning process. The social worker requires a diagnosis. By this I mean that the social worker needs to be able to understand what was the stage of emotional development of the infant or child when loss occurred, so that the type of reaction to loss may be assessed. Obviously where the child is near to a capacity for mourning then there is more hope that the child will be able to be helped even though there may be severe clinical illness. On the other hand where very primitive mechanisms have been invoked the social worker may have to recognize an essential limitation in regard to the help that can be given.

This is not exactly the place for an enumeration of the reactions to loss which are primitive and which indicate a maturity which is insufficient for mourning to take place. Examples may be given, however. It is possible sometimes to demonstrate that the loss of the breast and the mother at the same time may result in a state of affairs in which the child loses not only the object but also the apparatus for using the object, that is to say the mouth. The loss may go deeper and involve the whole creative capacity of the individual so that there is not so much a hopelessness about rediscovery of the object as a hopelessness based on an incapacity to go out to find an object.

In between the extremes of the very primitive reactions to loss and mourning there are all degrees of tantalizing communication failures. In this area there is to be observed clinically the whole symptomatology of the antisocial tendency and here stealing appears as a sign of hope, perhaps quite temporary, but positive while it lasts, and before there is a reversion to hopelessness. In the midway between the two extremes described there is a type of reaction to loss which indicates an undoing of what Melanie Klein calls the establishment of the depressive position in emotional development. When things go well, the object which is the mother or mother-figure remains over a period of time while the infant comes to a full recognition of the object at the moment of instinctual experience as a part of the mother who is constantly present. In this phase there is a gradual building-up of a sense of concern in the individual. The loss of the mother during this phase leads to a reversal of the process. The mother not being there when the infant feels concerned leads to an undoing of the integrating process, so that the instinctual life becomes either inhibited or dissociated from the general relationship of the child to the child care which is provided. The sense of concern in such a case becomes lost whereas when the object, that is to say, the mother, continues to exist and to play her part, the sense of concern gradually becomes strengthened. It is the flowering of this process which results in that mature thing which is called the capacity to mourn.

16 Aggression, guilt and reparation

(A talk given to the Progressive League, 8 May, 1960)

I wish to draw on my experience as a psychoanalyst to describe a theme which comes over and over again in analytic work and which is always of great importance. It has to do with one of the roots of constructive activity. It has to do with the relationship between construction and destruction. You may immediately recognize this theme as one which has been developed chiefly by Melanie Klein who has gathered together her ideas on the subject under the heading 'the depressive position in emotional develop-ment'. Whether this is a good name or not is beside the point. The main thing is that psychoanalytic theory evolves all the time and it was Mrs Klein who took up the destructiveness that there is in human nature and started to make sense of it in psychoanalytic terms. This was an important development that came in the decade after the First World War and many of us feel that our work could not have been done without this important addition to Freud's own statement of the emotional development of the human being. Melanie Klein's work extended Freud's own statement, and did not alter the analyst's way of working.

It might be thought that this subject belongs to the teaching of the psychoanalytic technique. If I judge the situation correctly you would not mind even this. I do believe, however, that the subject is of vital importance to all thinking people especially as it enriches our understanding of the meaning of the term 'a sense of guilt', by joining up the sense of guilt on the one hand to destruct-iveness and on the other hand to constructive activity.

It all sounds rather simple and obvious. Ideas of destroying an object turn up, a sense of guilt appears, and constructive work results. But what is found is very much more complex and it is important when attempting a comprehensive description to remember that it is an achievement in the emotional development of an individual when this simple sequence begins to make sense or to be a fact or to be significant.

It is characteristic of psychoanalysts that when they try to tackle a subject like this they always think in terms of *the developing individual*. This means going back very early and looking to see if the point of origin can be determined. Certainly it would be possible to think of earliest infancy as a state in which the individual has not a capacity for feeling guilty. Then one can say that at a later date we know that (in health) a sense of guilt can be felt, or experienced without perhaps being registered as such in consciousness. In between these two things is a period in which the capacity for a sense of guilt is in process of becoming established, and it is with this period that I am concerned in this paper.

It is not necessary to give ages and dates but I would say that parents can sometimes detect the beginnings of a sense of guilt before their infant is a year old, though no-one would think that before the age of 5 there has become firmly established in a child a technique for accepting full responsibility for destructive ideas. In dealing with this development we know we are talking about the whole of childhood and particularly about adolescence, and if we are talking about adolescence we are talking about adults because no adults are all the time adult. This is because people are not just their own age, they are to some extent every age, or no age.

In passing I would like to say that it seems to me that it is comparatively easy for us to get at the destructiveness that is in ourselves when this is linked with anger at frustration or hate of something we disapprove of or when it is a reaction to fear. The difficult thing is for each individual to take full responsibility for the destructiveness that is personal, and that inherently belongs to a relationship to an object that is felt to be good; in other words that is related to loving.

Integration is a word that comes in here because if one can conceive of a fully integrated person then that person takes full responsibility for *all* feelings and ideas that belong to being alive. By contrast it is a failure of integration when we need to find the things we disapprove of outside ourselves and do so at a price, this price being the loss of the destructiveness which really belongs to ourselves.

I am talking therefore about the development which has to take place in every individual of the capacity to take responsibility for the whole of that individual's feelings and ideas, the word 'health' being closely linked with the degree of integration which makes it possible for this to happen. One thing about a healthy person is that he or she does not have to use in a big way the technique of projection in order to cope with his or her own destructive impulses and thoughts.

You will understand that I am passing over the earliest stages, the things that one can call the primitive aspects of emotional development. Shall I say I am not talking about the first weeks or months. A breakdown in this area of basic emotional development leads to mental hospital illness, that is to say schizophrenia, with which I am not dealing in this lecture. In this paper I assume that in each case the parents have made the essential provision which has enabled the infant to start leading an individual existence. What I want to say could apply equally to the care of a normal child during a certain stage of development or to a phase in the treatment of a child or an adult, for in psychotherapy nothing really new ever happens; the best that can happen is that something that was not completed in an individual's development originally becomes to some extent completed at a later date, in the course of the treatment.

My intention now is to give you some examples from analytic treatments. I shall leave out everything except the details that are relevant to the idea I am trying to put forward.

Case 1

One example comes from the analysis of someone who is himself doing psychotherapy. He started off a session by telling me that he had been to see one of his own patients performing, that is to say he had gone outside the role of therapist dealing with the patient in the consulting room and had seen this patient at work. This work involved very quick movements and was highly skilled and the patient was very successful in this peculiar job in which he uses quick movements, which in the therapeutic hour make no sense but which move him round on the couch as if he were possessed. My patient (who is the therapist of this man) was doubtful about what he had done, whether it was good or not, although he felt that probably it was a good thing for him to see this man at work. He then made a reference to his own activities in the Easter holidays. He has a country house and he very much enjoys physical labour and all kinds of constructive activity, and he likes gadgets, which he really uses. He then went on to describe events in his home life. I need not pass these on with all their emotional colouring, but I will simply say that he returned to a theme which has been important in the recent analysis in which various kinds of engineering tools have played a large part. On his way to the analytic session he often stops and gazes at a machine tool in a shop window near my house. This has the most splendid teeth. This is my patient's way of getting at his oral aggression, the primitive love impulse with all its ruthlessness and destructiveness. We could call it eating. The trend in his treatment is towards this ruthlessness of primitive loving, and, as can be imagined, the resistance against getting to it is tremendous. (Incidentally this man knows the theory, and could give a good account of all these processes in an intellectual way, but he comes for postgraduate analysis because he needs to get truly in touch with his primitive impulses as a matter not of the mind but of instinctual experience and of bodily feeling.) There was much else in the hour's content, including a discussion of the question: can one eat one's cake and have it?

The only thing I want to pull out of this is the observation that when this new material came up relating to primitive love and to the destruction of the object *there had already been* some reference to constructive work. When I made the interpretation that the patient needed from me, about his destruction of me (eating) I could remind him of what he had said about construction. I could remind him that just as he saw his patient performing, and the performance made sense of the jerky movements, so I might have seen him working in his garden, using gadgets in order to improve the property. He could cut through walls and trees, and it was all enjoyed tremendously, but if this had come apart from the constructive aim it would have been a senseless maniacal episode. This is a regular feature in our work, and it is the theme of my talk this evening.

Perhaps it is true to say that human beings cannot tolerate the destructive aim in their very early loving. The idea of it can be tolerated however if the individual who is getting towards it has evidence of a constructive aim already at hand of which he or she can be reminded.

I am thinking here of the treatment of a woman. Early on in the treatment I made a mistake which nearly ended everything. I interpreted this very thing, oral sadism, the ruthless eating of the object belonging to primitive loving. I had plenty of evidence, and indeed I was right, but the interpretation was given 10 years too soon. I learned my lesson. In the long treatment that followed the patient re-organized herself and became a real and integrated person who could accept the truth about her primitive impulses. Eventually she became ready for this interpretation after 10 or 12 years of daily analysis.

Case II

A man patient came into my room and saw a tape-recorder that had been lent me. This gave him ideas, and he said as he lay down and as he gathered himself together for the work of the analytic hour: 'I would like to think that when I have finished treatment what has happened here with me will be of value to the world in some way or other.' I made a mental note that this remark *might* indicate that the patient was near to one of those bouts of destructiveness with which I had had to deal repeatedly since the treatment started two years ago. Before the end of the hour the patient had truly reached a new acquaintance with his envy of me for my being some good as an analyst. He had the impulse to thank me for being good, and for being able to do what he needed me to do. We had had all this before, but he was now more than he had been on previous occasions in touch with his destructive feelings towards what might be called a good object. When all this had been thoroughly established I reminded him of his hope, expressed as he came in and saw the tape-recorder, that his treatment might of itself prove valuable, something that would contribute in, to the general pool of human need. (It was not of course *necessary* for me to remind him of this because the important thing was what had happened, not the discussion of what had happened.)

When I linked these two things he said that this felt right, but how awful it would have been if I had interpreted on the basis of his first remark. He meant, if I had taken up his wish to be of use and told him that this indicated a wish to destroy. He had to reach to the destructive urge first, and he had to reach it in his own time and in his own way. No doubt it was his capacity to have an idea of ultimately contributing in that was making it possible for him to get into more intimate contact with his destructiveness. But constructive effort is false and worse than meaningless unless, as he said, he has first reached to the destruction. He felt that his work hitherto had been without proper foundation, and indeed (as he reminded me) it was for this that he came to me for treatment. Incidentally, he has done very good work, but always as he gets towards success he feels an increasing sense of futility and falseness, and a need to prove his worthlessness. This has been his life pattern.

Case III
A woman colleague is talking about a man patient. This man reaches to material which can properly be interpreted as an impulse to steal from the analyst. He in fact says to her, after experiencing a good piece of analytic work, 'I now find I hate you for your insight, the very thing I need of you; I have the impulse to steal from you whatever there is in you that makes you able to do this work.' Now, just before this he had said (in passing) how nice it would be to earn more money so as to be able to pay a higher fee. You will see the same thing here, a platform of generosity reached and used so that from it a glimpse might be gained of the envy, the stealing and the destructiveness of the good object, that which underlies the generosity, and which belongs to primitive loving.

Case IV
The next snippet comes out of a long case description of an adolescent girl who is having treatment from someone who is at the same time looking after the child in her own home, along with her own children. This arrangement has advantages and disadvantages.

The girl has been severely ill and, at the time of the incident I shall recount, she was emerging from a long period of regression to dependence and to an infantile state. It could be said that now the girl is not regressed in her relation to the home and the family but is still in a very special state in the limited area of the treatment sessions. These occur at a set time in the evenings.

A time came when this girl expressed the very deepest hate of Mrs X (who is both caring for her and doing her treatment). All was well in the rest of the 24 hours but in the treatment area Mrs

X was destroyed utterly and repeatedly. It is difficult to convey the degree of her hate of Mrs X, the therapist, and in fact her annihilation of her. Here it was not a case of the therapist going out to see the patient at work, for Mrs X had the girl in her care all the time and there were two separate relationships going on between them simultaneously. In the day all sorts of new things began to happen, the girl began to want to help to clean the house, to polish the furniture, to be of use. This helping was absolutely new and had never been a feature in this girl's personal pattern in her own home, even before she became acutely ill.

I should think that there must be few adolescents who have in fact done so little at home to help, and she had not even helped with the washing-up. So this helping was quite a new feature and it happened silently (so to speak) alongside the utter destructiveness that the child began to find in the primitive aspects of her loving which she reached in her relation to the therapist in the therapy sessions.

You see the same idea repeating itself here. Naturally the fact that the patient was becoming conscious of the destructiveness made possible the constructive activity which appeared in the day. But it is the other way round that I want you to see just now. The constructive and creative experiences were making it possible for the child to get to the experience of her destructiveness.

You will observe a corollary which is that the patient needs opportunity for contributing in, and this is where my subject links up with ordinary living. Opportunity for creative activity, for imaginative playing, and for constructive working, this is just what we try to give equally for everyone. I shall refer to this again.

I now want to try to put together the ideas that I have put forward in the form of case material.

We are dealing with one aspect of the sense of guilt. It comes from toleration of one's destructive impulses in primitive loving. Toleration of one's destructive impulses results in a new thing, the capacity to enjoy ideas, even with destruction in them, and the bodily excitements that belong to them, or that they belong to. This development gives elbow room for the experience of concern, which is the basis for everything constructive.

You will see that various pairs of words can be used according to the stage of emotional development that is being described.

annihilation	creating
destruction	re-creating
hating	reinforced loving
being cruel	being tender
soiling	cleaning
damaging	mending
and so on.	

Let me put my thesis this way. If you like, you can look at the way a person mends, and you can cleverly say: 'Aha, that means unconscious destruction.' But the world is not helped on much if you do this. Alternatively you may see in someone's mending that he or she is building up a self strength which makes possible a toleration of the destructiveness that belongs to that person's nature. Say you somehow block the mending, then to some extent that person becomes unable to take responsibility for his or her destructive urges, and clinically the result is either depression or else a search for relief by the discovery of destructiveness else-where, that is to say by the mechanism of projection.

To end this brief exposition of a vast subject let me list some of the everyday applications of the work that underlies what I have said:

(a) Opportunity for contributing in, in some way or other, helps each one of us to accept the destructiveness that is part of ourselves, basic, and belonging to loving, which is eating.

(b) Providing opportunity, being perceptive when people have constructive moments, does not necessarily work, and we can see why this should be so.

(c) We give opportunity to someone for contributing in, and we may get three results:

(1) That is just what was needed.
(2) The opportunity is falsely used, and eventually the constructive activities become withdrawn because they are felt to be false.
(3) Opportunity offered to someone who is unable to get to the personal destructiveness is felt as a reproach and the result is disastrous clinically.

(d) We may use the ideas I have discussed in order to enjoy some intellectual understanding of the way a sense of guilt works, being at the point of transformation of destructiveness into constructiveness. (It must be pointed out here that ordinarily the sense of guilt that I am talking about is silent, not conscious. It is a potential sense of guilt, annulled by the constructive activities. Clinical sense of guilt that is a conscious burden is rather another matter.)

(e) From this we reach some understanding of the compulsive destructiveness which may appear anywhere, but which is a special problem of adolescence, and a regular feature of the antisocial tendency. Destructiveness, though compulsive and spoof, is more honest than constructiveness when the latter is not properly founded on the sense of guilt that arises out of acceptance of one's personal destructive urges directed towards the object that is felt to be good.

(f) These matters relate to the tremendously important things that are going on in rather an obscure fashion when a mother and a father are giving their new baby a good start in life.

(g) Finally: we arrive at the fascinating and philosophic question: can one eat one's cake and have it?

17 *Struggling through the doldrums*

(Based on a lecture given to the senior staff of the London County Council Children's Department, February, 1961. Revised and published in 1963.)

The present world-wide interest in adolescence and in the problems of the adolescent indicates the special conditions of the times we live in. If we wish to explore this area of psychology we may as well first ask ourselves, do adolescent boys and girls wish to be understood? The answer, I think, is no. In fact adults should hide among themselves what they come to understand of adolescence. It would be absurd to write a book for adolescents on the subject of adolescence, because this period of life is one which must be lived. It is essentially a time of personal discovery. Each individual is engaged in a living experience, a problem of existing, and of the establishment of an identity.

In fact there exists only one real cure for adolescence: maturation. This and the passage of time do, in the end, result in the emergence of the adult person. The process cannot be hurried up, though indeed it can be broken into and destroyed by clumsy handling; or it can wither up from within when there is psychiatric illness in the individual. We do sometimes need to be reminded that although adolescence is something we always have with us, each adolescent boy or girl grows up in the course of a few years into an adult. Irritation with the phenomena of adolescence can easily be evoked by careless reference to adolescence as a permanent problem, forgetting that each individual is in the process of becoming a responsible society-minded adult.

If we examine the maturational processes we see that the boy or girl in this age phase is having to deal with important changes associated with puberty. A boy or girl develops sexual capacity and secondary sexual manifestations appear. The way in which the individual copes with these changes and deals with the anxieties arising out of them is based, to quite a large extent, on the pattern organized in early childhood when there was a similar phase of rapid emotional and physical growth. In this earlier phase those who were well cared for and who were healthy did develop what is called the Oedipus complex, that is to say, the capacity to be able to deal with triangular relationships – to accept the full force of the capacity to love and the complications that result.

The healthy child comes to adolescence already equipped with a personal method for dealing with new feelings, for tolerating distress, and for warding off situations which involve intolerable anxiety. Also derived from the experiences of each adolescent's early infancy and childhood are certain inherited and acquired personal characteristics and tendencies, residual illness patterns associated with failure rather than success in the management of feelings that belong to infancy and the toddler age. Patterns which have been formed in relation to infantile and early childhood experiences necessarily include a great deal that is unconscious and there is also much that the child does not know because it has not yet been experienced.

Always the question arises, how shall this personality organization meet the new instinctual capacity? How will the pubertal changes be accommodated in the personality pattern that is specific to the boy or girl in question? Moreover, how shall each one deal with something that really is new: the power to destroy and even to kill, a power which did not complicate the feelings of hatred that were experienced at the toddler age?

The part played by the environment is immensely significant at this stage, so much so that in a descriptive account it is best to assume the continued existence and interest of the child's own father and mother and the wider family organization. A great deal of the work of a psychiatrist concerns the troubles that arise relative to environmental failures at some stage or other, and this fact only emphasizes the vital importance of the environment and of the family setting. In the case of the vast majority of adolescents the environment can be assumed to be good enough. Most adolescents do in fact achieve adult maturity, even if in the process they give their parents headaches. But even in the best circumstances where the environment facilitates the maturational processes the individual adolescent still has many personal problems and many difficult phases to negotiate.

The isolation of the individual

The adolescent is essentially an isolate. It is from a position of isolation that he or she launches out into what may result in relationships. It is the individual relationships, one by one, that eventually lead to socialization. The adolescent is repeating an essential phase of infancy, for the infant too is an isolate, at least until he or she has been able to establish the capacity for relating to objects that are outside magical control. The infant becomes able to recognize and to welcome the existence of objects that are not part of the infant, but this is an achievement. The adolescent repeats this struggle.

It is as if the adolescent must start from a state of isolation. Relationships must first be tried out on subjective objects. In this way we sometimes see young adolescents as collections of isolates, attempting at the same time to form an aggregate through the adoption of mutual ideas, ideals, and ways of dressing and living. It is as if they can become grouped on account of their mutual interests and concerns. They can of course achieve a group if they are attacked as a group, but this is a grouping that is reactive, and after the end of the persecution the grouping ceases. It is therefore not satisfactory because it has no dynamic from within.

The sexual experiences of the younger adolescents are coloured by this phenomenon of isolation, and by the need that exists for association on the basis of mutual interest. Also is it not true that the boy or girl at this stage does not yet know whether he or she will be homosexual, heterosexual, or just narcissistic? It can indeed be painful for a young adolescent to realize that he only loves himself, and this can be worse for a boy than for a girl because society tolerates narcissistic elements in a girl but is impatient of self love in a boy. Often there is a long period of uncertainty in the boy or girl as to whether a sex urge will turn up at all.

Urgent masturbatory activity may be at this stage a repeated getting rid of sex rather than a form of sex experience. That is to say, it may be a repeated attempt to deal with a purely physiological problem which becomes urgent before the full meaning of sex dawns. Indeed, compulsive heterosexual or homosexual activities may also serve the purpose of getting rid of sex tension at a time when there has not yet developed a capacity for union between whole human beings. Union between whole human beings is more likely to appear first in aim inhibited sex play or in affectionate behaviour with the accent on dependence or interdependence. Here again is a personal pattern waiting to join up with the new instinctual developments, but in the long meanwhile adolescents have to find relief from sex tension, so that compulsive masturbation is to be expected, and it may bother the young adolescent because of its senselessness.

It is not even necessarily pleasurable, and it produces its own complications. The investigator, of course, seldom gets to know the truth about these matters, which are very secret, and indeed a good motto for the investigator would be: whoever asks questions must expect to be told lies.

The time for adolescence

Is it not a sign of the health of society that teenagers are able to be adolescent at the right time, that is to say at the age that covers pubertal growth? Among primitive peoples the pubertal changes are either hidden under taboos or else the adolescent is turned into an adult in the space of a few weeks or months by certain rites and ordeals. At present in our society adults are being formed by natural processes out of adolescents who move forward because of growth tendencies. This may easily mean that the new adults of today have strength and stability and maturity.

Naturally, there must be a price to pay in toleration and patience; and also this development puts a new strain on society, for it is distressing for adults who have been themselves defrauded of adolescence to watch the boys and girls all round them in a state of florid adolescence.

For me there are three main social developments that, together, have altered the whole climate for adolescents.

Venereal disease no deterrent

Venereal disease is no longer a bogy. The spirochaete and the gonococcus are no longer (as they certainly were felt to be 50 years ago) agents of a punishing God. Now they can be dealt with by penicillin and by appropriate antibiotics. I remember very clearly a girl somewhere after the First World War. She told me that it was only the fear of venereal disease that had kept her from being a prostitute. She was horrified at the idea I put forward in a simple conversation that venereal disease might one day be preventable or curable. She said she could not imagine how she could have got through her adolescence (and she was only just coming through it) without this fear which she had used in order to keep straight. She is now the mother of a large family and you would call her a normal sort of person; but she had yet to engage in her adolescent struggle and the challenge of her own instincts. She had a difficult time. She did a bit of thieving, and lying, but she emerged an adult.

Contraception

The development of contraceptive techniques has given the adolescent the freedom to explore. This freedom is new, the freedom to find out about sexuality and sensuality when there is not only an absence of a wish for parenthood, but also a wish to avoid bringing into the world an unwanted and unparented baby. Of course, accidents happen and will happen, and these accidents lead to unfortunate and dangerous abortions or to the birth of illegitimate children.

But in examining the problem of adolescence we must accept the fact, I suggest, that the modern adolescent can explore, if he or she has a mind to, the whole area of sensuous living, without suffering the mental agony that accidental conception involves. This is only partly true because the mental agony associated with the fear of an accident remains, but the problem has been altered in the course of the last 30 years by this new factor. The mental agony, we can now see, comes not so much from fear as from the individual child's guilt sense. I do not mean that every child has an inborn guilt sense, but I mean that in health the child develops in a very complicated way a sense of right and wrong and a capacity for experiencing a sense of guilt; and each child has ideals, and has an idea of what he or she wants for the future.

Very strong conscious and unconscious factors are involved, conflicting feelings and fears that can only be explained in terms of the individual's total fantasy. For instance, one girl felt compelled to plant two illegitimate children on her mother before settling down to have her own family in marriage. The motivation included revenge related to the girl's place in her own family, and it also included the idea that she owed her mother two babies and that she must discharge this debt before getting on with establishing her own life. There can be extremely complex motivations for behaviour at this age – and indeed at all ages – and any simplification violates the truth. It is fortunate that in most cases of adolescent difficulty the family attitude (which is in itself complex) restrains wild acting out and takes the boy or girl past awkward episodes.

An end of fighting

The hydrogen bomb is perhaps producing more profound changes even than the first two of the characteristics of our age that I have listed here. The atom bomb affects the relationship between adult society and the adolescent tide which seems to be for ever coming in. It is not so much that this new bomb symbolizes a maniacal episode, a moment of infantile incontinence expressed in terms of fantasy that has become true – rage that has turned into actual destruction. Gunpowder already symbolized all this and the deeper aspects of madness, and the world was long ago altered by the invention of gunpowder which gave reality to magic. The more general result of the threat of nuclear war is that in effect it means that *there is not going to be another war*. It can be argued that there might be a war any minute in some place or other in the world, but because of the new bomb we know we can no longer solve a social problem by organizing for a new war. Nothing exists any longer therefore that can justify our providing strong military or naval discipline. We cannot supply this for our young men and we cannot justify supplying it for our children unless we call on something in ourselves which must be called cruelty or revenge.

If it makes no sense any longer to deal with our difficult adolescents by preparing them to fight for their king and country, we have lost something that we have been in the habit of using, and so we are thrown back on this problem, that there is adolescence, a thing in itself, with which society must learn to live.

Adolescence could be said to be a state of prepotency. In the imaginative life of man potency is not just a matter of the active and passive of intercourse; it includes the idea of man's victory over man, and the girl's admiration of the victor. All this, I am suggesting, now has to be wrapped up in the mystique of the coffee bar and in the occasional disturbance with knives. Adolescence now has to contain itself, to contain itself in a way it has never had to do before, and we have to reckon that adolescence has pretty violent potential.

When we think of the occasional atrocities of modern youth we must weigh them against the deaths that belong to the war that is no more to take place, and against all the cruelty that belongs to the war that is not going to be, and against all the free sexuality which belongs to every war that has ever been but is not going to be again. So adolescence has come to stay, and along with it the violence and sex that is inherent in it.

These three changes that I have listed are among those that are having an effect on our social concern, and one of the first lessons that we have to learn is that adolescence is not something that can be hustled off the stage by false manoeuvres.

The struggle to feel real

Is it not a prime characteristic of adolescents that they do not accept false solutions? They have a fierce morality which accepts only that which feels real, and this is a morality that also characterizes infancy. It is a morality that goes much deeper than wickedness, and has as its motto, 'to thine own self be true'. The adolescent is engaged in trying to find the self to be true to.

This is linked with the fact that, as I have said, the cure for adolescence is the passage of time, a fact which has very little meaning for the adolescent who rejects one cure after another on account of some false element in it. Once he can admit that compromise is allowable, he may discover various ways in which the relentlessness of essential truth can be softened. For instance, there is the solution by identification with parent figures, and there can be a premature maturity in terms of sex, and there can be a shift of emphasis from violence to physical prowess in athletics or from the bodily functions to intellectual attainment or achievement. In general, adolescents reject these helps, because they have not yet become able to accept compromise; instead they have to go through what might be called a doldrums area, a phase in which they feel futile.

I think of a boy who lives with his mother in a small flat. He is very intelligent, but he wastes his grammar school opportunities. He lies in bed threatening to take an overdose of something, and playing lugubrious jazz on the record player. He sometimes locks his mother out, and she has to get the police to help her into her own flat. He has many friends, and suddenly the flat comes to life when they all come round and bring their own beer and food; the party may go on all night or a whole weekend. There is a good deal of sex and the boy himself has a firm girl friend, and his suicidal impulses are related to ideas of her being indifferent to him.

He lacks a father figure, but he does not really know this. He does not know what he wants to be, and this increases his sense of futility. Opportunities come his way but he neglects them. He cannot leave his mother although she and he are tired of each other.

An adolescent who entirely avoids compromise, especially the use of identifications and vicarious experience, must start from scratch, ignoring all that has been worked out in the past history of our culture. Adolescents can be seen struggling to start again as if they had nothing they could take over from anyone. They can be seen to be forming groups on the basis of minor uniformities, and on the basis of some sort of group appearance which belongs to locality and to age. They can be seen searching for a form of identification which does not let them down in their struggle, the struggle for identity, the struggle to feel real, the struggle not to fit into an adult-assigned role, but to go through whatever has to be gone through. They feel unreal except in so far as they are refusing the false solutions, and feeling unreal leads them to do certain things which are only too real from the point of view of society. Society does in fact get very much caught up with this curious thing about adolescents: the mixture of defiance and dependence which characterizes them. Those who look after adolescents will find themselves puzzled how it can be that a boy or girl can be defiant to a degree and at the same time so dependent as to be childish, even infantile. Moreover parents find themselves paying out money to enable children to be defiant, although of course it is the parents who suffer from the defiance. This is a good example of the way in which those who theorize and write and talk are operating in a layer that is different from the one in which adolescents live. Parents or parent substitutes are faced with urgent problems of management. They are not concerned with theory but with the impact of the one on the other, the adolescent and the parent.

So it is possible to gather together a list of what we may think are some of the needs of adolescents:

The need to avoid the false solution: the need to feel real or to tolerate not feeling at all;
the need to defy – in a setting in which their dependence is met and can be relied on to be met;
the need repeatedly to prod society so that society's antagonism is manifest, and can be met with antagonism.

Health and illness

That which shows in the normal adolescent is related to that which shows in various kinds of ill persons. For instance, the idea of the repudiation of the false solution corresponds with the schizophrenic patient's inability to compromise; and in contrast with this there is psychoneurotic ambivalence and also the deceptiveness and self deception to be found in healthy people. Again, the need to feel real corresponds with the feelings of unreality associated with psychotic depression, with depersonalization. And the need to defy corresponds with one aspect of the antisocial tendency as it appears in delinquency.

From this it follows that in a group of adolescents the various tendencies tend to be represented by the more ill members of the group. One member of a group takes an overdose of a drug, another lies in bed in a depression, another is free with the flick knife. In each case there are grouped a band of adolescent isolates behind the ill individual whose extreme symptom has impinged on society. Yet in the majority of these individuals, whether or not they get involved, there was not enough drive behind the tendency to bring the symptom into inconvenient existence and to produce a social reaction. The ill one had to act for the others.

To repeat: if the adolescent is to get through this developmental stage by natural process, then there must be expected a phenomenon which could be called adolescent doldrums. Society needs to include this as a permanent feature and to tolerate it, to go to meet it, but not to cure it. The question is, has our society the health to do this?

Complicating this issue is the fact that some individuals are too ill (either with psychoneurosis or with depression or with schizophrenia) to reach a stage of emotional development that could be called adolescence, or they can only reach this in a highly distorted way. It has not been possible to include in this brief statement a picture of severe psychiatric illness as it appears at this age level. Nevertheless there is one type of illness that cannot be set aside in any statement about adolescence: delinquency.

Here again, there is a close relationship between the normal difficulties of adolescence and the abnormality that may be called the antisocial tendency. The difference between these two states does not lie so much in the clinical picture each presents as in the dynamics – in the origin – of each. At the root of the antisocial tendency there is always a deprivation. It may simply be that the mother, at a critical time, was in a withdrawn state or depressed, or it may be that the family broke up. Even a minor deprivation occurring at a difficult moment in the life of a child may have a lasting result by overstraining the available defences. Behind the antisocial tendency there is always a history of some health and then an interruption, after which things were never the same again. The antisocial child is searching in some way or other, violently or gently, to get the world to acknowledge its debt, trying to make the world reform the framework which got broken up. In the root of the antisocial tendency is deprivation.

In the root of healthy adolescence in general it is not possible to say that there is inherently a deprivation, but still there is something in a diffused way which is the same but in a degree just not strong enough to overstrain the available defences. This means that in the group that the adolescent finds to identify with, the extreme members of the group are acting for the total group. All sorts of things in the adolescent's struggle, the stealing, the knives, the breaking out and the breaking in; all these have to be contained in the dynamic of this group sitting round listening to blue jazz, or whatever is on.

If nothing happens, the individual members begin to feel unsure of the reality of their protest, and yet they are not in themselves disturbed enough to do an antisocial act. But if in the group there is an antisocial boy or girl who is willing to do the antisocial thing which produces a social reaction, this makes all the others cohere, makes them feel real, and temporarily gives the group a structure. Each will be loyal and will support the individual who will act for the group, although not one of them would have approved of the thing that the extreme antisocial did.

I think that this principle applies to the use of other kinds of illness. The suicide attempt of one of the members is very important to all the others. Or, one of them cannot get up, he is paralysed with depression. The others all know this is happening. Such happenings belong to the whole group and the group is shifting and the individuals are changing their groups, but somehow the individual members of the group use the extremes to help themselves to feel real, in their struggle to endure this doldrums period.

It comes down to a problem of: how to be adolescent during adolescence? This is an extremely brave thing for anybody to be. It does not mean that we grown-ups have to be saying: 'Look at these dear little adolescents having their adolescence; we must put up with everything and let our windows get broken.' This is not the point. The point is that we are challenged and we meet the challenge as part of the function of adult living. But we meet the challenge rather than set out to cure what is essentially healthy.

The big threat from the adolescent is the threat to the bit of ourselves that has not really had its adolescence. This bit of ourselves makes us resent these people being able to have their phase of the doldrums and makes us want to find a solution for them. There are hundreds of false solutions. Anything we say or do is wrong. We give support and we are wrong, we withdraw support and that is wrong too. We dare not be 'understanding'. But in the course of time we find that this adolescent boy and this adolescent girl has come out of the doldrums phase and is now able to begin identifying with society, with parents, and with wider groups, and to do so without feeling threatened with personal extinction.

18 Youth will not sleep

(Written for *New Society*, 1964)

I would there were no age between sixteen and twenty-three or that youth would sleep out the rest; for there is nothing in between but getting wenches with child, wronging the ancientry, stealing, fighting.

'A Winter's Tale'

This apt quotation recently appeared in an otherwise inept correspondence in *The Times* on the subject of young hooligans. There is real danger in the present situation, and the worst result of today's adolescent tendency to group violence would be the beginning of a movement comparable with the beginning phase of the Nazi regime, when Hitler solved the adolescent problem overnight by offering youth the role of superego to the community. This was a false solution, as we can see when we look back, but it did temporarily solve a social problem which in some ways resembled the one in which we are involved now.

Everyone asks: what is the solution? Important people offer solutions. The fact remains, however, that there is no solution, except that *each adolescent boy or girl in the course of time* (unless ill) *does grow up into an adult.* An unhealthy reaction comes from those who do not understand, in the way that Shakespeare did, that a time factor is involved. Indeed, most of the loud-speaking comes from individuals who are unable to tolerate the idea of a solution in time instead of a solution through immediate action.

There are, of course, favorable factors if one takes in the total scene. The factor that gives most hope is the capacity of the vast majority of teenagers themselves to tolerate their own position of 'not knowing whither'. They devise all sorts of interim activities for coping with the here and now, while each individual waits for a sense of existing as a unit and the socialization of this to turn up worked well enough through childhood and through what is sometimes called the 'latency period'. As can be gathered from watching children playing the game *I'm the King of the Castle/ You're the Dirty Rascal!* this becoming an individual and enjoying the experience of full autonomy is an inherently violent business.

Publicity is given to every act of hooliganism because the public does not really want to hear or read about those teenage pursuits that are free from an antisocial bias. Moreover, when a miracle happens, like the Beatles, there are those adults who wince when they could sigh the sigh of relief – that is, if they were free from envy of the teenager in this teenage age.

A headline in *The Observer* (24 May) is worth remarking: *Rockers Held*. This headline soberly reports the functioning of authority, with the police 'holding' and society containing phenomena that are inherent in the eternal dialectic of individuals growing up in a society of adults who have achieved, by hook or by crook, an identification with society. (Sometimes this achievement is precarious, depending on the existence of a social subgroup.)

The fact that there is a positive element in antisocial acting out can really help in the consideration of the antisocial element that is actual in some, and potential in nearly all, teenagers. This positive element belongs to the antisocial individual's total personal history; and where the acting out is strongly compulsive, it relates to an environmental letdown in the particular individual's experience. Just as in stealing there is (if one allows for the unconscious) a moment of hope of reaching back over a gap to a legitimate claim on a parent, so in violence there is an attempt to reactivate a firm holding, which in the history of the individual was lost at a stage of childhood dependence. Without such a firm holding a child is unable to discover impulse, and only impulse that is found and assimilated is available for self-control and socialization.

When violence starts in a gang because of the compulsive activities of a few truly deprived boys and girls, then there is always the potential violence in the group-loyal teenager waiting for the age which Shakespeare (in the quotation) places at twenty-three. Nowadays we would probably wish 'that youth would sleep' from twelve to twenty rather than from sixteen to twenty-three. But youth will not sleep, and society's permanent task in relation to youth is to hold and to contain, avoiding both the false solution and that moral indignation which stems from jealousy of youthfulness. Infinite potential is youth's precious and fleeting possession. This generates envy in the adult who is discovering in his own living the limitations of the actual.

Or, to quote Shakespeare again, some have '*nor youth nor age/ But, as it were, an after-dinner's sleep/Dreaming on both*' ('Measure for Measure').

Part III
The Social Provision

Editors' introduction

Part III is in many ways a continuation of Part I, being mainly concerned with the practical management of difficult children. It also emphasizes the need for the professional worker to have some knowledge of normal emotional development. It begins with a letter written to a Juvenile Court magistrate in 1944 suggesting that (with the help of professional workers) he look at the juvenile delinquent from the point of view of which type of existing social provision would be of most help in the individual case. There is special emphasis on the need for hostels and for magistrates to be involved in running them. The second paper is a leading article from the *British Medical Journal* (1951) which discusses Bowlby's World Health Organisation monograph, *Maternal Care and Mental Health*, and its conclusions, derived from statistical studies, about the effects on children of separation from parents and home. It suggests that these conclusions could be used as a kind of preventive medicine.

The next two chapters, 'The Deprived Child and How He Can Be Compensated for Loss of Family Life' (1950) and 'Group Influences and the Maladjusted Child' (1955), are specifically about children taken into care and are written for those responsible for them. The first lays down guidelines for assessing both the personal and social factors in deprivation and talks about the type of provision according to individual diagnosis. The second sets forth the basis of group formation in terms of individual integration and contrasts the mature grouping with the group that needs superimposed cover (as in the hostels and homes for the maladjusted child) in order for its individual members to become self-sufficient. It ends with a table for the classification of children according to the degree of personal integration achieved. Each of these papers presents a clear account of a certain aspect of the theory of normal emotional development: the first is especially interesting in that it contains a very early formal description of the use of transitional objects and transitional phenomena, the concept for which Winnicott is perhaps most widely known. We have included the review of Sheila Stewart's autobiography here because it deals in a lighter vein with Winnicott's belief that a good-enough beginning can enable a child to cope with loss of family life.

The unpublished paper, 'Comments on the Report of the Committee on Punishment in Prisons and Borstals' (1961) discusses the conflict between ideas of punishment and ideas of therapy, and contains a plea for a theoretical consideration of the subject of punishment. It also has something to say about tobacco trafficking, absconding, and interference from outside in the management of Borstals.

The chapter about progressive schools (1965) consists of a talk given to a conference at Dartington Hall and some notes that Winnicott made in the train on the way home from it. It points out the need for personal and social diagnosis of children attending these schools, so that the staff may be aware of the number of cases in which they are doing therapy with antisocial children. The meaning of the word 'progressive' is investigated in its positive, negative, and practical aspects, and the nature of destructiveness is considered.

The final chapter, hitherto unpublished, is the David Wills Lecture given in 1970 to the Association of Workers for Maladjusted Children. It was the last public lecture given by Dr Winnicott, and it is easy to see why it was immensely enjoyed. It is a backward look at a war-time hostel, picking out aspects that are of lasting importance in the care of deprived children, and making a final assessment of that most demanding of all social work, residential care.

19 *Correspondence with a magistrate*

(Letters appearing in *The New Era in Home and School*, January, 1944, in consequence of an earlier article, May, 1943)

Fincham Farm,
Rougham,
King's Lynn, Norfolk.

Dear Dr. Winnicott,
  I write in reference to your article on 'Delinquency Research' and the short paper on the same subject by Dr. Kate Friedlander, which was sent me by the Institute for the Scientific Treatment of Delinquency, to which I subscribe. I have always been interested in the application of Psycho-Analysis to crime and delinquency, and since I have been appointed a magistrate and chairman of Quarter Sessions my interest has become very practical. I am interested in what you say about environment and external factors, because to change the environment of a delinquent is the most usual procedure by a magistrates' court. It is very difficult, outside London, to arrange for a delinquent to be analysed, and the court must therefore consider the alternatives of a fine, imprisonment, probation, borstal, sending to an approved school, or binding over with or without some condition imposed. The trouble is that the magistrate – I speak for myself here, but believe I am typical – knows practically nothing about borstal, or the approved schools, and not very much about the methods and skill of the probation officer; in his case one can only judge by results. What is wanted at present is a bridge between modern psycho-analytical knowledge, as exemplified in your article, and ordinary criminal court procedure and practice. In your consulting room you can concentrate on the good of the patient; in court we have to think of the good of the community as well, and this complicates matters. Our tools, in court, are very crude and

blunt, and it is difficult to balance the desire to turn the person before one into a valuable member of society, and the desire to deter other wrong-doers. I am not a great believer, myself, in the deterrent effect of punishment, but a number of magistrates are, and I have to take account of their views. It is discouraging when, as happened the other day, a youth of about 17 who committed various thefts and was given a talking-to by me and treated leniently, comes up before the court again very soon after for exactly the same type of crime. What is one to do in this sort of case? Being in a thinly populated part of the country, over 100 miles from London, one's choice of action is limited.

If ever you have time to consider these rather general, but extremely practical, problems, and write me your views, I should be most grateful.

Yours, etc.,
Roger North

44 Queen Anne Street,
London, W.1.

Dear Mr. North,

I am glad to learn that you, as a magistrate, have been interested in my comments on delinquency and Dr. Friedlander's article, and I do very clearly recognize that the psychologist has little to offer the magistrates. Indeed, I made these points in my article: that the magistrate has to express the unconscious revenge of the public (legal procedure being an attempt to prevent lynch law), and that the psychologist has much research to do before he can fully understand the good work that is done intuitively by the right kind of magistrate, probation officer, etc., and that it is doubtful whether the actual psychoanalytic treatment of delinquents and criminals will ever become valuable to the community, because so much has to be done in order fundamentally to alter an individual. It is only from the point of view of research that the psychoanalysis of a delinquent is sociologically justifiable, and it is for this reason that I am very strongly in favour of it. May I emphasize once more that we recognize that we psychoanalysts have a limited *quantity* of help to offer magistrates in the way of direct therapy!

Your letter stimulates me to make a few suggestions of a more practical nature which could perhaps actually help the magistrate who is, like yourself, trying to understand the deeper issues involved. The fact is that, whatever the Court does that is useful always turns out to be something very personal. All sorts of schemes and ideas can be thought out, but in practice the good work is always done by some individual in intimate contact with the child who is in difficulties.

As far as I can see it, a court can only do one of the following things:

(1) In a few instances, the child's home is good; in this case the child is best left there where a strong and united father and mother are able and willing to manage him. When a child gets into trouble in such circumstances, it is usually because he has been led astray by some less fortunate child. Although this solution is seldom available, it should always be remembered that it is the best one, and that parents are the proper guardians of their own children.

(2) Much more frequently the child's home is only just good enough for the child to be left there while under the personal care of a good probation officer, who then becomes the person who makes the difference. The probation officer supplies something missing in the home – love backed by strength (in this case the strength of the law).

It should not be forgotten that the probation officer can undertake only a certain number of cases because of the emotional strain that the work involves, and that he (or she) needs definite and compulsory off time and holidays.

(3) Frequently the child's home is not good enough for him to be left there, even with the help of a probation officer. In this case a hostel must be found – a good one – which can supply the love and the strong management which these children absolutely need. At the present moment almost the only hostels suitable are those set up for evacuated children who are difficult to billet. In my opinion it is important and significant that these hostels are sponsored by the Ministry of Health, and not by the Home Office, which means that public revenge is not involved.

(4) A proportion of children coming before the Courts are too far gone for a hostel to be able to manage them, and they can be

controlled only through strong management which would be very bad for those who are not so ill. Here public revenge has become involved, and the Home Office must be responsible.

It is in the matter of hostels (third alternative) that the psychologist should be able to give practical help to a magistrate, for a psychologist can formulate the principles involved, and also can make practical suggestions in regard to hostel set-up and management.

I would strongly advise a magistrate to get involved in the setting up and management of a hostel, such as one of those that already exist for evacuated children who are difficult to billet, for only in this way can he become acquainted with the real issues involved in the approved schools to which he must somewhat blindly send so many of the boys and girls who come under the jurisdiction of his Court. He could draft to such a hostel some of those children who come under category (3) in the above classification.

Those of us who have had practical experience of such hostels and who have gone through failures, and partial failures, to comparative success, can help the magistrate to go ahead with some promise of immediate success, which means that through the use of the hostel a number of children can be saved from actually being sent to an approved school.

This does not mean that Approved Schools are all bad, though they cannot avoid being (like prisons) institutions for the spread of criminal education, but there is a very big waiting list for the approved school, and nothing is worse for a child than an indefinite stay in a Remand Home.

It can be said at once that a hostel has to be small to be valuable – 12 to 18 children – that the policy should be to keep the children till they leave school, and that everything depends on the Warden. He should be a married man, and he and his wife should be joint wardens. These two must be strong enough to be able to show deep love. Sentimentality is absolutely ruled out.

The Warden and all the staff should be personally visited, and informal talks about the children are essential. Only by this means can the child be thought of by the staff as a whole human being with a history of development and a home environment, and a present-day problem.

The choice of the cook and of the gardener is second in importance only to the choice of the Warden, and indeed each member of the staff, charwoman included, is either a great help or a great hindrance.

The children must be carefully sorted before being drafted to the hostel; one unsuitable child can upset the applecart, and lead to the rapid degeneration of a hostel situation that is otherwise well in hand. Classification is better built on an assessment of the child's home (that is to say, on the existence or non-existence of the home and on relative stability of the parental inter-relationship) than on the badness of the actual symptoms or misdemeanour for which the child has been referred to the Court.

It would obviously be impossible for the magistrate to be entirely responsible for the hostel, whose interests would not be identical with those of the Court, and whose failures must not be able to damage the Court's dignity. But I should have thought that the Home Office would be glad to support the idea of the magistrates' interest in such a hostel, sponsored by the Ministry of Health, and the magistrate could then be a member of the Hostel's House Committee.

These and many other general principles could be easily written down, and it is in this way that I think the psychologist has something definite and practical to offer the keen magistrate of a Juvenile Court.

Yours, etc.,
D. W. Winnicott.

20 The foundation of mental health

(Leading article in the *British Medical Journal*,
16 June, 1951)

Mental hygiene, although an extension of ordinary public-health work, goes further in that it alters the kind of people that compose the world. It is significant that the report[1] of the second session of W.H.O.'s Expert Committee on Mental Health concerns itself mainly with the management of infancy and childhood, thus taking for granted something which might not have been accepted by doctors 50 years ago – namely, that the basis of adult mental health is laid down in infancy and childhood, and of course in adolescence. The introduction to the report begins with the statement: 'The most important single long-term principle for the future work of W.H.O. in the fostering of mental health, as opposed to the treatment of psychiatric disorders, is the encouragement of the incorporation into public-health work of the responsibility for promoting the mental as well as physical health of the community.' The report then discusses the maternity services, the management of the infant and the pre-school child, the dependence of the pre-school child on the mother, school health in its wider aspects, and the emotional problems arising from physical handicap and from the isolation of children suffering from infectious diseases such as leprosy and tuberculosis. The committee recognizes that the mental health worker in training has more to do than to learn. The student is faced with 'an emotional problem because of the nature of the subject matter quite apart from any intellectual difficulty in understanding the facts. Its initial emotional impact is far greater than that of the dissecting room or the operating theatre.'

Along with the publication of this report there comes a W.H.O. monograph on 'Maternal Care and Mental Health,' written by Dr.

---

[1] *W.H.O. tech. Rep. Ser.*, No. 31, 1951, Geneva.

John Bowlby, consultant in mental health to W.H.O., as a contribution to the United Nations programme for the welfare of homeless children.[2] Dr. Bowlby, in his work at the Tavistock Clinic, has already shown that he appreciates the need for presenting psychological concepts in a form which appeals to the scientific worker trained to make the statistical approach, and it can be said at once that he has been successful in writing a remarkably interesting and valuable report. Compared with the amount of individual psychotherapy that is being done all over the world the investigations giving clear-cut results are few and far between: perhaps there are aspects of psychology which cannot yield results for the statistician. The success of this monograph is due in part to the choice of subject – the effect of the separation from their homes, and specifically from their own mothers, on the emotional development of infants and children, who, as Dr. Bowlby writes, 'are not slates from which the past can be rubbed by a duster or a sponge, but human beings who carry their previous experiences with them and whose behaviour in the present is profoundly affected by what has gone before.' Quoting convincing figures, he is able to show how separation can augment the tendency to the development of a psychopathic personality. Bowlby found that almost all workers in this field had arrived at the same conclusion: 'What is believed to be essential for mental health is that the infant and the young child should experience a warm, intimate, and continuous relationship with the mother (or permanent mother-substitute) in which both find satisfaction and enjoyment.' This is not new: it is what mothers and fathers feel, and it is what those who work with children have found. But what is new in this report is the attempt to translate the idea into figures.

There are three main sources of information: studies by direct observation of infants and small children; studies based on the investigation of early histories of those who are ill; and follow-up studies of groups of deprived children in various categories. Perhaps the main result of these inquiries, especially when they have been confirmed and amplified, will be to serve as a lesson for the medical profession, including the administrators. It must always be difficult for those who are making physical health their

[2] *Maternal Care and Mental Health*, Geneva, 1951.

speciality to keep the greater importance of mental health in mind. Emotional development can so easily be disturbed: the child in hospital who has forgotten its mother and who has reached the stage of making friends with anyone who comes along may be delightful to have in the ward, but it is a fact that a child, and especially a small child, cannot forget a parent without damage to the personality. Happily in children's wards and children's hospitals there is now a tendency to allow daily visiting. Admittedly this presents great difficulties to the nurses, but even the small amount of carefully controlled work which Bowlby is able to report on this limited aspect of the subject shows how worthwhile the extra trouble is.

Naturally the effect on the child of separation from its mother will depend on the degree of deprivation and also on the age of the child. The care of infants brought up in an institution from their earliest days was obviously due for reform, and in this country public opinion was firmly behind the Curtis Committee and the Children Act which followed in 1948. It is now becoming generally accepted that no child should be removed from the mother's care if this can be avoided – and this simple statement must not be obscured by the subsidiary fact that a minority of parents are themselves ill (in a psychiatric sense) and therefore bad for their children.

It would be a large task to teach the parents of the world how to be good parents, especially as most of them already know much better than we can ever tell them. It is appropriate therefore that W.H.O should start at the other end in its consideration of mental hygiene, at the end at which teaching can have effect. The two important conclusions are that the impersonal upbringing of children tends to produce unsatisfactory personalities and even active antisocial characters and, secondly, that when there is anything like a good relationship between the developing infant or child and the parent the continuity of this relationship must be respected and must never be broken without good cause. Bowlby likens the acceptance of these facts to the acceptance of certain facts on the physical side of paediatrics, such as the importance of vitamins in the prevention of scurvy and rickets. Acceptance of the principle to which Bowlby's statistics point could lead to a reduction of antisocial tendencies and the suffering that lies behind them, exactly as vitamin D has lessened the incidence of rickets. Such a result would be a great achievement of preventive medicine, even without taking into account the deeper aspects of emotional development, such as richness of personality, strength of character, and the capacity for full, free, and mature self-expression.

21 *The deprived child and how he can be compensated for loss of family life*

(A lecture to the Nursery School Association, July, 1950)

By way of introduction to the subject of providing for the child who has been deprived of family life, let us remember this: that the chief concern of a community should be for its healthy members. It is the usual run of good homes that need priority, for the simple reason that the children who are being nurtured in their own homes are the ones that reward; it is the care of these children that pays the dividends.

Two things follow, if this be accepted. First, provision for the ordinary home of a basic ration of housing, food, clothing, education, and recreation facilities, and what could be called cultural food, has first claim on our attention. Second, we must see that we never interfere with a home that is a going concern, not even for its own good. Doctors are especially liable to get in the way between mothers and infants, or parents and children, always with the best intentions, for the prevention of disease and the promotion of health; and doctors are by no means the only offenders in this respect. For example:

A mother who had been divorced asked me for advice in the following situation. She had a six-year-old daughter, and a religious organization with which the father of this child was connected wished to take the child away from the mother and put her in a boarding school – for holidays as well as term-time – because this organization did not approve of divorce. The fact that the child was quite settled and secure with the mother and her new husband was to be ignored, and a state of deprivation was to be created for this child because of a principle: a child must not live with a divorced mother.

A great number of deprived children are in fact engineered in one way or another, and the remedy lies in avoidance of bad management.

Nevertheless, I have to face up to the fact that I am myself a deliberate home-breaker, like many others. We are all the time sending children away from their homes. In my clinic alone we have cases every week in which it is urgently necessary to get the child away from home. It is true that such children are seldom under the age of four. Everyone working in this field knows the type of case in which, for one reason or another, a state of affairs has arisen of such a nature that, unless the child is removed within a few days or weeks, the home will break up or the child will certainly get to the courts. Often one can predict that the child will do well away from home or that the home will do well with the child away. There are many distressing cases that mend themselves if one can immediately bring about these separations, and it would be a great pity if all that we are doing to avoid the unnecessary destruction of good homes should in any way weaken the efforts of the authorities that are responsible for the provision of short-term and long-term accommodation for the kind of children that I am considering here.

When I say that in my clinic we have these cases each week, I am implying that in the great majority of cases we manage to help the child in the setting which already exists. This is of course our aim, not only because it is economical but also because when the home is good enough the home is the proper place for the child to grow up in. The vast majority of the children who need psychological help are suffering from disturbances in respect of *internal* factors, disturbances in the emotional development of the individual, disturbances which are largely inherent because life is difficult. These disturbances can be treated with the child at home.

Assessment of deprivation

In order to discover how we can best help a deprived child we first have to determine what amount of normal emotional development was made possible in the beginning by a good-enough environment ((i) infant-mother relationship, (ii) triangular father-mother-child relationship); and then in the light of this to try to assess the damage done by the deprivation, when it began and as it subsequently persisted. The history of the case is therefore important.

The following six categories may be found useful as a way of classifying cases of broken home:

(a) Ordinary good home, broken by an accident to one or both parents.

(b) Home broken by the separation of the parents, who are good as parents.

(c) Home broken by the separation of the parents, who are not good as parents.

(d) Home incomplete, because there is no father (child illegitimate). The mother is good; grandparents may take over parental role, or help to some extent.

(e) Home incomplete, because there is no father (child illegitimate). The mother is not good.

(f) There never was a home.

In addition, cross-classifications will be made:

(a) according to the age of the child; and the age at which a good-enough environment ceased;

(b) according to the child's nature and intelligence;

(c) according to the child's psychiatric diagnosis.

We avoid making any assessment of the problem on the basis of the child's symptoms, or the nuisance value of the child, or the feelings roused in us by the child's plight. These considerations lead us astray. Often the history is lacking or deficient in essential parts. Then, and in fact commonly, the only way to determine the fact of an early good-enough environment is to supply a good environment and see what use the child can make of it.

Here special comment is needed on the meaning of the words 'what use the child can make of a good environment'. A deprived child is ill, and it is never so simple a matter that environmental readjustment will bring about a changeover in the child from ill to healthy. At best, the child who can benefit from a simple environmental provision begins to get better, and as the change takes place from ill to less ill the child becomes increasingly able to be angry about the past deprivation. Hate of the world is there somewhere, and health has not arrived unless the hate has been felt. In a small proportion of cases the hate is felt, and even this small complication can cause difficulties. However, this favourable result comes about only if everything is relatively available to the child's *conscious* self, and this is but seldom the case. To some extent, or to a very great extent, the feelings belonging to the environmental failure are not available to consciousness. Where deprivation occurs on top of a satisfactory early experience something like this *can* happen and the hate appropriate to the deprivation can be reached. The following example illustrates this kind of situation:

> Here is a girl of seven. Her father died when she was three but she negotiated this difficulty all right. The mother cared for her excellently and married again. This remarriage was successful and the child's stepfather was very fond of her. All was well until the mother became pregnant. At this point the father completely changed in his attitude to the stepdaughter. He became orientated towards his own baby and withdrew affection from the stepchild. After the birth of the baby things got worse, and the mother was in a position of divided loyalties. The child could not thrive in this atmosphere but, removed to a boarding school, she may quite possibly be able to do well and even to understand the difficulty that occurred in her own home.

On the other hand, the next case shows the effects of an unsatisfactory early experience:

> A mother brings her little boy of two and a half. He has a good home but he is only happy when having the personal attention of his mother or father. He cannot leave his mother and therefore cannot play on his own, and the approach of strangers is felt by him to be terrifying. What has gone wrong in this case, considering that the parents are ordinary normal people? The fact is that the boy was adopted at five weeks, and already by that time he was ill. There is some evidence that the matron of the home in which he was born made a special pet of him, since she seems to have tried to hide him from these parents who were looking for an infant to adopt. The transfer at five weeks

caused a severe upset in the emotional development of the infant, and the adopting parents are only beginning to be able gradually to overcome the difficulties – which they certainly did not expect, taking over a baby at so early a date. (They had in fact tried very hard to get a baby even earlier, in the first week or two of the infant's existence, because they were aware of the complications that could arise.)

We have to know what sort of things happen in the child when a good setting is broken up and also when a good setting has never existed, and this involves a study of the whole subject of the emotional development of the individual. Some of the phenomena are well-enough known: hate is repressed or the capacity to love people is lost. Other defensive organizations become set up in the child's personality. There may be regression to some early phases of the emotional development which were more satisfactory than others, or there may be a state of pathological introversion. Much more commonly than is generally thought, there is a splitting of the personality. In the simplest form of this splitting, the child presents a shop-window or out-turned half, built up on a basis of compliance, and the main part of the self containing all the spontaneity is kept secret and is all the time involved in hidden relationships to idealized fantasy objects.

Although it is difficult to make a simple and clear statement of these phenomena, an understanding of them is necessary if we are to see what are the favourable signs in the case of deprived children. If we do not understand what is there when the child is very ill, we cannot see, for instance, that a depressed mood in a deprived child may be a favourable sign, especially when not accompanied by strong persecution ideas. A simple depressed mood indicates at any rate that the child has retained unity of personality and has a sense of concern, and is indeed taking responsibility for all that has gone wrong. Also, antisocial acts, such as bed-wetting and stealing, indicate that at any rate momentarily there can be hope – hope of rediscovering a good-enough mother, a good-enough home, a good-enough inter-parental relationship. Even anger may indicate that there is hope, and that for the moment the child is a unit and able to feel the clash between what is conceivable and what is actually to be found in what we call shared reality.

Let us consider the meaning of the antisocial act, for instance, stealing. When a child steals, what is sought (by the total child, i.e. the unconscious included) is not the object stolen; what is sought is the person, the mother, from whom the child has the right to steal because she is the mother. In fact every infant at the start can truly claim the right to steal from the mother because the infant invented the mother, thought her up, created her out of an innate capacity to love. By being there the mother gave her infant, gradually, bit by bit, the person of herself as material for the infant to create into, so that in the end his subjective self-created mother was quite a lot like the mother we can agree about. In the same way, the child who wets the bed is looking for the mother's lap that is meet to be wetted in the early stages of the infant's existence.

The antisocial symptoms are gropings for environmental recovery, and indicate hope. They fail not because they are wrongly directed, but because the child is unconscious of what is going on. The antisocial child needs therefore a specialized environment that has a therapeutic aim, and that can give a reality response to the hope that is expressed in the symptoms. This has to be spread over a long period, however, to become effectual as a therapeutic, since, as I have said, much is unavailable to the child as conscious feeling and memory; and also the child has to gain great confidence in the new environment, in its stability and its capacity for objectivity, before the defences can be given up – defences against intolerable anxiety that is always liable to be reactivated by new deprivation.

We know, then, that the deprived child is an ill person, a person with a past history of traumatic experience, and a personal way of coping with the anxieties roused; and a person with a capacity for recovery greater or less according to the degree of loss of consciousness of the appropriate hate and of the primary capacity to love. What practical measures can be undertaken to help such a child?

Providing for the deprived child

Obviously someone has to care for the child. The community no longer denies responsibility for children who are deprived; indeed, the swing is right in the other direction today. Public opinion demands that the best that is possible shall be done for the child whose own family life is lacking. Many of our troubles at the present time come from the practical difficulties that arise in the application of the principles deriving from the new attitude.

It is not possible to do the right thing for a child by passing a law or by setting up administrative machinery. These things are necessary but are only the first miserable stage. In every case a proper management of a child involves *human beings*, and these human beings have to be of the right kind; and there is a distinct limit to the number of such people who are immediately available. This number is much increased if in the administrative machinery there is a provision for *intermediate* persons, who can on the one hand deal with the overriding authorities and on the other hand keep in touch with the persons actually doing the work, appreciating their good points, acknowledging success where it occurs, enabling the educative process to leaven and make interesting the job, discussing failures and the reasons for failure, and being available to give relief where necessary by removal of a child from a foster home or hostel, perhaps at short notice. The care of a child is very much a whole-time process, and leaves the person who is doing the work with little emotional reserve for coping with administrative procedure or with the wide social issues represented in certain cases by the police. Conversely, the person who is able to keep one eye firmly on administration or on the police is unlikely to be first-rate in the care of a child.

Coming now to more specific matters, it is necessary to keep in mind the psychiatric diagnosis of every child for whom provision has to be made. As I have pointed out, this diagnosis can be made only after a carefully taken history or perhaps after a period of observation. The point is that a child deprived of family life can have had a good start in infancy and can even have had the beginnings of a family life. The foundation of the mental health of the child may in such a case have been well laid down, so that the illness secondary to the deprivation supervenes on health. On the other hand, another child, not perhaps looking worse, has no healthy experience which can be rediscovered and reactivated by the child in a new environment; and, further than that, there may have been such a poor or complex management of early infancy that the foundations for mental health in terms of personality structure and reality sense may be deficient. In such extreme cases the good environment has to be created for the first time, or a good environment may have no chance at all because the child is fundamentally unsound, perhaps with the addition of a hereditary tendency to insanity or instability. In the extreme cases the child is insane, although this word is not used in respect of children.

It is important to recognize this part of the problem, otherwise those who are assessing results will be surprised to find that with the very best management there are always failures, and always children who grow up eventually to become insane or at best antisocial.

The diagnosis of the child having been made, in terms of the presence or absence of positive features in the early environment and the child's relation to it, the next thing to consider is procedure. I want to emphasize here (and I write as a psycho-analyst of children) that the clear principle of the management of the deprived child is not the provision of psychotherapy. Psychotherapy is something which eventually, one hopes, may be added in some instances to whatever else is done. At the present time, generally speaking, personal psychotherapy is not practical politics. The essential procedure is the provision of an alternative to the family. We can classify what we provide in the following way:

(i) Foster parents, who wish to give the child a family life like that which the child could have been provided with by the actual parents. It is generally acknowledged that this is the ideal, but one must quickly add that it is essential that children sent to foster parents must be children who can respond to something so good. This practically means that they must have had something of a good-enough family life somewhere in their past and have been able to respond to it. In this foster home they have a chance to rediscover something they have had and have lost.

(ii) Next come the small homes in the care, if possible (but not necessarily), of married wardens, each home containing children in various age groups. Such small homes can conveniently be grouped together, with advantages both from the administrative point of view and from the point of view of the children, who acquire cousins, so to speak, as well as siblings. Here again, the best is being attempted, and therefore it is essential that children who cannot benefit from something so good shall be kept away. One unsuitable child can spoil the good work of a whole group. It must be remembered that good work is emotionally more difficult than less good work, and only too easily, if there is a failure, those in charge give up the best and slip over into the easier and less valuable types of management.

(iii) In the third category the groups are larger. The hostel perhaps contains eighteen. The wardens can keep in personal touch with all the children but they have assistants, and the management of the assistants is an important part of their job. Loyalties are divided and the children have opportunity for putting the grown-ups against each other and playing on latent jealousies. We are already in the direction of the less good management. On the other hand, we are also in the direction of the type of management that can deal with the less satisfactory type of deprived child. The way in which things are worked is less personal, more dictatorial, and the demands made on each child are less. A child in such a home is less in need of a previous good experience which can be revived. In such homes there is less need than there is in the small homes for the child to grow towards the ability to identify with the home while retaining personal impulsiveness and spontaneity. The intermediate thing is good enough in the larger homes, that is to say, a merging of identity with the other children in the group. This involves both loss of personal identity and loss of identification with the total home setting.

(iv) Next in our classification comes the larger hostel, in which the wardens are mainly engaged in the management of the staff and only indirectly concerned with the minute-to-minute management of the children. Here there are advantages in that a larger number of children can be accommodated. The fact that there is a larger staff means that there is more opportunity for discussion among the staff; there are also advantages for the children in that there can be teams competing with each other. I think it can be claimed that this hostel is further in the direction of the type of management that can cope with the more ill children, i.e. those whose good experiences at the beginning were small. The rather impersonal chief can be in the background as a representative of authority which such children need; which they need because within themselves they are incapable of holding both the spontaneity and the control at the same time. (Either they must be identified with authority and turn into miniature gauleiters, or else they must be impulsive, relying entirely on external authority for control.)

(v) Beyond this is the still larger institution which does its best for children under impossible conditions. For some time there will have to be such institutions. They have to be run by dictatorship methods, and what is good for the individual child has to be subordinated on account of the limitations of that which society can provide immediately. Here is a good form of sublimation for potential dictators. One can even find other advantages in this undesirable state of affairs, for, the accent being on dictatorship methods, quite hopelessly difficult children can be managed in such a way that they do not get into trouble with society over long periods. Really ill children can be happier here than in better homes, and they can become able to play and learn, so much so that the uninformed observer must be impressed. It is difficult in such institutions to recognize the children who become ripe to be removed to a more personal type of management, where their growing capacity to identify with society without losing their own individuality can be catered for.

Therapeutics and management

I now want to contrast the two extremes of management, the one being the foster home and the other the large institution. In the former, as I have said, the aim is truly therapeutic. It is hoped that the child will recover in the course of time from the deprivation which, without such management, would not only leave a scar but would actually leave crippling. If this is to happen, much more is needed than the child's response to the new environment.

At first the child is apt to make a quick response and those concerned are apt to think that their troubles are over. When the child gains confidence, however, there follows a growing capacity for anger with the previous environmental failure. It is unlikely, of course, that what happens will exactly look like this, especially since the child is not conscious of the main revolutionary changes which are taking place. The foster parents will find that they themselves periodically become the target of the child's hate. They will have to take over the anger which is beginning to be able to be felt and which belongs to the failure in the child's own home. It is very important for foster parents to understand this, otherwise they get disheartened; and child care officers must know about it, otherwise they will blame foster parents and believe the children's stories about ill treatment and starvation. If the foster parents receive a visit from an officer who is looking for signs of trouble, they may become over-anxious, and this makes them try to seduce the child into being friendly and happy, thus depriving the child of a most important part of recovery.

Sometimes a child will very cleverly bring about specific ill treatment, in an attempt to bring into the actual present a badness that can be met by hate; the cruel foster parent is then actually loved because of the relief that the child feels through transformation of 'hate versus hate' locked up within into hate meeting external hate now. Unfortunately at this point the foster parents are liable to become misunderstood in their social group.

There are ways out. For instance, some foster parents will be found to work on the rescue principle. For them the child's parents were hopelessly bad, and they say so over and over again out loud to the child, and thus they divert the child's hate from themselves. This method may work fairly well but it ignores the reality situation, and in any case disturbs something which is a feature in deprived children, that they tend to idealize their own home such as it is. No doubt it is more healthy when the foster parents can take the periodical waves of negative feeling and survive them, reaching each time to a new, more secure (because less idealized) relation to the child.

In contrast, the child in the big institution is *not* being managed with the aim of curing him of his illness. The aims are, first, to provide housing and food and clothing for children who are neglected; second, to devise a type of management in which the children live in a state of order rather than chaos; and third, to keep as many of the children as possible from a clash with society until they must be let loose on the world somewhere about the age of sixteen. It is no good mixing things up and pretending that at this end of the scale an attempt is being made to create normal human beings. A strict management in such cases is essential, and if to this can be added some humanity so much the better.

It must be remembered that even in very strict communities, as long as there is consistency and fairness the children can discover humanity among themselves, and they can even come to value the strictness because of the fact that it implies stability. Understanding men and women working this kind of system can find ways of introducing more humane moments. Something can be done, for instance, by selecting suitable children for regular contacts with reliable aunt and uncle substitutes in the outside world. People can be found who will write on the child's birthday, and who will ask the child home to tea three or four times a year. These are only examples but they show the sort of thing that can be done and that is done without disturbance of the strict setting in which the children live. It has to be remembered that if the strict setting is the basis, then it is disturbing to the children if this strict setting has exceptions and loopholes. If there has to be a strict setting, then let it be consistent, reliable, and fair, so that it can have positive value. Besides, there will always be those children who abuse privileges, and then the children who could use them will have to suffer.

In this type of large institution, for the sake of peace and quiet, the accent is put on management on behalf of society. Within this framework the children must lose their own individuality to a greater or lesser extent. (I am not ignoring the fact that in the intermediate institutions there is room for a gradual growth of the children who are healthy enough to grow, so that they become increasingly able to identify with society without loss of identity.)

There will still be some children who, because they are what I want to call mad (although one must not use such a word), are failures even if dictated to. For such children there must be the equivalent of the mental hospital which caters for adults, and I think we have not yet determined what is the best that society can do for these extreme cases. Such children are so ill that those who are looking after them easily recognize that when they begin to become antisocial this means that they are beginning to get better.

I conclude this section by referring to matters which are of great importance in a consideration of the needs of the deprived child.

Importance of child's early history

The first of these very much concerns the child care worker, especially in her capacity of boarding out and of keeping a watchful eye on the new situation. If I were a child care officer, as soon as a child came into my care I would immediately want to collect together every particle of information that could be found about that child's life up to the present moment. This is always urgent because the passage of every day makes it less easy for anyone to come by the essential facts. How distressing it was in the second world war, when the failures of the evacuation scheme were being dealt with, and there were children about whom one could never find out anything!

We know how normal children sometimes say as they are going to bed, 'What did I do today?', and then the mother says, 'You woke up at half past six, and you played with your teddy, singing nursery rhymes until we woke, and then you got up and went out into the garden, and then you had breakfast, and then . . .', and so on, until the whole scheme of the day has been integrated from outside. The child has all the information there but likes to be helped to be aware of it all. This feels good and real and helps the child to distinguish reality from the dream and from imaginative play. The same thing writ large would be represented by the way the ordinary parent has of going over the past life of the child, including what the child only just remembers and also what the child does not know anything about.

The lack of this simple thing is a serious loss for the deprived child. At any rate there should be someone who has gathered together whatever is available. In the very favourable case the child care officer will be able to have a long interview with the actual mother, letting her gradually unfold the whole history from the moment of birth, even perhaps giving important details about her experiences during pregnancy and the experiences leading up to conception, which may or may not have determined much of her attitude to the child. Often, however, the worker will have to go here and there and everywhere to collect information; even the name of a friend that the child had in the institution before last may be valuable. There will follow the task of organizing a contact with the child, when the social worker gains the child's confidence. Some way may be found of letting the child know that here or in a file in the office of the children's officer there is the saga of the child's life as lived hitherto. The child may not want to be told anything for the time being, but later on details may be needed. It is particularly the illegitimate and the child with a broken home who eventually need to be able to get to the facts – that is, if health is to be reached, and I assume that in the case of the fostered child the aim is to produce a healthy child. The child at the other extreme, managed by dictatorial methods in a large group, is less likely to become well enough to assimilate the truth about the past.

Because this is so, and because there is an acute shortage of workers, the start should be made at the more normal end. Even so, child care workers are likely to feel that, much as they would like to do this kind of thing, it is impossible because of their case load. My point is that child care workers must decide absolutely that they will not take more cases than they can manage. There is no half and half business about the care of children. It is a matter of dealing with a few children well and handing the others over to the large institution with dictatorial methods until society can manage something better. Good work has to be personal, or it is cruel and tantalizing both to the child and to the child care worker. *The work is only worth doing if it is personal and if those who are doing the work are not overburdened.*

It must be remembered that if child care workers accept too much work they will be bound to have failures, and eventually statisticians will come along and prove that the whole thing is wrong, and that the dictatorial methods are more effectual in providing factories with workers, and homes with domestic servants.

Transitional phenomena

The other point that I wish to make can be got at again by first looking at the normal child. How is it that ordinary children can be deprived of their homes and of all that is familiar to them without becoming ill? Every day children go into hospital and come out again, not only physically mended but also undisturbed and even enriched by the new experience. Over and over again children go away to stay with aunts and uncles, and in any case they go away with their parents from familiar surroundings to strange ones.

This is a very complex subject, which we may approach in the following way. Let us think of any child whom we know well, and ask ourselves what it is that the child takes to bed to help in the transition from waking to dream life: a doll; several dolls perhaps;

a teddy; a book; a bit of mother's old dress; a corner of an eider-
down; a bit of old blanket; or it may be a handkerchief which was
substituted for a napkin at a certain stage in the infant's development. In some cases it may be that there was no such object, but
the child simply sucked what was available, a fist, and then the
thumb or two fingers; or perhaps there was a genital activity to
which the word masturbation is more easily applied; or the child
may lie on the tummy or make rhythmic movements, showing the
orgiastic nature of the experience by sweating in the head. In
some cases from early months the infant will have demanded
nothing less than the personal appearance of a human being,
probably the mother. There is a wide range of possibilities which
can be commonly observed. Among the various dolls and teddies
belonging to a child, there may be one particular, probably soft,
object that was introduced to the infant at about ten, eleven, or
twelve months, which the infant treats in a most brutal as well as a
most loving manner, and without which the infant could not
conceive of going to bed; this thing would certainly not have to be
left behind if the child had to go away; and if it were lost it would
be a disaster for the child and therefore for those caring for him or
her. It is unlikely that such an object would ever be given away to
another child, and in any case no other child would want it;
eventually it becomes smelly and filthy and yet one dare not wash
it.

I call this thing a transitional object. By this means I can illustrate that one difficulty every child experiences is to relate
subjective reality to shared reality which can be objectively
perceived. From waking to sleeping the child jumps from a
perceived world to a self-created world. In between there is a need
for all kinds of transitional phenomena – neutral territory. I would
describe this precious object by saying that there is a tacit understanding that no one will claim that this real thing is a part of the
world, or that it is created by the infant. It is understood that both
these things are true: the infant created it and the world supplied
it. This is the continuation forward of the initial task which the
ordinary mother enables her infant to undertake, when by a most
delicate active adaptation she offers herself, perhaps her breast, a
thousand times at the moment that the baby is ready to create
something like the breast that she offers.

Most of the children who come into the category of the maladjusted either have not had an object of this kind, or they have lost it. There must be someone for the object to stand for, which means that the condition of these children cannot be cured simply by giving them a new object. A child may, however, grow to such confidence in the person who is caring for him or her that objects that are deeply symbolical of that person will appear. This will be felt as a good sign, like being able to remember a dream, or to dream of a real event.

All these transitional objects and transitional phenomena enable the child to stand frustrations and deprivations and the presentation of new situations. Do we make sure in our management of deprived children that we respect such transitional phenomena as do exist? I think that if we look at the use of toys, of auto-erotic activities, of bedtime stories and nursery rhymes in this way, we can see that, by means of these things, children have got a capacity for being deprived to some extent of what they are used to and even of what they need. A child removed from one home to another or from one institution to another may manage or may not manage according to whether a bit of cloth or a soft object can go with him or her from one place to the other; or whether there are familiar rhymes to be said at bedtime that link the past with the present; or whether the auto-erotic activities can be respected and tolerated and even valued because of their positive contribution. Surely with children whose environments are disturbed these phenomena have a special importance, and the study of them should enable us to increase our capacity to give help to these human beings who are being bandied about before they have been able to accept that which we accept only with the greatest difficulty: that the world is never as we would create it and that the best that can happen for any one of us is that there shall have been sufficient overlap of external reality and what we can create. We accept the idea of an identity between the two as an illusion.

It may be hard for people who have had fortunate environmental experiences to understand these things; nevertheless, the infant or the little child who is being moved about from one place to another is coping with exactly this problem. If we deprive a child of the transitional objects and disturb the established transitional phenomena, then the child has only one way out, which is a split in the personality, with one half related to a subjective world and the other reacting on a compliance basis to the world which impinges. When this split is formed and the bridges between the subjective and the objective are destroyed, or have never been well formed, the child is unable to operate as a total human being.[1]

To some extent this state of affairs can always be found in the child who comes under our care because of being deprived of family life. In the children that we hope to send to foster parents or to the small sensitive hostel there will certainly be found in every case some degree of this splitting. The subjective world has the disadvantage for the child that although it can be ideal it can also be cruel and persecutory. At first the child will translate whatever is found in these terms, and either the foster home is wonderful and the real home is bad, or vice versa. In the end, however, if all goes well, the child will be able to have a fantasy of good and bad homes and to dream and talk about them and to draw them, and at the same time to perceive the real home provided by the foster parents as it is actually.

The actual foster home has the advantage of not swinging violently from good to bad and from bad to good. It remains more or less just middlingly disappointing and middlingly reassuring. Those who are managing deprived children can be helped by recognizing that each child does to some extent bring a capacity for accepting a neutral territory, localized in some way or other into masturbation or the use of a doll or the enjoyment of a nursery rhyme or something like that. So, from the study of what normal children enjoy, we can learn what these deprived children absolutely need.

---

[1] For a fuller development of this theme, see 'Transitional Objects and Transitional Phenomena', Chapter XVIII in *Collected Papers* by D. W. Winnicott (London: Tavistock Publications, 1958; Hogarth Press, 1975).

22 Group influences and the maladjusted child: the school aspect

(A lecture to the Association of Workers for Maladjusted Children, April, 1955)

My purpose in this section is to study certain aspects of the psychology of groups, which may help towards a better understanding of the kind of problems that are involved in the group management of maladjusted children. Let us think first of the normal child, who lives in a normal home, has aims, and goes to school actually wanting school to teach; who finds his or her own environment, and even helps to maintain or develop or modify it. In contrast, the maladjusted child needs an environment that has the accent on management rather than on teaching; the teaching is a secondary matter and may at times be a specialized affair, more of the nature of remedial teaching than of instruction in school subjects. In other words, in the case of the maladjusted child, 'school' has the meaning of 'hostel'. For these reasons, those who are concerned with the management of antisocial children are not schoolteachers who add a dash of human understanding here and there; they are in fact group psychotherapists who add a dash of teaching. And so a knowledge of the formation of groups is highly important for their work.

Groups and the psychology of groups constitute a vast subject, out of which I have selected one main thesis for presentation here: namely, that the basis of group psychology is the psychology of the individual, and especially of the individual's personal integration. I start therefore with a brief statement of the task of individual integration.

Individual emotional development

Psychology emerged from a hopeless muddle with the now accepted idea that there is a continuous process of emotional development, starting before birth, and continuing throughout life, till (with luck) death from old age. This theory underlies all the various schools of psychology and provides a useful agreed principle. We may differ violently here and there, but this simple idea of continuity of emotional growth joins us all together. From this base we can study the manner of the process, and the various stages at which there is danger, either from within (instincts) or from without (environmental failure).

We all accept the general statement that the earlier we go in the examination of this process of individual growth, the more important we find the environmental factor. This is an acceptance of the principle that the child goes from dependence towards independence. In health we expect the individual to become gradually able to identify with wider and wider groups, and to identify with groups without loss of sense of self and of individual spontaneity. If the group is too wide the individual loses touch; if it is too narrow there is a loss of sense of citizenship.

We take much trouble to provide *gradual* extensions of the meaning of the word group in our provision of clubs and other organizations suitable for adolescents, and we judge success by the way in which each boy or girl can identify with each group in succession, without too great a loss of individuality. For the pre-adolescent we provide scouts and guides; for the latency child, cubs and brownies. At the first school age, school gives an extension and a widening of the home. If school is to be provided for the toddler then we see that it is integrated in with the home, and that it does not place too much value on actual teaching, because what a toddler needs is organized opportunity for play and controlled conditions for the beginnings of a social life. For the toddler we recognize that the true group is the child's own home, and for the infant we know that it is a disaster if a break in the continuity of home management becomes necessary. If we look at the earlier stages of this process we see the infant very dependent on the mother's management, and on her continued presence and her survival. She must make a good-enough adaptation to the infant's needs, else the infant cannot avoid developing defences that distort the process; for instance, the infant must take over the environmental function if the environment is not reliable, so that there is a hidden true self, and all that we can see is a false self engaged in the double task of hiding the true self and of complying with the demands that the world makes from moment to moment.

Still earlier, the infant is held by the mother, and only understands love that is expressed in physical terms, that is to say, by live, human holding. Here is absolute dependence, and environmental failure at this very early stage cannot be defended against, except by a hold-up of the developmental process, and by infantile psychosis.

Let us look now at what happens when the environment behaves well enough, all along well enough according to the needs that are specific to the moment. Psychoanalysis concerns itself (and it must do so) primarily with the meeting of instinctual needs (the ego and the id), but in this context we are more concerned with the environmental provision that makes all the rest possible; that is to say, we are more concerned here and now with the mother *holding* the baby than with the mother *feeding* the baby. What do we find in the process of individual emotional growth when the holding and the general management are good enough?

Of all that we find, that which chiefly concerns us here is that part of the process which we call integration. Before integration the individual is unorganized, a mere collection of sensory-motor phenomena, collected by the holding environment. After integration the individual IS, that is to say, the infant human being has achieved unit status, can say I AM (except for not being able to talk). The individual has now a limiting membrane, so that what is not-he or not-she is repudiated, and is external. The he or the she has now an inside, and here can be collected memories of experiences, and can be built up the infinitely complex structure that belongs to the human being.

It does not matter if this development happens in a moment or gradually over a long period of time; the fact is that there is a before and an after, and the process deserves a name all to itself.

No doubt the instinctual experiences contribute richly to the integration process, but there is also all the time the good-enough environment, someone holding the infant, and adapting well enough to changing needs. That someone cannot function except through the sort of love that is appropriate at this stage, love that carries a capacity for identification with the infant, and a feeling that adaptation to need is worth while. We say that the mother is devoted to her infant, temporarily but truly. She likes to be pre-occupied in this way, until the need for her wanes.

I suggest that this I AM moment is a raw moment; the new individual feels infinitely exposed. Only if someone has her arms round the infant at this time can the I AM moment be endured, or rather, perhaps, risked.

I would add that at this moment it is convenient when the psyche and the body have the same places in space, so that the limiting membrane is not only metaphorically a limit to the psyche, but also it is the skin of the body. 'Exposed' then means 'naked'.

Before integration there is a state in which the individual only exists for those who observe. For the infant the external world is not differentiated out, nor is there an inner or personal world or an inner reality. After integration the infant begins to have a self. Whereas before, what the mother can do is to be ready to be repudiated, afterwards what she can do is to supply support, warmth, loving care, and clothes (and soon she starts catering for instincts).

Also in this period before integration there is an area between the mother and the infant that is *both* mother and infant. If all goes well, this very gradually splits into two elements, the part that the infant eventually repudiates and the part that the infant eventually claims. But we must expect relics of this intermediate area to persist. We do indeed see this later in the infant's first affectionately held possession – perhaps a bit of cloth derived from a blanket, bedcover, or shirt; or a napkin, mother's handker-chief, etc. Such an object I like to call a 'transitional object', and the point of it is that it is both (and at the same time) a creation of the infant and a part of external reality. For this reason parents respect this object even more than they do the teddies and dolls and toys that quickly follow. The baby who loses the transitional object at the same time loses both mouth and breast, both hand and mother's skin, both creativity and objective perception. The object is one of the bridges that make contact possible between the individual psyche and external reality.

In the same way it is unthinkable that an infant should exist, before integration, without good-enough mothering. Only after integration can we say that if the mother fails the infant dies of cold, or falls infinitely down, or flies off and away, or bursts like a hydrogen bomb and destroys the self and the world in one and the same moment.

The newly integrated infant is, then, in the first *group*. Before this stage there is only a primitive pre-group formation, in which unintegrated elements are held together by an environment from which they are not yet differentiated. This environment is the holding mother.

A group is an I AM achievement, and it is a dangerous achievement. In the initial stages protection is needed, else the repudiated external world comes back at the new phenomenon and attacks from all quarters and in every conceivable way.

If we continued this study of the individual's evolution, we would see how the more and more complex personal growth complicates the picture of group growth. But at this point let us follow up the implications of our basic assumption.

The formation of groups

We have reached the stage of *an integrated human unit*, and at the same time someone who might be called *mother who supplies covering*, knowing full well the paranoid state that is inherent in the newly integrated state. I can hope to be understood if I use the two terms 'individual unit' and 'maternal covering'.

Groups may have origin in either of the two extremes implied in these terms:

 (i) Superimposed units
 (ii) Covering.

(i) The basis of mature group formation is the multiplication of individual units. Ten persons, who are personally well integrated, loosely superimpose their ten integrations and to some degree share a limiting membrane. The limiting membrane is now representative of the skin of each individual member. The organization that each individual brings in terms of personal integration tends to maintain the group entity from within. This means that the group benefits from the personal experience of the individuals, each of whom has been seen through the integration moment, and has been covered until able to provide self-cover.

The group's integration implies at first an expectation of persecution, and for this reason persecution of a certain type can artificially produce a group formation, but not a stable group formation.

(ii) At the other extreme a collection of relatively unintegrated persons can be given covering, and a group may be formed. Here the group work does not come from the individuals but from the covering. The individuals go through three stages:

(a) They are glad to be covered and they gain confidence.
(b) They begin to exploit the situation, becoming dependent, and regressing to unintegration.
(c) They begin, independently of each other, to achieve some integration, and at such times they use the cover offered by the group which they need because of their expectation of persecution. Great strain is placed on the cover mechanisms. Some of these individuals do achieve personal integration, and so become ready to be moved to the other type of group in which the individuals themselves provide the group work. Others cannot be cured by cover-therapy alone, and they continue to need to be managed by an agency without identification with that agency.

It is possible to see which extreme predominates in any one group that is examined. The word 'democracy' is used to describe the most mature grouping, and democracy only applies to a collection of adult persons of whom the vast majority have achieved personal integration (as well as being mature in other ways).

Adolescent groups may achieve a kind of democracy under supervision. It is a mistake, however, to expect democracy to ripen among adolescents, even when each individual is mature. With younger healthy children the cover aspect of any group must be in evidence, while every chance is given to the individuals to contribute to the group cohesion through the same forces that promote cohesion within the individual ego structures. The limited group gives opportunity for individual contribution.

Group work with the maladjusted child

The study of group formations composed of healthy adults, adolescents, or children throws light on the problem of group management where the children are ill, illness here meaning maladjustment.

This ugly word – maladjustment – means that at some early date the environment failed to adjust appropriately to the child, and the child is therefore compelled either to take over the cover-work and so to lose personal identity, or else to push round in society forcing someone else to act cover, so that a chance may come for a new start with personal integration.

The antisocial child has two alternatives – to annihilate the true self or to shake society up till it provides cover. In the second alternative if cover is found then the true self can re-emerge, and it is better to exist in prison than to become annihilated in meaningless compliance.

In terms of the two extremes that I have described, it is evident that no group of maladjusted children will adhere because of the personal integration of the boys and girls. This is partly due to the fact that the group is composed of adolescents or children, immature human beings, but chiefly because the children are all more or less unintegrated. Each boy or girl therefore has an abnormal degree of need for cover because each is ill in just that way, having been overstrained in this matter of the integration process at some point or other in early childhood or in infancy.

How, then, can we provide for these children in such a way as to ensure that what we offer them will be adapted to their changing needs as they progress towards health? There are two alternative methods:

(i) By the first, a hostel keeps the same group of children and is responsible for seeing them through; it provides what is necessary at the various stages of their development. In the beginning the staff provide cover, and the group is a cover-group. In this cover-group the children (after the honeymoon period) become worse, and with luck they reach a rock-bottom of unintegration. They do not all do this at one moment, fortunately, and they use each other, so that one child is usually much worse than the others at any one time. (How tempting it is to be always getting rid of the one, and so to be always failing at the critical point!)

Gradually one by one the children begin to achieve personal integration, and in the course of five to ten years they are the same children but they have become a new kind of group. Cover technique can be lessened, and the group starts to integrate by the forces that make for integration within each individual.

The staff are always ready to re-establish cover, as when a child steals in the first job, or in some other way shows symptoms of the fear that belongs to a belated attainment of the I AM state, or relative independence.

(ii) By the other method, a group of hostels work together. Each hostel is classified according to the kind of work it is doing, and it maintains its type. For example:

A hostel gives 100 per cent cover
B hostel gives   90 per cent cover
C hostel gives   65 per cent cover
D hostel gives   50 per cent cover
E hostel gives   40 per cent cover

The children know the various hostels in the group through visits that are deliberately planned, and there are interchanges of assistants also. When a child in A hostel achieves some sort of personal integration he or she moves up one. In this way the children who improve progress towards E hostel, which is able to cover the child's adolescent plunge into the world.

The group of hostels is itself covered, in such a case, by some authority and by a hostels committee.

The awkward thing about this second method is that the hostel staffs will fail to understand each other unless they meet and are kept fully informed as to the method employed and the way it is working out. The B hostel that gives 90 per cent cover and does all the dirty work will be looked down on; there will be alarms and excursions at this hostel. Hostel A will be better placed because here there will be no room at all for individual freedom; all the children will look happy and well fed, and visitors will like it the best of all the five. The warden will need to be a dictator and he will no doubt think that the failures in the other hostels are due to lax discipline. But the children in Hostel A have not yet started. They are getting ready to start.

In Hostels B and C, where children lie about on the floor, cannot get up, refuse to eat, mess their pants, steal whenever they feel a loving impulse, torture cats, kill mice and bury them so as to have a cemetery where they can go and cry, in these hostels there should be a notice: visitors not admitted. The wardens of these hostels have the perpetual job of covering naked souls, and they see as much suffering as can be seen in a mental hospital for adults. How difficult it is to keep a good staff under these conditions!

Summary

Of all that can be said about hostels as groups I have chosen to speak of the relation of the group work to the plus or minus quantity of the personal integration of the individual children. I believe this relationship to be basic: where there is a plus sign the children bring their own integrating forces with them; when there is a minus sign the hostel provides cover, like clothes for a naked child and like the personal human holding of an infant newly born.

When there is a muddle of classification in respect of the factor of personal integration, then a hostel cannot find its place. The illnesses of the ill children dominate, and the more normal children who could be contributing to the group work cannot be given opportunity, since cover must be provided all the time and everywhere.

I believe that my over-simplification of the problem in this way will be justified if it can give a simple language for the better classification of children and of hostels. Those who work in such hostels are being all the time avenged for innumerable early environmental failures which were not their doing. If they are to stand the terrific strain of tolerating this and even in some cases of correcting the past failure through their tolerance, then they must at least know what it is that they are doing, and why it is that they cannot all the time succeed.

Classification of cases

On the basis of acceptance of the ideas that have been put forward, it is possible gradually to enter into the complexity of the problem of groups. I conclude with a rough classification of types of case.

(a) Those children who are ill in the sense that they have not become integrated into units, and who therefore cannot contribute to a group.

(b) Those children who have developed a false self which has the function of making and maintaining contact with the environment and at the same time of protecting and hiding the true self. In these cases there is a deceptive integration which breaks down as soon as it is taken for granted and called upon for a contribution.

(c) Those children who are ill in the sense of being withdrawn. Here the integration has been achieved and the defence is along the lines of a rearrangement of benign and malign forces. These children live in their own inner worlds which are artificially benign although alarming because of the operation of magic. Their outer worlds are malign or persecutory.

(d) Those children who maintain a personal integration by over-emphasis of integration, and a defence from threat of disintegration which takes the form of establishment of a strong personality.

(e) Those children who have known good-enough early management and who have been able to employ an intermediate world with objects that derive importance through representing at one and the same time external and internal objects of value. They have nevertheless suffered from an interruption of the continuity of their management to a degree which broke up the use of intermediate objects. These children are the ordinary 'deprived complex' children, whose behaviour develops antisocial qualities whenever they begin to hope again. They steal and crave for affection and claim that we shall believe their lies. At their best they regress in a general way, or in a localized way as in bed-wetting, which represents a momentary regression in relation to a dream. At their worst they force society to tolerate their symptoms of hope although they are unable immediately to benefit from their symptoms. They do not find what they want by stealing but they may eventually (because someone tolerates their stealing) reach some degree of new belief in having a claim on the world. In this group is the whole range of antisocial behaviour.

(f) Those children who have had a tolerably good early start but who suffer from the effects of parental figures with whom it is unsuitable for them to identify. There are innumerable sub-groups here, examples of which are:

(i) Mother chaotic
(ii) Mother depressed
(iii) Father absent
(iv) Mother anxious
(v) Father appearing as stern parent without earning the right to be stern
(vi) Parents quarrelling, which joins up with overcrowded conditions and the child sleeping in the parents' room, etc.

(g) Children with manic-depressive tendencies, with or without a hereditary or genetic element.

(h) Children who are normal except when in depressive phases.

(i) Children with an expectation of persecution and a tendency to get bullied or to become bullies. In boys this can form the basis of homosexual practice.

(j) Children who are hypomanic, with the depression either latent or hidden in psychosomatic disorders.

(k) All those children who are sufficiently integrated and socialized to suffer (when they are ill) from the inhibitions and compulsions and organizations of defence against anxiety, which are roughly classed together under the word psycho-neurosis.

(l) Lastly, the normal children, by which we mean children who, when faced with environmental abnormalities or danger situations, can employ any defence mechanism, but who are not driven towards one type of defence mechanism by distortions of personal emotional development.

23 *The persecution that wasn't*

(Review of *A Home from Home* by Sheila Stewart, 1967)

As an addict to autobiography I welcome this book: it has value as good reading. As a clinician I note with relief that Sheila Stewart, this child of misfortune, found that the world gradually shaped her into a happy person. One can see in the story all the awful environmental conditions that persecute so many who are illegitimate and who have good cause to complain, but for Sheila somehow the persecutions failed to persecute. Consequently the reader is not side-tracked into withers-wringing, and is free to glean truths from every little episode and from the sequence of events. For instance, the gradual development in Sheila of sex into a real in-love relationship and a marriage is highly instructive. Much depended on the exercise of a parental function, often harsh, offered by the matron of her church home; and there could scarcely be a better advertisement than this for a certain Church Society.

It is the little things that make the story ring true for me. For example, describing collecting money for the home, evacuated in the war to Ascot: 'I did not mind painting the huge notices CAR PARK 10/-, but I felt like a pauper selling our home-made, fresh flower buttonholes or sprays to all the grand gentlemen and ladies . . .' and ''Ere, catch! – Put it in yer moonay box! I caught the crumpled ball of paper and held it tightly in my hot resentful hand until all the vehicles had gone . . . I knew the £5 note was not mine; with the rest of my tips I handed it over to Matron. It belonged to the Family "moonay box".'

Compare this with the Robert Graves incident recounted in (of all places!) his LSE Annual Oration 1963, entitled *Mammon*: 'A holiday incident from my North Wales childhood comes to mind. We had bought teas at a lakeside farm; afterwards I went to play in the farmyard. When a wagonette drove up with more visitors, I ran to open the gate. Someone tossed me a sixpence, and though I did not throw it back, the idea that my disinterested courtesy had been mistaken for money making shocked me . . .' Common denominators can be very simple units.

As a clinician I must add an opinion as to why the persecutory elements failed to persecute. Sheila had a basically good first experience on the North Devon coast with her winkle-picking Danma, her fisherman Danpa and the freedom of the sea-shore. So the happy ending is an echo of the opening phrase of the book: 'I sat contentedly on the sea wall swinging my bare feet. I was tired of picking up the winkles and running over the wet sand to put them in the buckets Danma had brought down to the shore . . .'

24 *Comments on the* Report of the Committee on Punishment in Prisons and Borstals *(1961)*

This seems to me to be a very valuable report and gives the impression of being made after full investigation. Especially welcome is the frank comment on tobacco trafficking by a prisoner, which rings true as it is printed with all its grammatical errors.

I find myself wanting to make five comments on the report; the first is a general one:

(1) I have drawn attention elsewhere to the fact that there is a danger in the modern tendency towards sentimentality whenever the punishment of offenders is being considered. As a psychoanalyst I feel inclined to regard every offender as ill and as a distressed person, although the distress is not always evident. From this point of view one could say that it is illogical to punish an offender. What he or she requires is treatment or remedial management. The fact remains, however, that the offender has committed an offence, that is to say, the community has to react somehow or other to the sum total of offences committed against it in a given length of time. It is one thing to be a psychoanalyst investigating the cause of thieving, and another thing to be a person from whom a bicycle is stolen at a critical moment. In fact there is another point of view. The psychoanalyst is also a member of society and joins in as a member of society in having to manage the reactions which are natural to the person hurt by the anti-social act. It is impossible to get away from the principle that the first function of the law is to express the unconscious revenge of society. It is quite possible for any individual offender to be forgiven and yet for there to be a reservoir of revenge and also of fear which we cannot afford to neglect; we cannot think only in terms of treating individual criminals, forgetting that society has

been wounded and also needs treatment. My own inclination, along with that of a very large number of people at the present time, is to widen as much as possible the range of offence which is treated as an illness. It is because of hope in this direction that I feel like making it quite clear that the law cannot suddenly give up the punishment of all criminals. Possibly if society's revenge feelings were fully conscious society could stand the treatment of the offender as ill, but so much of the revenge is unconscious that allowance must be made all the time for the need for punishment to be kept up to some extent even when it is not useful in the treatment of the offender.

There is a conflict here which we cannot avoid by pretending it is non-existent. We have to be able to feel the conflict as something essential to any serious consideration of the subject of punishment. It is important that these matters should be constantly brought to the fore, otherwise there will be reaction against the treatment of offenders as ill even though it can be shown that this is a good thing, as in the case of children.

At the present time the tendency is to do the best for the delinquent or antisocial boy or girl rather than to avenge. Except in the case of really serious crime the adolescent and young adult also come into this category. Perhaps in time other sections of the antisocial community can be treated as ill rather than as subjects for punishment, and the report mentions that at least 5 per cent of the present prison population would be considered by most doctors to be psychiatric cases, and notably manic depressives.

To sum up, those of us who are working for the extension of the principle of treatment rather than punishment must not blind ourselves to the great danger of producing a reaction by ignoring society's need to be avenged, not for any one particular crime, but for criminality in general.

The report deals more clearly with the need of the public for protection and with society's fear than it does with the unconscious revenge reservoir and indeed I am fully aware that it is a very unpopular thing at the present time to postulate such feeling. Whenever I put forward this point of view I know that I shall be misunderstood and shall be thought to be calling for punishment rather than for the treatment of these ill people, the antisocials.

(2) I have already mentioned that perhaps the most valuable part

of the report is the inclusion in it of the prisoner's statement about tobacco. There is room I think for comment on the need to smoke. One does not have to be a psychoanalyst to know that smoking is not just something done for pleasure. It is something which has a very great importance in the lives of many people, and which cannot be given up without substitution of something else. Smoking can be vitally important to individuals, especially when there is widespread hopelessness in a community. The psycho-analyst is able to watch at close quarters the use of tobacco and indeed there is a great deal of research to be done on this subject before it can be properly understood. Without waiting for clear understanding it is possible already to state that smoking is one of the ways in which individuals can just hold on to sanity, when without smoking and especially if alcohol and other drugs are withheld, the sense of reality is lost and the personality tends to disintegrate. There is of course a great deal more in smoking than this, but I think it should be appreciated by those who deal with the subject of smoking in prisons that the fact that so much trafficking in tobacco goes on in spite of all regulations and in spite of every possible effort on the part of the authorities to curb it, confirms one theory, which is that criminals are on the whole in a state of great distress and in constant fear of madness.

There are many who have not experienced the fear of madness and for them it is impossible to imagine what it can be like to be kept without proper occupation over a big chunk of the life span, always on the edge of delusions, hallucinations, disintegration of the personality, feelings of unreality, loss of sense that one's body is one's own, and so on.

A superficial investigation will not reveal these things. It will only reveal the excitement that belongs to the acquiring of tobacco and the skill and cunning that belongs to the whole racket. One would not have to go very deep, however, to discover the fear of madness. I cannot claim to have made any study of adult prisoners, but from a close study of a very large number of the children who eventually form the prison population I know that fear of madness is ever present, and that the antisocial set-up is on the whole a complex defence against delusions of persecution, hallucinations, and a going to pieces without hope of recovery. I am speaking of something which is worse than unhappiness, and on the whole one would feel pleased when an antisocial child, or adult for that matter, reaches the stage of unhappiness. At this point there is hope and there is also a possibility of providing help. The hardened antisocial has to defend himself even from hope because by experience he knows that the pain of losing hope again and again is unbearable. In one way and another tobacco provides something which enables the individual to hang on and to postpone life until living makes sense again.

A practical suggestion comes out of this. In the report it is suggested that wages to prisoners should be increased on the grounds really that the price of tobacco has gone up and wages have remained stationary. The rise will not, however, enable the prisoner to smoke 1 oz. of tobacco a week. There is a quantity (which could be worked out) which would make life bearable for the prisoner and in my opinion there is a great deal to be said for making it possible for each prisoner to have at least this minimal quantity.

As there may be some non-smokers it would seem to be more sensible to allow tobacco to be sold as in the navy out of bond rather than to raise wages. Speaking theoretically, the latter process (raising wages) must seem to put the non-smoker in a very strong position for becoming a tobacco baron because he will be a rich man in the prison community. Perhaps the reason why the suggestion of having tobacco out of bond in prisons is not made is that the public might think that the prisoner is now going to have a wonderful time and from what I have said in the first paragraph it can be seen that I appreciate that the public must know that prisoners are not being pampered. Nevertheless in so far as the public can be educated this should be attempted and I think that most people can see, if it is pointed out to them, that for the long-term prisoner smoking makes the difference between life being just bearable and life being one continuous mental torture.

(3) When it comes to a consideration of the borstals, the visiting committee was obviously horrified by the state of some of the boys seen. Apparently they had matted hair and did not spring to attention when passing officers. It may be that the public really demands that military discipline should be observed in borstals, but it is not certain, and I feel that this part of the report may do a good deal of harm. The committee definitely states that it is not asking for military discipline; nevertheless there are probably

only the two alternatives: one is military discipline rather after the Nazi pattern and this keeps everything nice and quiet because the boys are so fully occupied that they have no time to think or to grow; and the other is a rather horrifying extreme of allowing the boys to reach down to the hopelessness which is the bottom of their illness, but which may be the beginning of their growth. If this cannot be explained in terms which the public can appreciate then military discipline will have to be instituted. The whole idea of borstal training, however, is to avoid precisely this. To be a governor of a borstal is a terrible job which can only be undertaken by someone with a mission, as the committee points out: indeed there was no criticism of the governors, the difficulty of whose job is fully recognized. Nevertheless if a governor is to be afraid that a member of a committee will turn up and see a boy with matted hair he must institute practically what amounts to military discipline. In the only other alternative there will always be some boys at some time or another who only feel honest if they look like tramps. When they get to this stage the future is not altogether obscure and the prognosis not altogether hopeless. Military discipline however makes every case hopeless because no young man can develop individual responsibility and personality in that atmosphere.

In my opinion those who are responsible for the borstals should have complete trust in the governor and then allow him to use his own judgement. If he has not the confidence of the authorities he should be removed, but if he is governor then he must be allowed to experiment and to feel his own way and to try the alternative to military discipline. In the course of this he will discover some boys who are unsuitable for anything but military discipline or prison and he should be relieved of these by some means or other. The committee mentions this and points out that an experimental borstal for the minority who spoil the work for the majority in the ordinary borstals should be set up immediately. This would seem to be urgent. If it is not done immediately then the whole borstal idea will fizzle out and discipline will take the place of therapy through management.

(4) The report deals with the subject of absconding, which it is pointed out is a better word than escaping, considering that borstals have no closed doors. What I miss, however, is a study of

the causes for absconding. It is not quite clear from the report that the members of the committee know that a good deal of work has been done on the psychology of absconding. In the hostels for evacuated children in the war many studies of absconding were made although perhaps not all were published. Children do not just run away because they are cowards or because the system by which they are managed is wrong. Often running away has positive features, and represents the growing confidence that they have found a place that would welcome them back after they have run away from it.

The machinery that the report describes for dealing with absconders on their return seems to me to leave little room for judgement on the part of the staff who may know perfectly well from their study of an individual case that the boy simply needs on return to be given a hug or, if that is too direct a show of feeling, to be allowed to slip back into the routine with a sigh of relief. Sometimes boys run away because they get a feeling of conviction that their mother has been run over or that their sister is in hospital with diphtheria or something like that. They have what seems to the observer to be an absurd idea that they can find out the truth. Actually by the time they get anywhere near their objective the main aim is lost so that often all that is *seen* is a boy running away and getting into bad company and stealing money for food. Among the abnormal children who constitute any anti-social group there are always many who develop astonishing ideas of what home is like when they have been away from it for a certain length of time. This is well known but bears repetition. A boy or girl who has been rescued from the most ghastly basement dwelling with cruel and drunken parents, after a few months in a hostel or institution can develop such a strong idea that home is the summation of all that is good that it becomes silly not to run away. In such cases all that is required is for the child to reach home and then to be gently led back sad and disillusioned and very much in need of a little affection. It is in all cases a most delicate thing, this management of the absconder on his return, and it can be done only by the persons who know the boy or girl well. It is unlikely that a visiting committee could act in the best way on such occasions.

(5) It would seem to be important in a report on punishment for there to be some sort of theoretical consideration of the subject of what punishment means to the individual and to the person administering the punishment. Perhaps such a theoretical chapter would have been out of place in this report but punishment is a subject requiring study and research just like any other subject. In all cases one can say that there are two aspects of the problem. Society demands that the individual be punished. The individual being ill is not in a state to derive benefit from punishment, and is indeed most likely to have to develop pathological trends, masochistic and other, for dealing with the punishment as it comes.

In a very favourable case punishment may succeed, that is to say, a boy who has come to doubt the existence of a father, his own father having been absent for some years because of the war, may recover the sense of having a father through the strong line taken by his father when he behaves in an antisocial way. This is a rare type of case, however, and is unlikely to be met with in a borstal. Punishment is only valuable when it brings alive a strong and loved reliable father figure for an individual who has lost just exactly that. All other punishment can be said to be a blind expression of the unconscious revenge of society. Certainly a very great deal more could be said about the theory of punishment, and while a report on punishment leaves out the theoretical background of the subject it cannot properly express the forward tendencies in modern society.

25 Do progressive schools give too much freedom to the child?

(A contribution to a conference on 'The Future for Progressive Education' held at Dartington Hall, 12–14 April, 1965)

In this paper it is necessary for me to deal with the subject that has been given me from the theoretical angle, since I have no first-hand experience of progressive schools, either as pupil or teacher.

My speciality being child-psychiatry, with psychoanalysis as a ground-base, I must look at this subject of progressive schools in terms of the work that I have done with innumerable ill children and sometimes ill parents.

Diagnosis

In all kinds of medical care the basis of action is diagnosis. This is certainly true of psychiatry and of child psychiatry. In psychiatry social diagnosis has its place alongside the diagnosis of the individual patient.

My thesis in this contribution to your discussion is that nothing can be said about Progressive Education except on a firm basis of diagnosis.

Education proper can perhaps be discussed in terms of putting across the Rs or introducing the principles of physics or presenting the facts of history, though even in this limited field the teacher must learn to know the pupil. Special education of any kind is, however, a different matter, and progressive schools have an aim that transcends the banality of teaching and enters the wider field of the individual need. It will easily be conceded, therefore, that those who discuss progressive schools cannot avoid having a vested interest in the study of the nature of each individual pupil.

What cannot be assumed is that an educationalist will have at hand a theoretical basis for the making of a diagnosis. Perhaps it is here that the child-psychiatrist can help.

In illustration, should illustration be needed, let me take another problem, the problem of corporal punishment. Often one hears or reads a discussion of the good or bad aspects of corporal punishment, and one knows that this discussion is doomed to remain futile because no attempt is being made to sort out the boys according to the state of their emotional growth. To take two extremes: in a school for normal boys from normal homes corporal punishment may be considered along with a number of other moderately important issues, whereas in a school designed to cater for children with behaviour disorders and, in a high proportion of cases, broken homes, then corporal punishment needs to be considered as a vital issue, and indeed as a detail of management that is always harmful.

Curiously enough it is in the management of the first group that corporal punishment can sometimes be ruled out by an edict, and it is in the management of the second group that corporal punishment may need to be kept as a possibility, something that could be employed if circumstances seem to warrant, i.e. not ruled out by a committee of management.

This is a relatively simple problem as compared with the wide subject of progressive schools and their place in the community. But perhaps the analogy can be used in the introduction.

It will be necessary to proceed step by step. (I must assume physical health.)

Classification A

Child normal (psychiatrically)
Child abnormal (psychiatrically)
    What is normal?

Normality or health has been discussed by many (including myself).[1] This state does not carry freedom from symptoms. It implies that in the personality structure of the child the defences are organized satisfactorily, but without rigidity. Rigidity of

---

[1] D. W. Winnicott *The Child and the Family*. London: Tavistock Publications, 1957. *The Child, the Family, and the Outside World*. London: Penguin, 1964.

defences hampers further growth, and disturbs the child's contact with the environment.

The positive sign of health is the continuing growth process, the fact of emotional change in the direction of development,

> development towards integration;
> development from dependence to independence;
> development in terms of instinct and,

add development in terms of richness in the personality.

Also: steadiness of rate of development is a positive feature. (It is difficult to assess health in terms of behaviour.) Social diagnosis now needs to be brought into play:

> Home intact, functioning.
> Home intact, lame functioning.
> Home broken.
> Home never established.

> *also*

> Home well integrated into a social grouping narrow.
> wide.

> Home establishing itself in society.
> Home withdrawn from society.
> Home ostracized by society.

It will perhaps be conceded that the majority of children in the community are:

> Healthy, with lives based on the intact family that is integrated into a social grouping (though this grouping may be narrow or even pathological in some aspect).

For these children schools are to be assessed according to their ability to facilitate:

> Personal: enrichment of personality.
> Familial: integration of home with school life.
> Social: initial interweaving with family's social grouping. Possible widening of social grouping of the individual child growing up to become an independent adult.

It is necessary to allow for the existence of a proportion of children who can be called normal or healthy in spite of their having broken families or families with awkward social connections. Among the healthy children will be found those who are ill in the sense of

Psycho-neurosis
Mood disorder
Pathological psycho-somatic interaction
Schizoid personality structure
Schizophrenia

Most of such children may be counted as normal or healthy if they belong to intact families that are socially integrated, and such children can be treated by management or by psychotherapy within the home–school setting. These are among the ordinary term-by-term troubles of home–school intercommunication, and they can be ranked with spring-term infectious diseases and acute appendicitis and other emergencies, and with the fractured bone that belongs to the playing of games.

Clearly extreme degrees of these illnesses may affect the type of school that is selected.

Diagnosis of deprivation

There is one kind of classification that is of vital importance to those who think in terms of educational systems, and yet this form of classification is not always given due place. It cuts right across the classification according to type of neurotic or psychotic defence organization, and it even includes (at one extreme) some boys and girls who are potentially normal. This classification is in terms of *deprivation*. The deprived or relatively deprived child has had environmental provision that was good enough so that there was a continuity of personal being, and then became deprived of this: deprived at an age (in emotional development) at which the process could be felt and perceived. The reaction to a deprivation (i.e. not to a privation) is one that holds the child in its grip – henceforth the world must be made to acknowledge and repair the injury. But as the process is largely working in the unconscious, the world does not succeed, or does so by paying heavily.

We call these children maladjusted. They are in the grip of the antisocial tendency. The clinical picture is to be observed in terms of:

(a) Stealing (lying, etc.), staking claims.
(b) Destruction, attempting to force the environment to re-constitute the framework, the loss of which made the child lose spontaneity, since spontaneity only makes sense in a controlled setting. Content is of no meaning without form.

The diagnosis along these lines is of utmost significance when the place of progressive schools is being discussed.

A group of deprived children can be said

(1) To need a Progressive School;
    and at the same time
(2) To be most likely to break it up.

In other words, the challenge to those who favour progressive schools is of the following nature. These schools will tend to be used by persons trying to place deprived children. Any idea of providing opportunity for creative learning, that is, of giving a better education to normal children, will be vitiated by the fact that a big proportion of the pupils will not be able to get down to learning because they are busy with a more important task, namely the discovery and establishment, each one, of his or her own identity (arising out of loss of sense of identity relative to deprivation).

A good result is often not to be measured in academic terms; it may be that all the school did was to keep a pupil (i.e. not expelling him or her) until the time came for passing him or her on to a wider area of living.

In this way, in some cases the school will have succeeded in curing or almost curing a deprived child of having a compulsion to go on being antisocial. Along with this must be some failures, tantalizing failures causing heartbreaks because the school has had the chance to see the best as well as the worst (or compulsive antisocial) side of the child's nature.

I think it is important that this aspect of the progressive school work should be stated as clearly as possible, otherwise those responsible get disheartened; and if those responsible become disheartened, then there tends to follow a gradual change over in the school towards being an ordinary school which is suitable for educating healthy children from intact families, but which is no longer progressive.

NOTES MADE IN THE TRAIN
(After the conference at Dartington Hall, April, 1965)

PART I

The label: PROGRESSIVE SCHOOLS = a legitimate nickname implying:

(1) 'Forward-reaching.'
(2) Operating from a creative if not actually *rebellious* element in someone's nature. This means that general acceptance has the effect of undermining motivation. Awkwardness in individuals may cause waste in terms of energy, but the advantage is to be measured in terms of originality, experimentation, tolerance of failure, leadership.

'Forward-reaching' means:

(a) Having a firm base in terms of an awareness of the actual here and now.
(b) To this here and now actuality add a forging ahead. (The establishment of won principles has to be left to the establishment. The look-out for backsliding may, however, be the concern of the creative rebel.)
(c) The meaning of the word *ahead* depends partly on

(1) the actual here and now;
(2) the temperament of the pioneer.

For the 'progressive' movement 'ahead' could have to do with:

Positive:

A. The dignity of the individual in his or her own right, and as a basis for social dignity.
B. A theory of individual emotional development that allows for:

(1) inherited potential;
(2) the (inherited) maturational process;
(3) dependence for maturational development on a facilitating environment;

(4) evolution in terms of DEPENDENCE-TOWARDS-INDEPENDENCE matched by evolution in terms of the environment that adapts and then fails to adapt (graduated change).

C. A theory of human failure (personality, character, behaviour) that takes into consideration both:

    (1) environmental abnormalities

and   (2) the difficulties inherent in human growth and self-establishment and self-expression.

Corollary: provision of facilities for personal psycho-therapy.

D. A theory that allows for the importance of the instinctual life, and that recognizes not only that which is not conscious but also that which is under *repression*, repression being an energy-absorbing defence.

E. A theory which sees society in terms of

    (1) history, past, and future

    (2) the contribution of the individual (through the family unit) to social groupings and functioning.

Negative:

A distaste for and suspicion of *indoctrination*, i.e.

    (1) blatant advertisement

or (2) teaching unrelated to creative learning

or (3) subtle propaganda techniques (affecting behaviour, politics, religion, morals, attitudes generally).

Practical matters – provision of opportunities

        countryside,
        equipment,
        contact with local industry,
        for service locally, etc.

A parental sharing of responsibility for a general attitude.
This is relatively direct (c.f. indirect sharing in the state school system via politics and via the Department of Education and the Teacher Training Centres).

Problems:

(1) How to teach better on basis of the individual's learning capacity.
(2) How to combine:
    (a) freedom to the individual

with (b) those controls that are necessary if the individual is not to set up crude primitive or even sadistic inner (unconscious) superego systems.

(3) How to assess failure and to profit by failures (failures being an essential element in experimentation).

How to avoid becoming a pioneer turned conservator and obstructionist?

Questions:

(1) Is the 'progressive' label absolutely linked with co-education, as it is with revolt relative to indoctrination? (I suggest that it is not.)
(2) Is the progressive label linked with intolerance of hate, meeting hate, aggression meeting control, of competition (polite name for war)?
(3) Is there a flight from fantasy in the attempt in some progressive schools to include everything, i.e. a failure to allow for personal inner psychic reality? (i.e. the withdrawn individual in uncouth surroundings may be having a more rich personal experience than some of the participants in a richly functioning here and now (extrovert) situation.) I suggest the answer is No, not in most instances, but possibly in some.

PART II

Development of theme of control

Axiom. It is not profitable to discuss control apart from a statement on the diagnosis of the child or adult who may possibly come under control (see relevant paragraph in my conference paper).

When considering the question of diagnosis of those subject to control an important factor will be the (relative) maturity of the individual as seen in the history and quality of the relationship to the primary love object that he or she has established. I suggest that we might profitably speculate in the following way:

What can a human being do with an object? At the beginning the relation is to a subjective object. Gradually subject and object become separated out, and then there is the relation to the object-ively perceived object. Subject destroys object.

This splits up into:
(1) subject preserves object;
(2) subject *uses* object;
(3) subject *destroys* object.

(1) This is idealization.
(2) Use of object: this is a sophisticated idea, an achievement of healthy emotional growth, not attained except in health and in the course of time.

Meanwhile there appears
(3) which appears clinically as a rendering down of the object from perfection towards some kind of badness. (Denigration, dirtying, tearing, etc.) This protects the object because it is only the perfect object that is worthy of destruction. This is not idealization but denigration.

In the course of the individual's growth it becomes possible for the destruction to have adequate representation in the (unconscious) fantasy that is an elaboration of body func-tioning and instinctual experiences of all kinds.

This aspect of growth enables the individual to become concerned about the destruction that goes with object-relating, and to experience guilt relative to the destructive ideas that go with loving. On the basis of this the individual finds the motivation for constructive effort and for giving and for mending (Klein's reparation and restitution).

The practical issue here arises out of the distinction between

(1) spoiling the good object to render it less good and so less under attack, and
(2) the destruction that is at the root of object relating and that becomes (in health) channelled off into the destruction that takes place in the unconscious, in the individual's inner

psychic reality, in the individual's dream life and play activities, and in creative expression.

The latter does not need control; what is needed here is for the provision of conditions that allow for the emotional growth of the individual, continuous from earliest infancy until the time when the complexities of fantasy and displacement become available to the individual in his or her search for a personal solution.

By contrast, the compulsive denigration, messing and destruction that belongs to the former, an alteration of the object aimed at making it less exciting and less worthy of destruction, this needs society's attention. For example: the antisocial person who enters an art gallery and slashes a picture by an old master is not activated by love of the painting and in fact is not being as destructive as the art-lover is when preserving the picture and using it fully and in unconscious fantasy destroying it over and over again. Nevertheless the vandal's one act of vandalism affects society, and society must protect itself. This rather crude example may serve to show the existence of a wide difference between the destructiveness that is inherent in object-relating, and the destructiveness that stems from an individual's immaturity.

In the same way, compulsive heterosexual behaviour has a complex aetiology, and is a very long way away from the capacity of a man and woman to love each other in a sexual way when they have decided to set up together a home for possible children. In the former case there is included the element of the spoiling of what is perfect or of being spoiled, and no longer perfect, in an effort to lessen anxiety.

In the latter case, relatively mature persons have dealt with destruction, with concern, and with the sense of guilt within themselves, and have become free to plan to use sex constructively, not denying the crude elements that hang around in the total sex fantasy.

It is a matter for surprise when one discovers how little the romantic lover, and how very little the teenage heterosexual, know *about the total sex fantasy*, conscious and unconscious, with its competitiveness, its cruelty, its pregenital elements of crude destruction and its dangers.

Those who wave the progressive flag in education do need to study these things otherwise they too easily mistake hetero-sexuality for health, and find it convenient when violence does not appear, or only shows as the irrational reactive pacifism of adolescence which bears but little relation to the crude realities of the actual world which one day these adolescents will enter as competitive adults.

26 *Residential care as therapy*

(The David Wills Lecture, given to the Association of
Workers for Maladjusted Children, 23 October, 1970. Dr
Winnicott died in January, 1971.)

A great deal of growing is growing downwards. If I live long
enough I hope I may dwindle and become small enough to get
through the little hole called dying. I do not need to go far to find
an inflated psychotherapist. There's me. In the decade called the
thirties I was learning to be a psychoanalyst, and I could feel that,
with a little more training, a little more skill, and a little more luck I
could move mountains by making the right interpretations at the
right moment. This would be therapy, well worth the five-a-week
sessions and the cost charged for such work, and the disruption
that the treatment of one member of a family can cause to the rest
of the family.

As my insight deepened I found that, like my colleagues, I could
make significant shifts in patients' material as presented in the
treatment hours; I could induce greater hope and therefore bigger
commitment and more and more valuable unconscious co-
operation, and indeed it was all very fine and dandy, and I
planned to spend the remainder of my professional life practising
psychotherapy. At one time I could have been heard saying that
there is no therapy except on the basis of fifty minutes five times a
week, going on for as many years as necessary, done by a trained
psychoanalyst.

I have made this sound silly, but I don't mean it to be so; I
simply mean that that's a kind of beginning. But sooner or later
the process of growing smaller starts, and it's painful at first, till
you get used to it. For me I think I started to grow smaller at the
time of my first contact with David Wills. David will not let
himself be proud of his work in an old Poor Law Institution in
Bicester. It was notable work, and I am proud for him.

The two chief characteristics of the place were the long baths built for the scrubbing of tall tramps, since the buildings were designed as a state hotel on the route from Oxford to Pershore, and also the champagne rhubarb which grew as a weed, and which was appreciated more by the staff (including myself as visiting psychiatrist) than by the boys.

It was exciting to be involved with the life of this wartime hostel for evacuation failures. Naturally it collected the most unmanageable boys in the area, and a familiar sound was like this: a car would drive up at some speed, the bell-pull would start up a clatter of bells, someone would open the front door; the door would bang to the accompaniment of a car whose engine had been left running making off as if chased by a fiend. It would be found that a boy had been slipped into the front door, often with no warning phone call, and a new problem had been put on the David Wills plate. Perhaps the boy had done no more than burn down a haystack or obstruct the railway line, but these things were frowned on in the phase of the war around Dunkirk and the knife-edge of outcome. Be that as it may behind the banged door there was always a new inmate.

What part did I play? Well, this is where I try to describe growing down. At first in my weekly visits I would see a boy or two, give each a personal interview in which the most astonishing and revealing things would happen. I would sometimes get David and some of his staff to listen while I told the story of the interview, in which I made smashing interpretations based on deep insight, relative to material breathlessly presented by boys who were longing to get personal help. But I could feel my little bits of sowing fall on stony ground.

Rather quickly I learned that the therapy was being done in the institution, by the walls and the roof; by the glass conservatory which provided a target for bricks, by the absurdly large baths for which an enormous amount of precious wartime coal had to be used up if the water was to reach up to the navel of the swimmers.

The therapy was being done by the cook, by the regularity of the arrival of food on the table, by the warm enough and perhaps warmly coloured bedspreads, by the efforts of David to maintain order in spite of shortage of staff and a constant sense of the futility of it all, because the word success belonged somewhere else, and not to the task asked of Bicester Poor Law Institution. Of course

the boys ran away, they stole from the houses in the neighbourhood, and they kept breaking glass till the committee really began
to get worried. The sound of breaking glass took on epidemic
proportions. Fortunately the champagne rhubarb was a long way
away, towards the west, where exhausted members of the staff
could stand in the quiet and watch the sunset.

When I came to look further into what was going on I found that
David was doing important things based on certain principles
which we are still trying to state and to relate to a theoretical
structure. It may be that what we are talking about is a kind of
loving, and I shall say more about this later. We have to examine
the things that come naturally in the home setting in order that we
may do these things deliberately and adapt what we do eco-
nomically to the special needs of individual children or meet
special situations as they arise.

I continue talking about David Wills not only because this is the
David Wills Lecture but also because for me watching his work
was one of the early educational knocks which made me understand that there is something about psychotherapy which is not to
be described in terms of making the right interpretation at the
right moment.

Naturally I needed to have had a decade in which I explored to
the full the use of the technique that really stems from Freud, the
technique which he devised for the investigation of the repressed
unconscious which obviously would not allow of a direct
approach. I began to see, however, that in psychotherapy it is
necessary for the boy or girl who is seen in personal interview to
be able to return from the interview to a personal type of care, and
that even in psychoanalysis itself, by which I mean work done on
a five-a-week basis, inviting the full force of the transference
development, something special was needed from the patient
which could be described as a measure of belief in people and in
available care and help.

One of the things that David was doing was of the nature of a
weekly session in which all the boys met and were free to talk. As
can be imagined, the behaviour of the boys was irregular and
often exasperating. They wandered round; they complained of
this and that and the other; and when asked to pronounce
judgement on an offender they would often be very harsh, even
cruel, in their verdicts. Nevertheless in the extremely tolerant

atmosphere which David was able to allow, very important things were expressed by certain of the children, and one could see how each individual was trying to establish an identity and not really succeeding except perhaps through violence. One could say that every individual boy, and it would be the same of girls, was screaming out for personal help, but personal help is not available for every individual and the work of this hostel was being done on the basis of group management.

I know that many have done this work before and since, and David would say that he had done it much better in other settings than he did do it at Bicester. Nevertheless from my point of view the work done was of a high order and not to be measured in terms of superficial success and failure. It is also true that this was an exceptionally difficult group of boys because they were neither hopeless nor hopeful. On the whole they had not given up hope but they could not see the direction in which they should look in order to get help. The easiest way to get help is provocatively and through violence, but there was this other alternative, different in the extreme, in which they could save up things to say at five o'clock on Tuesdays.

Now it is necessary to look in detail at therapy that is provided by residential care. First I would like to say, however, that residential care is not just something that becomes necessary because there are not enough people properly trained to treat individuals. The therapy of residential care comes into being because there are children who lack one or both of two features essential for individual therapy. One is that the only setting that can deal with them adequately as individuals is the residential establishment; and the other is that they bring with them a low quantity of what Willi Hoffer[1] called an internal environment, that is to say an experience of good-enough environmental provision which has become incorporated and fitted into a system of a belief in things. In each case it is a matter of both personal and social diagnosis.

In residential care it is possible to provide certain environmental conditions which in fact we need to understand when we are doing even quite classical psychoanalysis. As it turns out

---

[1] See W. Hoffer, *The Early Development and Education of the Child*. London: Hogarth Press, 1981.

psychoanalysis is not just a matter of the verbalization of material brought by the patient in unconscious co-operation just ready to be verbalized, though we know that each time this is successfully accomplished the patient becomes that much less occupied with keeping something under repression, which is always a waste of energy, and which gives rise to troublesome symptoms. Even in a suitable case for classical psychoanalysis the main thing is the provision of conditions in which this particular kind of work can be done and in which the patient's unconscious co-operation can be gained to produce the material for verbalization. In other words it is the development of trust, or whatever word is best used, which is the prerequisite if a classical and correct interpretation is to be effectual.

In residential work we may leave out the verbalization and the material that is just ready for interpretation because the accent is on the total provision which is the setting. It can readily be seen that certain features are essential. I will enumerate a few.

(1) *Reliability*. There is a general attitude in the residential home, if it is a good one, which contains built-in reliability. You will want me to say quickly that this reliability is human and not mechanical. It might be mechanical in the sense that it helps if meals are on time by the clock; but whatever rules are laid down, reliability is relative because human beings are unreliable. It is possible for a psychoanalyst to be reliable for fifty minutes five times a week, and this is of extreme importance in spite of the fact that in his private life he or she is just as unreliable as anyone else. The same can be said of a nurse or a social worker or anyone dealing with human beings. The point about residential work when it is looked on as a therapy is that the children live in the private lives of the workers. They therefore get the unreliability which is human. Nevertheless there is some professional orientation even in a 24-hour service, and in any case staff must be encouraged to take time off and given opportunity to develop a private life. When one looks at the rationale of reliability as therapy one sees that a big proportion of children who are candidates for residential homes have been brought up in an environment which was chaotic either in a general way or else at a specific phase, or both. The chaotic environment for the child means *unpredictability*. Unpredictability means that the child must always expect trauma and the sacred

central area of the personality must be hidden away where nothing can do it either good or bad. The tantalizing environment produces mental confusion and the child may develop along the lines of being always confused, never organized, in the sense of orientation. Clinically we call these children restless and say they have no power of concentration and that they do not persevere. They cannot think of something they will be when they grow up. Actually they will spend their lives hiding something which could be called a true self. Perhaps they will live some kind of life in terms of the false self fringe, but the sense of existing will be linked with an un-get-at-able central true self. The complaint, if the child is given the chance to complain, is that nothing feels real or essentially important, or truly a manifestation of the self. Such children may find a solution in *compliance*, with violence always latent; sometimes manifest. Behind the acute mental confusion lies the memory of unthinkable anxiety when at least once the central core of the self was found and wounded. Such anxiety is physical and is intolerable to the individual. We describe it in terms of falling forever, going to pieces, absence of orientation, and so on, and we need to know that children who carry the memory of something like this around with them are not the same as children who because they were cared for well enough at the beginning do not have this hidden threat always to be reckoned with.

In residential care reliability of a human kind can in the course of time undo quite a severe sense of unpredictability and a great deal of the therapy of residential care can be stated in these terms.

(2) An extension of this idea can be expressed in terms of *holding*. Holding is at first physical; the egg and the baby in the womb; and then psychology is added; the baby is in somebody's arms. Then if things go well there is the family and so on. If the residential care needs to provide holding of a very early kind then the task indeed is difficult or impossible, but very frequently the residential therapy lies in the fact that the child rediscovers in the institutional environment a good-enough holding situation which got lost or broken up at a certain stage. James and Joyce Robertson have made all this abundantly clear to us through their films and writing, and John Bowlby has done more than one man's share of drawing the world's attention to the sacredness of the early

holding situation and the extreme difficulties that belong to the work of those who try to mend it. It always has to be remembered that where the child is hopeless then the symptomatology is not very troublesome. It is when the child is hopeful that the symptoms begin to include stealing and violence and ultimate claims which it would be unreasonable to meet except in terms of the recovery of that which is lost which is the claim of the very small child on the parents.

(3) You will want me to mention the fact that the therapy done in a residential setting has nothing to do with a moralistic attitude. The worker may have his or her own ideas of right and wrong. A child will certainly have a personal moral sense either latent and waiting for a chance to become a feature of the child's personality, or else present and fiercely punitive.

The residential worker, however, does no therapy by linking symptomatology with sin. There is nothing to be gained from using a moralistic category instead of a diagnostic code, the latter being based truly on aetiology, i.e. in the person and character of the individual child.

Punishment of awkward children may be needed but it has to do with the inconvenience of the symptomatology and the irritation that it engenders in those who are trying to make the home look nice for visiting members of the management committee who represent society which provides the necessary financial support. In any case children may like a limited punishment because it is so much less awful than the punishment that they are expecting, which is certainly vindictive. Vindictiveness has no place whatever in child care and in residential work. Nevertheless we are all human and in the course of a year it might be found that almost anyone has had a vindictive moment. This would just be a human failure and outside the therapeutic approach.

(4) There are many more broad principles but one of them has to do with gratitude. I suggest that in so far as therapy is the byword you are not expecting gratitude. All these things are deliberate professional attitudes based on natural home matters and any parent who expects a baby to be grateful is looking for something false. We all know that parents wait a long time before they make a

child say 'ta', and when they do they are not making a demand that the child shall mean 'thank you'. This is nicely ridiculed in the Beatles' song: 'Thank you very much'. Children find that 'thank you' is a part of compliance and puts people in a good temper. Gratitude is something quite sophisticated and may turn up according to the way that the development of the child's personality takes. We could often say that in any case we suspect gratitude, especially if it is exaggerated, knowing how easily it can be a manifestation of appeasement. Naturally I am not asking anyone to turn down a gift. I am simply saying that you do not do your work in order to receive the gratitude of the children. In a sense it is you who are grateful to them. The Provost of Derby recently at a meeting of social workers quoted from St Vincent de Paul who said to his followers, 'Pray that the poor may forgive us for helping them'. I think this contains the idea that I am putting forward that we could expect to thank children for being in need even though in making use of the therapy we provide they can be a nuisance and can wear us out.

(5) It is very much a part of the therapy of our work that when children do well they discover themselves and they become a nuisance. They go through phases in which violence and stealing are the manifestations of hope that they can manage to show. In the case of every child receiving therapy in a residential care setting there must be a phase in which the child becomes a candidate for the role of scapegoat. 'If only that child could be got rid of we would be all right.' This is the critical time. At such a time you will agree I think that your job is not to cure the symptoms or to preach morality or to offer bribes. Your job is to survive. In this setting the word survive means not only that you live through it and that you manage not to get damaged, but also that you are not provoked into vindictiveness. If you survive, then and then only you may find yourself used in quite a natural way by the child who is becoming a person and who is newly able to make a gesture of a rather simplified loving nature.

You might even occasionally hear the word 'thank you', but you have certainly earned it because you have been trying to do something that should have been done when the child was at an early stage of development and has been lost through untoward breaks in the continuity of the child's own home life. You must have a proportion of failures, and this again is something you have to survive in order to enjoy the occasional success.

It can be seen, I hope, from what I have said, that from my point of view residential care can be a very deliberate act of therapy done by professionals in a professional setting. It may be a kind of loving but often it has to look like a kind of hating, and the key word is not treatment or cure but rather it is survival. If you survive then the child has a chance to grow and become something like the person he or she would have been if the untoward environmental breakdown had not brought disaster.

Part IV
Individual therapy

Editors' introduction

The first chapter in Part IV, which has not previously been published, contains a brief description of psychoanalysis and discusses in simple language the difference in the therapeutic needs of the psychotic, the psychoneurotic and the antisocial individual. The second chapter is specifically devoted to the individual therapy of character disorders, linking them with deprivation and relating the therapy of the antisocial individual to the two main trends in the antisocial tendency. Two clinical examples are given. This paper also shows very clearly how Winnicott's theory of the antisocial tendency fits in with psychoanalytic theory as it had developed up to this time. Finally there is a description of a complete therapeutic consultation with a young girl who stole at school. This shows how lying is intimately connected with stealing. It also reveals in a most vivid and dramatic way, through the spontaneous drawings of the child, the nature of a specific deprivation.

27 Varieties of psychotherapy

(A talk given to MIASMA (Mental Illness Association Social and Medical Aspects), Cambridge, 6 March, 1961)

You will more often hear discussed varieties of illness than varieties of therapy. Naturally the two are interrelated, and I shall need to talk about illness first and therapy later.

I am a psychoanalyst, and you will not mind if I say that the basis of psychotherapy is the psychoanalytic training. This includes the personal analysis of the student analyst. Apart from such a training it is psychoanalytic theory and psychoanalytic metapsychology that influences all dynamic psychology, of whatever school.

There are, however, many varieties of psychotherapy, and these should depend for their existence not on the views of the practitioner but on the need of the patient or of the case. Let us say that where possible we advise psychoanalysis, but where this is not possible, or where there are arguments against, then an appropriate modification may be devised.

Of the many patients who come to me one way or another, only a very small percentage do in fact get psychoanalytic treatment, although I work at the centre of the psychoanalytic world.

I could talk about the technical modifications that are called for when the patient is psychotic or borderline, but it is not this that I wish to discuss here.

My special interest here is in the way in which a trained analyst can do something other than analysis and do it usefully. This is important when, as is usual, a limited amount of time is available for treatment. Often these other treatments can look better than the treatments that I personally feel have a more profound effect – i.e. psychoanalysis.

First let me say that one essential of psychotherapy is that no other treatment shall be mixed up with it. It is not possible to do the work if the idea of a possible shock therapy is looming large, as this alters the whole clinical picture. The patient either fears or secretly longs for the physical treatment (or both) and the psychotherapist never meets the patient's real personal problem.

On the other hand I must take for granted adequate physical care of the body.

The next thing is, what is our aim? Do we wish to do as much as possible or as little? In psychoanalysis we ask ourselves: how much can we do? At the other extreme, in my hospital clinic, our motto is: how little need we do? This makes us always aware of the economic aspect of the case; also it makes us look for the central illness in a family, or for the social illness, so that we may avoid wasting our time and someone's money by giving treatments to the secondary characters in a family drama. There is nothing original in this, but you will perhaps like to hear a psychoanalyst say this since analysts are especially liable to get bogged down in long treatments in the course of which they may lose sight of an adverse external factor.

And then, how much of the patient's difficulties belong simply to the fact that no-one has ever intelligently listened? I very quickly discovered as long as forty years ago that the taking of case-histories from mothers is in itself a psychotherapy if it be well done. Time must be allowed and a non-moralistic attitude naturally adopted, and when the mother has come to the end of saying what is in her mind, she may add: now I understand how the present symptoms fit into the whole pattern of the child's life in the family, and I can manage now, simply because you let me get at the whole story in my own way and in my own time. This is not only a matter that concerns parents who bring their children. Adults say this about themselves, and psychoanalysis could be said to be one long, very long, history-taking.

You know of course of the transference in psychoanalysis. In the psychoanalytic setting patients bring samples of their past and of their inner reality and expose them in the fantasy that belongs to their ever-changing relationship to the analyst. In this way the unconscious can gradually be made conscious. Once this process has started up and the unconscious co-operation of the patient has been gained, there is always much to be done; hence the length of the average treatment. It is interesting to examine the first interviews. If a psychoanalytic treatment is starting the analyst is careful not to be too clever at the beginning; and there is a good reason for this. The patient brings to the first interviews all his belief and all his suspicion. These extremes must be allowed to find real expression. If the analyst does too much at the beginning the patient either runs away or else, out of fear, develops a most splendid belief and becomes almost as if hypnotized.

Before I go further I must mention some other assumptions. There can be no reserved area in the patient. Psychotherapy does not prescribe for a patient's religion, his cultural interests or his private life, but a patient who keeps part of himself completely defended is avoiding the dependence that is inherent in the process. You will see that this dependence carries with it a corresponding thing in the therapist, a professional reliability which is even more important than the reliability of the doctor in ordinary medical practice. It is interesting that the Hippocratic oath which founded the medical practice recognized this with crude clarity.

Again, by the theory that underlies all our work a disorder that is not physically caused and that is therefore psychological represents a hitch in the individual's emotional development. Psychotherapy aims simply and solely at undoing the hitch, so that development may take place where formerly it could not take place.

In another though parallel language, psychological disorder is immaturity, immaturity of the emotional growth of the individual, and this growth includes the evolution of the individual's capacity to be related to people and to the environment generally.

In order to make myself clear I must give you a view of psychological disorder, of the categories of personal immaturity, even if this involves a gross simplification of a highly complex matter. I make three categories. The first of these brings to mind the term psycho-neurosis. Here are all the disorders of individuals who were well enough cared for in the early stages to be in a position, developmentally, to meet and to fail to some extent to contain the difficulties that are inherent in the full life, a life in which the individual rides and is not ridden by the instincts. I must include in with this the more 'normal' varieties of depression.

The second of these categories brings to mind the word psychosis. Here something went wrong in the area of the very early details of infant nurture, the result being a disturbance of the basic structuring of the individual's personality. This basic fault, as

Balint[1] has called it, may have produced an infantile or childhood psychosis, or difficulties at later stages may have exposed a fault in ego-structure which had passed unnoticed. Patients in this category were never healthy enough to become psycho-neurotic.

The third category I reserve for the in-betweens, those individuals who started well enough but whose environment failed them at some point, or repeatedly, or over a long period of time. These are children or adolescents or adults who could rightly claim: 'all was well until . . ., and my personal life cannot be developed unless the environment acknowledges its debt to me', but of course it is not usual for the deprivation and the suffering it produced to be available to consciousness, so that instead of the words we find clinically an attitude, one which displays an anti-social tendency, and which may crystallize into delinquency and into recidivism.

For the moment, then, you are looking at psychological illness through the wrong end of three telescopes. Through one telescope you see reactive depression, which has to do with the destructive urges that accompany loving impulses in two-body relationships (basically, infant and mother) and also you see psychoneurosis, which has to do with ambivalence, that is to say co-existing love and hate, which belongs to triangular relationships (basically child and two parents), the relationship being experienced both heterosexually and homosexually, in varying proportions.

Through the second telescope you see the very early stages of emotional development becoming distorted by faulty infant care. I admit that some infants are more difficult to nurture than others are, but as we are not out to blame anyone we can ascribe the cause of illness here to a failure in nurture. What we see is a failure of the structuring of the personal self, and the capacity of the self for relating to objects that are of the environment. I would like to dig this rich seam with you but I must not do so.

Through this telescope we see the various failures which produce the clinical picture of schizophrenia, or which produce the psychotic under-currents that disturb the even flow of life of many of us who manage to get labelled normal, healthy, mature.

When we look at illness in this way we only see exaggerations of

---

[1] M. Balint, *The Basic Fault*. London: Tavistock Publications, 1968.

elements in our own selves, we do not see anything which would put psychiatrically ill people in a place apart. Hence the strain inherent in treating or in nursing ill people psychologically, rather than by drugs and by the so-called physical treatments.

The third telescope takes our attention away from the difficulties inherent in life to disturbances which have a different nature, for the deprived person is prevented from getting at his or her own inherent problems by a grudge, a justified claim for a mending of an almost remembered insult. We in this room are probably not in this category, not even slightly. Most of us can say of our parents: they made mistakes, they constantly frustrated us and it fell to their lot to introduce us to the Reality Principle, arch-enemy of spontaneity, creativity, and the sense of Real; BUT, they never really let us down. It is this being let down that constitutes the basis for the antisocial tendency, and however much we dislike our bicycles being stolen, or having to use the police to prevent violence, we do see, we understand, why this boy or that girl forces us to meet a challenge, whether by stealing or by destructiveness.

I have done as much as I can allow myself to do to build up a theoretical background for my brief description of some varieties of psychotherapy.

CATEGORY I (psycho-neurosis)

If illness in this category needs treatment we would like to provide psychoanalysis, a professional setting of general reliability in which the repressed unconscious may become conscious. This is brought about as a result of the appearance in the 'transference' of innumerable samples of the patient's personal conflicts. In a favourable case the defences against anxiety that arises out of the instinctual life and its imaginative elaboration become less and less rigid, and more and more under the patient's deliberate control system.

CATEGORY II (failure in early nurture)

In so far as illness of this kind needs treatment, we need to provide opportunity for the patient to have experiences that properly belong to infancy under conditions of extreme dependence. We see that such conditions may be found apart from organized psychotherapy, for instance in friendship, in nursing care that may be provided on account of physical illness, in cultural experiences including for some those that are called religious. A family that continues to care for a child provides opportunities for regression to dependence even of a high order, and it is indeed a regular feature of family life, well embedded in a social milieu, this going on being available to re-establish and to emphasize elements of care that belong initially to infant care. You will agree that some children enjoy their families and their growing independence, while others continue to use their families psychotherapeutically.

Professional social work comes in here, as an attempt to give professionally the help which would be provided non-professionally by parents and by families and by social units. The social worker on the whole is not a psychotherapist in the sense described under patients in Category I. The social worker is a psychotherapist, however, in meeting Category II needs.

You will see that a great deal that a mother does with an infant could be called 'holding'. Not only is actual holding very important, and a delicate matter that can only be delicately done by the right people, but also much of infant nurture is an ever-widening interpretation of the word holding. Holding comes to include all physical management, in so far as it is done in adaptation to an infant's needs. Gradually a child values being let go, and this corresponds with the presentation to the child of the Reality Principle, which at first clashes with the Pleasure Principle (omnipotence abrogated). The family continues this holding, and society holds the family.

Casework might be described as the professionalized aspect of this normal function of parents and of local social units, a 'holding' of persons and of situations, while growth tendencies are given a chance. These growth tendencies are present all the time in every individual, except where hopelessness (because of repeated environmental failure) has led to an organized withdrawal. The tendencies have been described in terms of integration, of the psyche coming to terms with the body, the one becoming linked with the other, of the development of a capacity for relating to objects. These processes go ahead unless blocked by failures of holding and of the meeting of the individual's creative impulses.

CATEGORY III (deprivation)

Where patients are dominated by a *deprivation* area in their past history the treatment needs to be adapted to this fact. As persons they may be normal, neurotic, or psychotic. One can hardly see what is the personal pattern because whenever hope begins to become alive the boy or girl produces a symptom (stealing or being stolen from, destructiveness or being destroyed) which forces the environment to notice and to act. Action is usually punitive, but what the patient needs, of course, is a full acknowledgement and full payment. As I have said, this very often cannot be done because so much is unavailable to consciousness, but it is important that a serious digging done in the early stages of an antisocial career quite frequently does produce the clue and the solution. A study of delinquency should be started as a study of the antisocial in relatively normal children whose homes are intact, and here I find it frequently possible to track down the deprivation and the extreme suffering that resulted and which altered the whole course of the child's development. (I have published cases, and I can give other examples if there is time.)

The point here is that society is left with all the untreated and untreatable cases in which the antisocial tendency has built up into a stabilized delinquency. Here the need is for the provision of specialized environments, and these must be divided into two kinds:

(1) those which hope to socialize the children they are holding,

and (2) those which are merely designed to keep their children in order to preserve society from them until these boys and girls are too old to be detained, and until they go out into the world as adults who will repeatedly get into trouble. This latter kind of institution may run most smoothly when very strictly administered.

Can it be seen that it is very dangerous to base a system of child-care on the work done in homes for the maladjusted, and especially on the 'successful' management of delinquents in detention centres?

On the basis of what I have said it is now perhaps possible to compare the three types of psychotherapy.

Naturally a practising psychiatrist needs to be able to pass easily from one kind of therapy to another, and indeed to do all kinds at one and the same time if necessary, as need arises.

Illness of psychotic quality (Category II) demands of us that we organize a complex kind of 'holding', including if necessary physical care. Here the professional therapist or nurse comes in when the patient's immediate environment fails to cope. As a friend of mine (the late John Rickman) said, 'Insanity is not being able to find anyone to stand you', and here there are two factors, the degree of illness in the patient and the ability of the environment to tolerate the symptoms. In this way there are some in the world who are more ill than some of those who are in mental hospitals.

Psychotherapy of the kind I am referring to can look like friendship, but it is not friendship because the therapist is paid and only sees the patient for a limited period by appointment, and moreover only over a limited course of time, since the aim in every therapy is to arrive at a point at which the professional relationship ends because the patient's life and living takes over and the therapist passes on to the next job.

A therapist is like other professional people in that in his job his behaviour is at a higher standard than it is in his private life. He is punctual, he adapts himself to his patient's needs and he does not live out his own frustrated urges in his contact with his patients.

It will be evident that patients who are very ill in this category do put a very great strain on the integrity of the therapist, since they do need human contact, and real feelings, and yet they need to place an absolute reliance on the relationship in which they are maximally dependent. The greatest difficulties come when there has been a seduction in the patient's childhood, in which case there must be experienced in the course of the treatment a delusion that the therapist is repeating seduction. Naturally, recovering depends on the undoing of this childhood seduction which brought the child prematurely to a real instead of an imaginary sexual life, and spoiled the child's prerequisite: unlimited play.

In therapy designed to deal with psycho-neurotic illness (Category I) the classical psychoanalytic setting devised by Freud can be easily attained, since the patient brings to the treatment a degree of belief and capacity to trust. With all this taken for granted the analyst has the opportunity to allow the transference to develop in its own way, and instead of the patient's delusions there come into the material of the analysis dreams, imagination, and ideas expressed in symbolic form which can be interpreted according to the process as it develops through the unconscious co-operation of the patient.

This is all I have time to say about the psychoanalytic technique, which can be learned, and which is difficult enough, but not as exhausting as therapy designed to meet psychotic disorder.

Psychotherapy designed to deal with an antisocial tendency in a patient only works, as I have said, if the patient is near the beginning of his or her antisocial career, before secondary gains and delinquent skills have become established. It is only in the early stages that the patient knows he (or she) is a patient, and actually feels a need to get to the roots of the disturbance. Where work is possible along these lines the doctor and the patient settle down to a sort of detective story, using any clues that may be available, including what is known of the past history of the case, and the work is done in a thin layer that is somewhere between the deeply buried unconscious and the conscious life and memory system of the patient.

This layer that is between the unconscious and the conscious is occupied in normal people by cultural pursuits, and the cultural life of the delinquent is notoriously thin, because there is no freedom in such a case except in a flight either to the un-remembered dream or to reality. Any attempt to explore the intermediate area leads not to art or religion or playing, but to antisocial behaviour that is compulsive and inherently un-rewarding to the individual as well as hurtful to society.

28   The psychotherapy of character disorders

(A paper read at the 11th European Congress of Child Psychiatry, Rome, May–June, 1963)

Although the title chosen for this paper is the 'Psychotherapy of Character Disorders', it is not possible to avoid a discussion of the meaning of the term 'Character Disorder'. As Fenichel[1] remarks,

> The question may be raised whether there is any analysis that is not 'character analysis'. All symptoms are the outcome of specific ego attitudes, which in analysis make their appearance as resistances and which have been developed during infantile conflicts. This is true. And to a certain degree, really, all analyses are character analyses.

And again,

> Character disorders do not form a nosological unit. The mechanisms at the basis of character disorder may be as different as the mechanisms at the basis of symptom neuroses. Thus a hysterical character will be more easily treated than a compulsive one, a compulsive one more easily than a narcissistic one.

It is clear that either the term is too wide to be useful, or else I shall need to use it in a special way. In the latter case I must indicate the use I shall make of the term in this paper.

First, there must be confusion unless it be recognized that the three terms: character, a good character, and a character disorder, bring to mind three very different phenomena, and it would be

---

[1] O. Fenichel, *The Theory of Neurosis*. New York: W. W. Norton, 1945.

artificial to deal with all three at one and the same time, yet these three are inter-related.

Freud wrote that 'a fairly reliable character' is one of the prerequisites for a successful analysis but we are considering *unreliability* in the personality, and Fenichel asks: can this unreliability be treated? He might have asked: what is its aetiology?

When I look at character disorders I find I am looking at *whole persons*. There is in the term an implication of a degree of integration, itself a sign of psychiatric health.

The papers that have preceded mine have taught us much, and have strengthened me in the idea of character as something that belongs to integration. Character is a manifestation of successful integration, and a disorder of character is a distortion of the ego structure, integration being nevertheless maintained. It is perhaps good to remember that integration has a time factor. The child's character has formed on the basis of a steady developmental process, and in this respect the child has a past and a future.

It would seem to be valuable to use the term character disorder in description of a child's attempt to accommodate his or her own developmental abnormalities or deficiencies. Always we assume that the personality structure is able to withstand the strain of the abnormality. The child needs to come to terms with the personal pattern of anxiety or compulsion or mood or suspicion, etc., and also to relate this to the requirements and expectations of the immediate environment.

In my opinion the value of the term belongs specifically to a description of personality distortion that comes about *when the child needs to accommodate some degree of antisocial tendency*. This leads immediately to a statement of my use of this term.

I am using these words which enable us to focus our attention not so much on behaviour as on those roots of misbehaviour that extend over the whole area between normality and delinquency. The antisocial tendency can be examined in your own healthy child who at the age of two takes a coin from his mother's handbag.

The antisocial tendency always arises out of a *deprivation* and represents the child's claim to get back behind the deprivation to the state of affairs that obtained when all was well. I cannot develop this theme here, but this thing that I call the antisocial tendency must be mentioned because it is found regularly in the dissection of character disorder. The child in accommodating the antisocial tendency that is his or hers may hide it, may develop a reaction formation to it, such as becoming a prig, may develop a grievance and acquire a complaining character, may specialize in day-dreaming, lying, mild chronic masturbating activity, bed-wetting, compulsive thumb-sucking, thigh-rubbing, etc., or may periodically manifest the antisocial tendency (that is his or hers) in a *behaviour disorder*. This latter is always associated with hope, and it is either of the nature of stealing or of aggressive activity and destruction. It is compulsive.

Character disorder, then, according to my way of looking at things, refers most significantly to the distortion of the *intact* personality that results from the antisocial elements in it. It is the antisocial element that determines society's involvement. Society (the child's family and so on) must meet the challenge, and must *like or dislike* the character and the character disorder.

Here then is the beginning of a description:

Character disorders are not schizophrenia. In character disorder there is hidden illness in the intact personality. Character disorders in some way and to some degree actively involve society.

Character disorders may be divided according to:

Success or failure on the part of the individual in the attempt of the total personality to hide the illness element. Success here means that the personality, though impoverished, has become able to socialize the character distortion to find secondary gains or to fit in with a social custom.
Failure here means that the impoverishment of the personality carries along with it a failure in establishment of a relation to society as a whole, on account of the hidden illness element.

In fact, society plays its part in the determination of the fate of a person with character disorder, and does this in various ways. For example:

Society tolerates individual illness to a degree.
Society tolerates failure of the individual to contribute-in.
Society tolerates or even enjoys distortions of the mode of the individual's contributing-in.

or Society meets the challenge of the antisocial tendency of an individual, and its reaction is being motivated by:

(1) Revenge.
(2) The wish to socialize the individual.
(3) Understanding and the application of understanding to prevention.

The individual with character disorder may suffer from:

(1) Impoverishment of personality, sense of grievance, un-reality, awareness of lack of serious purpose, etc.
(2) Failure to socialize.

Here then is a basis for psychotherapy, because psychotherapy relates to individual *suffering* and need for help. But this suffering in character disorder only belongs to the early stages in the individual's illness; the secondary gains quickly take over, lessen the suffering, and interfere with the drive of the individual to seek help or to accept help offered.

It must be recognized that in respect of 'success' (character disorder hidden and socialized) *psychotherapy makes the individual ill*, because illness lies between the defence and the individual's health. By contrast, in respect of 'unsuccessful' hiding of character disorder, although there may be an initial drive in the individual to seek help at an early stage, because of society's reactions, this motive does not necessarily carry the patient through to the treatment of the deeper illness.

The clue to the treatment of character disorder is given by the part the environment plays in the case of *natural cure*. In the slight case the environment can 'cure' because the cause was an environmental failure in the area of ego-support and protection at a stage of the individual's dependence. This explains why it is that children are regularly 'cured' of incipient character disorder in the course of their own childhood development simply by making use of home life. Parents have a second and third chance to bring their children through, in spite of failures of management (mostly inevitable) in the earliest stages when the child is highly dependent. Family life is the place therefore that offers the best opportunity for investigation into the aetiology of character disorder; and indeed it is in the family life, or its substitute, that the child's *character* is being built up in positive ways.

Aetiology of character disorder

In considering the aetiology of character disorder it is necessary to take for granted both the maturational process in the child, the conflict-free sphere of the ego (Hartmann), also forward movement with anxiety drive (Klein), and the function of the environment which facilitates the maturational processes. Environmental provision must be 'good' enough if maturation is to become a fact in the case of any one child.

With this in mind, one can say that there are two extremes of distortion, and that these relate to the stage of maturation of the individual at which environmental failure did actually overstrain the ego's capacity for organizing defences:

At one extreme is the ego hiding *psycho-neurotic* symptom-formations (set up relative to anxiety belonging to the Oedipus complex). Here the hidden illness is a matter of conflict in the individual's personal unconscious.

At the other extreme is the ego hiding *psychotic* symptom-formations (splitting, dissociations, reality side-slipping, depersonalization, regression and omnipotent dependencies, etc.). Here the hidden illness is in the ego structure.

But the matter of society's essential involvement does not depend on the answer to the question: is the hidden illness psycho-neurotic or psychotic? In fact, in character disorder there is this other element, *the individual's* correct perception at a time in early childhood that at first all was well, or well enough, and then that all was not well. In other words, that there happened at a certain time, or over a phase of development, an actual failure of ego-support that held up the individual's emotional development. A reaction in the individual to this disturbance took the place of simple growth. The maturational processes became dammed up because of a failure of the facilitating environment.

This theory of the aetiology of character disorder, if correct, leads to a new statement of character disorder at its inception. The individual in this category carries on with two separate burdens. One of these, of course, is the increasing burden of a disturbed and in some respects stunted or postponed maturational process. The other is the hope, a hope that never becomes quite extinguished, that the environment may acknowledge and make up for the specific failure that did the damage. In the vast majority of cases the parents or the family or guardians of the child recognize the fact of the 'let-down' (so often unavoidable) and by a period of special management, spoiling, or what could be called mental nursing, they see the child through to a recovery from the trauma.

When the family does not mend its failures the child goes forward with certain handicaps, being engaged in

(1) arranging to live a life in spite of emotional stunting, and
(2) all the time liable to moments of hope, moments when it would seem to be possible to force the environment to effect a cure (hence: acting-out).

Between the clinical state of a child who has been hurt in the way that is being described here and the resumption of that child's emotional development, and all that that means in terms of socialization, there is this need to make society acknowledge and repay. Behind a child's maladjustment is always a failure of the environment to adjust to the child's absolute needs at a time of relative dependence. (Such failure is initially a failure of nurture.) Then there can be added a failure of the family to heal the effects of such failures; and then there may be added the failure of society as it takes the family's place. Let it be emphasized that in this type of case the initial failure can be shown to have happened at a time at which the child's development had made it just possible for him or her to perceive the fact of the failure and to perceive the nature of the environment's maladjustment.

The child now displays an antisocial tendency, which (as I have said) in the stage before the development of secondary gains is always a manifestation of hope. This antisocial tendency is liable to show in two forms:

(1) The staking of claims on people's time, concern, money, etc. (manifested by stealing).
(2) The expectation of that degree of structural strength and organization and 'comeback' that is essential if the child is to be able to rest, relax, disintegrate, feel secure (manifested by destruction which provokes strong management).

On the basis of this theory of the aetiology of character disorder I can proceed to examine the matter of therapy.

Indications for therapy

Therapy of character disorder has three aims:

(1) A dissection down to the illness that is hidden and that appears in the character distortion. Preparatory to this may be a period in which the individual is invited to become a patient, to become ill instead of hiding illness.

(2) To meet the antisocial tendency which, from the point of view of the therapist, is evidence of hope in the patient; to meet it as an S.O.S., a *cri de coeur*, a signal of distress.

(3) Analysis that takes into consideration both the ego distortion and the patient's exploitation of his or her id-drives during attempts at self-cure.

The attempt to meet the patient's antisocial tendency has two aspects:

The allowance of the patient's claims to rights in terms of a person's love and reliability.

The provision of an ego-supportive structure that is relatively indestructible.

As this implies, the patient will from time to time be acting-out, and as long as this has a relation to the transference it can be managed and interpreted. The troubles in therapy come in relation to antisocial acting-out which is outside the total therapeutic machinery, that is to say, which involves society.

In regard to the treatment of hidden illness and of ego distortion, the need is for psychotherapy. But at the same time the antisocial tendency must be engaged, as and when it appears. The aim in this part of the treatment is to arrive at the original trauma. This has to be done in the course of the psychotherapy or, if psychotherapy is not available, in the course of the specialized management that is provided.

In this work the failures of the therapist or of those managing the child's life will be real and they can be shown to reproduce the original failures, in token form. These failures are real indeed, and especially so in so far as the patient is either regressed to the dependence of the appropriate age, or else remembering. The acknowledgement of the analyst's or guardian's failure enables the patient to become appropriately angry instead of traumatized.

The patient needs to reach back through the transference trauma to the state of affairs that obtained before the original trauma. (In some cases there is a possibility of quick arrival at deprivation trauma in a first interview.) The reaction to the current failure only makes sense in so far as the current failure *is* the original environmental failure from the point of view of the child. Reproduction in the treatment of examples as they arise of the original environmental failure, along with the patient's experience of anger that is appropriate, frees the patient's maturational processes; and it must be remembered that the patient is in a dependent state and needing ego-support and environmental management (holding) in the treatment setting, and the next phase needs to be a period of emotional growth in which the character builds up positively and loses its distortions.

In a favourable case the acting-out that belongs to these cases is confined to the transference, or can be brought into the transference productively by interpretation of displacement, symbolism, and projection. At one extreme is the common 'natural' cure that takes place in the child's family. At the other extreme are the severely disturbed patients whose acting-out may make treatment by interpretation impossible because the work gets interrupted by society's reactions to stealing or destructiveness.

In a moderately severe case the acting-out can be managed provided that the therapist understands its meaning and significance. It can be said that acting-out is the alternative to despair. Most of the time the patient is hopeless about correcting the original trauma and so lives in a state of relative depression or of dissociations that mask the chaotic state that is always threatening. When, however, the patient starts to make an object relationship, or to cathect a person, then there starts up an antisocial tendency, a compulsion either to lay claims (steal) or by destructive behaviour to activate harsh or even vindictive management.

In every case, if psychotherapy is to be successful, the patient must be seen through one or many of these awkward phases of manifest antisocial behaviour, and only too often it is just at these awkward points in the case that treatment is interrupted. The case is dropped not necessarily because the situation cannot be tolerated, but (as likely as not) because those in charge do not know that these acting-out phases are inherent, and that they can have a positive value.

In severe cases these phases in management or treatment present difficulties that are so great that the law (society) takes over, and at the same time psychotherapy goes into abeyance. Society's revenge takes the place of pity or sympathy, and the individual ceases to suffer and be a patient, and instead becomes a criminal with a delusion of persecution.

It is my intention to draw attention to *the positive element in character disorder.* Failure to achieve character disorder in the individual who is trying to accommodate some degree of anti-social tendency indicates a liability to psychotic breakdown. Character disorder indicates that the individual's ego structure can bind the energies that belong to the stunting of maturational processes and also the abnormalities in the interaction of the individual child and the family. Until secondary gains have become a feature the personality with character disorder is always liable to break down into paranoia, manic depression, psychosis or schizophrenia.

To sum up, a statement on the treatment of character disorder can start with the dictum that such a treatment is like that of any other psychological disorder, namely, psychoanalysis if it be available. There must follow the following considerations:

(1) Psychoanalysis may succeed, but the analyst must expect to find *acting-out* in the transference, and must understand the significance of this acting-out, and be able to give it positive value.

(2) The analysis may succeed but be difficult because the hidden illness has psychotic features, so that the patient must become ill (psychotic, schizoid) before starting to get better; and all the resources of the analyst will be needed to deal with the primitive defence mechanisms that will be a feature.

(3) The analysis may be succeeding, but as acting-out is not confined to the transference relationship the patient is removed from the analyst's reach because of society's reaction to the patient's antisocial tendency or because of the operation of the law. There is room for great variation here, owing to the variability of society's reaction, ranging from crude revenge to an

expression of society's willingness to give the patient a chance to make late socialization.

(4) In many cases incipient character disorder is treated and treated successfully in the child's home, by a phase or by phases of special management (spoiling) or by especially *personal* care or strict control by a person who loves the child. An extension of this is the treatment of incipient or early character disorder without psychotherapy by management in groups designed to give what the child's own family cannot give in the way of special management.

(5) By the time the patient comes to treatment there may already be a fixed antisocial tendency manifest, and a hardened attitude in the patient fostered by secondary gains, in which case the question of psychoanalysis does not arise. Then the aim is to provide firm management by understanding persons, and to provide this as a *treatment* in advance of its being provided as a *corrective* by court order. Personal psychotherapy can be added if it is available.

Finally,

(6) The character disorder case may present as a court case, with society's reaction represented by the probation order, or by committal to an approved school or a penal institution.

It can happen that early committal by a court proves to be a *positive* element in the patient's socialization. This corresponds again to the natural cure that commonly takes place in the patient's family; society's reaction has been, for the patient, a practical demonstration of its 'love', that is of its willingness to 'hold' the patient's unintegrated self, and to meet aggression with firmness (to limit the effects of maniacal episodes) and to meet hatred with hatred, appropriate and under control. This last is the best that some deprived children will ever get by way of satisfactory management, and many restless antisocial deprived children change from ineducable to educable in the strict regime of a remand home. The danger here is that because restless antisocial children thrive in an atmosphere of dictatorship this may breed dictators, and may even make educationalists think that an atmosphere of strict discipline, with every minute of the child's day filled, is good educational treatment for normal children, which it is not.

Girls

Broadly speaking, all this applies equally to boys and girls. At the stage of adolescence, however, the nature of the character disorder is necessarily different in the two sexes. For example, at adolescence girls tend to show their antisocial tendency by prostitution, and one of the hazards of acting-out is the production of illegitimate babies. In prostitution there are secondary gains. One is that girls find they contribute-in to society by being prostitutes, whereas they cannot contribute-in by any other means. They find many lonely men, who want a relationship rather than sex, and who are ready to pay for it. Also, these girls, essentially lonely, achieve contacts with others of their kind. The treatment of adolescent antisocial girls who have started to experience the secondary gains of the prostitute, presents *insuperable difficulties.* Perhaps the idea of treatment does not make sense in this context. In many cases it is already too late. It is best to give up all attempts to cure prostitution, and instead to concentrate on giving these girls food and shelter and opportunity for keeping healthy and clean.

Clinical illustrations

A common type of case

A boy in later latency (first seen at ten years) was having psychoanalytic treatment from me. His restlessness and liability to outbreaks of rage started from a very early date, soon after his birth and long before he was weaned at eight months. His mother was a neurotic person and all her life more or less depressed. He was a thief and given to aggressive outbursts. His analysis was going well, and in the course of a year of daily sessions much straightforward analytic work was accomplished. He became very excited, however, as his relationship to me developed significance, and he climbed out on to the clinic roof and flooded out the clinic and made so much noise that the treatment had to stop. Sometimes there was danger to me; he also broke into my car outside the clinic and drove off in bottom gear by using the self-starter, thus obviating the need for a car key. At the same time he started stealing again and being aggressive outside the treatment setting, and he was sent by the Juvenile Court to an approved school just at a time when the treatment by psycho-analysis was in full spate. Perhaps if I had been much stronger than he I might have managed this phase, and so have had opportunity to complete the analysis. As it was I had to give up.

(This boy did moderately well. He became a lorry driver, which suited his restlessness. He had kept his job fourteen years at the time of the follow-up. He married and had three children. His wife divorced him, after which he kept in touch with his mother, from whom the details of the follow-up were obtained.)

Three favourable cases

A boy of eight started stealing. He had suffered a relative deprivation (in his own good home setting) when he was two, at the time his mother conceived, and became pathologically anxious. The parents had managed to meet this boy's special needs and had almost succeeded in effecting a natural cure of his condition. I helped them in this long task by giving them some understanding of what they were doing. In one therapeutic consultation when the boy was eight it was possible for me to get this boy into feeling-contact with his deprivation, and he reached back to an object relationship to the good mother of his infancy. Along with this the stealing ceased.

A girl of eight years came to me because of stealing. She had suffered a relative deprivation in her own good home at the age of 4–5 years. In one psychotherapeutic consultation she reached back to her early infantile contact with a good mother, and at the same time her stealing disappeared. She was also wetting and messing and this minor manifestation of the antisocial tendency persisted for some time.

A boy of thirteen years, at a public school a long way from his good home, was stealing in a big way, also slashing sheets and up-setting the school by getting boys into trouble and by leaving obscene notes in lavatories, etc. In a therapeutic consultation he was able to let me know that he had been through a period of intolerable strain at the age of six when he went away to boarding school. I was able to arrange for this boy (middle child of three) to be allowed a period of 'mental nursing' in his own home. He used this for a regressive phase, and then went to day school. Later he went to a boarding school in the neighbourhood of his home. His antisocial symptoms ceased abruptly after his one interview with me and follow-up shows that he has done well. He has now passed through a university, and is establishing himself as a man. Of this case it is particularly true to say that the patient brought with him the understanding of his case, and what he needed was for the facts to be acknowledged and for an attempt to be made to mend, in token form, the environmental failure.

Comment. In these three cases in which help could be given when secondary gains had not become a feature the general attitude of myself as psychiatrist enabled the child in each case to state a specific area of relative deprivation, and the fact that this was accepted as real and true enabled the child to reach back over the gap and make anew a relationship with good objects that had been blocked.

A case on the borderline between character disorder and psychosis

A boy has been under my care over a period of years. I have only seen him once, and most of my contacts have been with the mother at times of crisis. Many have tried to give direct help to the boy, who is now twenty, but he quickly becomes uncooperative.

This boy has a high I.Q. and all those whom he has allowed to teach him have said that he could be exceptionally brilliant as an actor, a poet, an artist, a musician, etc. He has not stayed long at any one school but by self-tuition has kept well ahead of his peers, and he did this in early adolescence by coaching his friends in their school-work, then keeping in touch.

In the latency period he was hospitalized and diagnosed schizo-phrenic. In hospital he undertook the 'treatment' of the other boys, and he never accepted his position as a patient. Eventually he ran away and had a long period without schooling. He would lie in bed listening to lugubrious music, or lock himself into the house so that no one could get to him. He constantly threatened suicide, chiefly in relation to violent love affairs. Periodically he would organize a party, and this would go on indefinitely, and damage was sometimes done to property.

This boy lived with his mother in a small flat and he kept her constantly in a state of worry, and there was never any possibility of an outcome since he would not go away, he would not go to school or to hospital, and he was clever enough to do exactly as he wanted to do, and he never became criminal, and so kept out of the jurisdiction of the law.

At various times I helped the mother by putting her in touch with the police, the probation service, and other social services, and when eventually he said he would go to a certain grammar school I 'pulled strings' to enable him to do this. He was found to be well ahead of his age group, and the masters gave him great encouragement because of his brilliance. But he left school before time, and obtained a scholarship for a good college of acting. At this point he decided that he had the wrong-shaped nose, and eventually he persuaded his mother to pay a plastic surgeon to alter it from retroussé to straight. Then he found other reasons why he could not go forward to any success, and yet he gave no one any opportunity to help him. This continues, and at present he is in the observation ward of a mental hospital, but he will find a way of leaving this and will settle in at home once more.

This boy has an early history that gives the clue to the antisocial part of his character disorder. In fact he was the result of a partnership that foundered soon after its unhappy start, and the father soon after separating from the mother himself became a paranoid casualty. This marriage followed immediately after a tragedy, and was doomed to failure because the boy's mother had not yet recovered from the loss of her much-loved fiancé whom, as she felt, was killed by the carelessness of this man whom she married and who became the father of the boy.

This boy could have been helped at an early age, perhaps six, when he was first seen by a psychiatrist. He could then have led the psychiatrist to the material of his relative deprivation, and he could then have been told about his mother's personal problem, and the reason for the ambivalence in her relationship to him. But instead the boy was placed in a hospital ward, and from this time on he hardened into a case of character disorder, becoming a person who compulsively tantalizes his mother and his teachers and his friends.

I have not attempted to describe a case treated by psychoanalysis in this series of short case-descriptions.

Cases treated by management alone are innumerable and include all those children who when deprived in one way or another are adopted, or fostered out, or placed in small homes that are run as therapeutic institutions and on personal lines. It would be giving a false impression to describe one case in this category. It is indeed necessary to draw attention to the fact that incipient character disorder is being treated successfully all the time, especially in the home, in social groups of all kinds, and quite apart from psychotherapy.

Nevertheless, it is intensive work with the few cases that throws light on the problem of character disorder as of other types of psychological disorders, and it is work of the psychoanalytic groups in various countries that has laid the basis for a theoretical statement and has begun to explain to the specialized therapeutic groups what it is that is being done in such groups that so often succeeds in the prevention or treatment of character disorder.

29 *Dissociation revealed in a therapeutic consultation*

(A chapter prepared for a book entitled *Crime, Law and Corrections*, 1965)

My purpose is to take one detail of the antisocial clinical picture and to discuss this detail which derives importance from the fact that it recurs regularly in case histories. In order to illustrate my meaning I shall describe a psychotherapeutic interview. This interview with a girl of eight years led to a cessation of stealing and presumably therefore it was significant. Towards the end of the interview there appears the detail that I make the subject of this study. The reader will need to keep this point in mind while digesting the whole of a long interview in which other things are being discussed.

Issue under discussion

Over and over again in the stories given by parents and school-masters there is a statement such as this: "The boy denied having stolen anything. He seemed to have no signs of guilt and no sense of responsibility. When faced, however, with fingerprint evidence, and after persistent enquiry, he admitted that he had stolen the goods." Usually at this point the child that is suspected begins to co-operate with the investigator and shows that he knew all the time what he denied that he knew. There is no difference whether it is a boy or girl who is suspected and investigated.

Example of a dissociation as reported in a case-history

The parents of a fourteen-year-old boy gave me the details of the boy's early history. In effect the boy's development was normal until the age of three years when he had a serious physical illness for which he was treated in a hospital. He seemed to recover from this. At the age of five years, when he changed school because his home had moved from the city to the country, his personality altered. For a time he met rough boys and he joined up with them and became very difficult. He lost all power of concentration and in fact stopped working, which he had been able to do well at his previous schools. He was liked by the headmistress but he plagued her. At this time he changed over from being easily related to women to being more closely in touch with his father, and he became intolerant of all females. Following this period of difficulty the parents sent him to a specialized school because he could not get accepted at an ordinary school owing to the combination of his intellectual backwardness and his roughness. At the same time there was always evidence of his having at least average intelligence.

The parents now knew that they had a problem, and they gave up their ambitions for their boy and found another highly specialized school for him in the hope that it would cure him of his difficulties. They brought him to me because this school did not bring about any improvement.

I asked about stealing. I was told that this had not been a feature. Nevertheless recently he had been found with money, and this money was travelling-money and should have been handed in. At first, when taken to task, *the boy denied all knowledge of what he had done.* When I asked about destruction there was the same story. He had gone to his father's gun cupboard and with an air gun had terrified everybody. When again taken to task he lied about this for a whole day. Eventually he gave in and owned up and said he had been stupid.

In this family there is no question of over-strict management. The parents are quite capable of taking responsibility without overdoing harshness. The trouble lies in the boy himself who finds he is compelled to act out of character. Now at the age of fourteen years he has been found smoking. His headmaster spoke to him about this and he owned up and agreed that he had contravened the rules; he said that he would not be doing this again. A few days later he was found smoking a second time and he had nothing whatever to say about this.

This boy is a deprived child living in his own good family. He is also somewhat paranoid. He does not make friends easily and it has been said of him that he craves friendship but cannot achieve it. When he was told that he could see a doctor he knew immediately what it was about, and he wrote home: "I hope the doctor will be able to straighten things out." He was aware of something that he was unable to avoid by deliberate effort; that is to say, he suffered from a compulsion which he could not explain, and he could not believe in what he found he had done under this compulsion.

My purpose is to instigate a study of this state of affairs which in fact draws our attention to interesting aspects of the theory of the antisocial behaviour.

Advance statement

My thesis is that such a case description provides an example of a *dissociation*. The parent or the schoolmaster is talking to a child about a dissociated part of that child and the child is not telling lies. By denying knowledge of what has happened the child is stating something that is true for the child as a whole, and the aspect of the self which committed the act is not a part of the total personality. Some would call this a personality split. It is perhaps better, however, to reserve the term splitting for the primitive defense mechanisms that underlie the symptomatology of schizophrenic or borderline personalities or persons with hidden schizophrenia, and to retain *dissociation* as a term to describe a case in which one can communicate with a main self about a fraction of the self.

This type of partial disintegration is characteristic of the antisocial boy or girl. If enquiry is pursued, a suspected person may eventually leave this area of true being and pass over into another kind of integration according to his or her capacity to achieve integration in the intellectual area of ego functioning.

Let it be noted that by the time the boy or girl has admitted that he or she has committed the act, the investigator is talking to an intellectual apparatus. Here integration is not difficult. The individual is able to know and to understand and to remember, and the forces producing the dissociation are no longer operative. Guilt is now admitted, *but it is not felt.*

Whereas the answer was no, it is now yes. Along with this change comes a change also in the relationship of the investigator to the suspect individual. The latter has become unavailable except in regard to the intellectualized aspect of the personality, and it is no longer of value for the investigator to pursue the investigation although sociologically the change may be convenient. It may be convenient to get at the facts, but these facts have no value if any attempt is being made to help the suspected person.

In short, in terms of psychotherapy there is a possibility of giving help while the individual is *quite honestly* saying no, because the help is needed by the main part of the personality. The whole person acted under a compulsion, the roots of which were unavailable to that person's conscious self, and it can be said that the individual suffers from a compulsive activity. Where there is suffering, there help can be given.

Further statement

A further development of this idea involves a statement or restatement of the theory underlying antisocial behaviour.

It is of value to postulate *an antisocial tendency*. The value of this term is that it covers not only that which makes a boy or girl into an antisocial character but also the delinquencies, minor and major, that belong to ordinary home life. In any family there are always minor delinquencies; in fact it is practically normal for a child of two and a half years to steal a coin from the mother's handbag, or for an older child to steal something rather special from the larder. Also all children do damage to household property. These things would be labelled antisocial behaviour only if the child were living in an institution.

Also enuresis and encopresis need to be brought under this heading, and the tendency that is very near to stealing, namely, pseudologia. These delinquencies are not sharply divided from the tendency of a child to expect to be allowed to make a certain amount of mess, to wear out clothes and shoes, to be careless about washing and personal hygiene, and (in infancy) to dirty innumerable napkins.

This term, the antisocial tendency, can be extended to cover any claim on the parents' or the mother's energy, time, credulity, tolerance, beyond that which seems reasonable. What seems reasonable to one parent seems unreasonable to another.

The fact can be allowed for that there is no sharp line between the compulsive antisocial behaviour of a recidivist at one extreme and the almost normal exaggerations of claims on parents which belong to everyday home life. When parents are spoiling a child it can usually be shown (unless they are spoiling a child for reasons of their own, and regardless of the child's needs) that they are doing psychotherapy, usually successful psychotherapy, of a child's antisocial tendency.

Simplified theoretical statement

In the simplest possible terms the antisocial tendency is an attempt to stake a claim. Normally the claim is allowed. In psychopathology the claim is a denial that the right to stake a claim has been lost. In pathological antisocial behaviour the antisocial boy or girl is driven to mend, and to make the family or society mend, the failure that has been forgotten. Antisocial behaviour belongs to a moment of hope in a child who is otherwise without hope. At the point of origin of the antisocial tendency is a deprivation, and the antisocial act aims at a mending of the effect of the deprivation by a denial of it. The difficulty that arises in the live situation has two aspects:

1. The child does not know what the original deprivation was.
2. Society is not willing to allow for the positive element in the antisocial activity, partly because society is (naturally) annoyed at being hurt, and partly because society is unaware of this important aspect of theory.

It must be emphasized that it is a deprivation, not a privation, that underlies the antisocial tendency. A privation produces a different result: the basic ration of facilitation environment being deficient, the course of the maturational process is distorted and the result is a personality defect, not a character defect.

In the aetiology of the antisocial tendency there was an initial period of satisfactory personal development; and then there was a failure of the facilitating environment, this failure being felt, even if not intellectually appraised, by the child. The child can know this sequence: I was doing well enough, and then I was not able to continue my development, and it was when I was living at . . . and I was . . . years old, and a change occurred. This understanding, based on memory, can be made actual in a child under special conditions, as in psychotherapy. It would not be true to say that the child usually goes around holding these ideas in consciousness, but sometimes this does actually happen, and it is common for a child to know clearly of the deprivation in terms of a *later version of deprivation*, for example, a period of intolerable loneliness experienced at seven years, associated with a bereavement, or with being away from home at a boarding school.

Clearly, the deprivation did not distort the ego organization (psychosis) but it gave the child a drive to force the environment to acknowledge the fact of the deprivation. The child must always try, except when feeling hopeless, to reach back over the area of intolerable distress to the *remembered* earlier period when dependence was taken for granted by the child and the parents, and when the child had a claim on the parents appropriate to the age of the child and the capacity of the parents to adapt to each child's needs.

The antisocial tendency may be a feature, then, in normal children, and in children of any type or any psychiatric diagnosis except schizophrenia, since the schizophrenic is not mature enough to suffer from deprivation, being in a state of distortion associated with privation. The paranoid personality fits the antisocial tendency very easily into the general tendency to feel persecuted, so that here in the paranoid personality there can be an overlap of personality and character disturbance.

Study of the antisocial tendency is best made in terms of the less ill child, the child who is truly puzzled at finding himself or herself saddled with a compulsion to steal, to lie, to do damage, and to produce social reactions of one kind or another. If such a study is combined, as it should always be, with therapeutics, then it is essential to arrange for early diagnosis and to do as much as possible quickly.

It is in fact necessary for the investigator to be in touch with a school or private group and to have children referred to him when they first display character defect, or when they manifest the first symptoms which provoke social reaction; that is, at the stage before punishment has entered into the picture. As soon as there is a clinch between the antisocial tendency and social reaction then secondary gains are initiated, and the case is on the way towards that *hardening* which we associate with delinquency.

The special detail of denial

It is at the early stage and in the less ill child, especially, that the child's denial can be treated as a symptom that indicates a degree of ego-organization and strength, and that therefore gives a positive loading in the assessment of prognosis. The child who does not acknowledge the antisocial act is the child who is in distress and who wants help and who can be helped. The child's distress belongs to the fact that he or she feels compelled to act; it is this compulsion from an unknown source that *feels mad* and that leads the child to welcome understanding and help at this early or predelinquent stage.

This extract from the report of an interview with an adolescent girl will illustrate this idea.

Girl of seventeen years

I asked her about stealing, and she said: "Well, only once when I was seven, I had a period in which I was constantly taking pennies, anything of that nature that was lying about the house. I have always felt extremely guilty about this and I've never told anyone at all. It's really very silly because it's so slight."

Here I made an interpretation. I spoke to her about the difficulty that she really does not know why she stole these pennies; in other words she was *under a compulsion*. She was very interested in this. She said: "I know that children steal when they have been deprived of something or other but I've never thought of this before, that of course the trouble is that I *had* to steal and I didn't know why, and it's just like that with lying. You see it's pathetically easy to deceive people and I'm a wonderful actress; I don't mean that I could act on the stage, but once I get caught up in a deceit I can carry it through so well that no one can know. The thing is, it's often compulsive and meaningless."

Psychotherapeutic interview

I now give a detailed and complete description of a psychotherapeutic interview with a girl of eight years who was brought on account of stealing. (There was also enuresis but this was not beyond the parents' understanding and tolerance.) It is at the end of this long description that the reader will find the illustration of denial representing a dissociation.

Referral. The school had made it clear that Ada's stealing was giving trouble, and Ada would have to leave if the symptom persisted.

It was practicable for me to see this girl once or even a few times, but she lived too far away for me to be able to think in terms of a treatment. It was therefore necessary for me to act on the basis that I must do everything possible in the first psychotherapeutic consultation.

This is not the place for a description of the technique for this type of consultation, but certain principles may be given:

1. The training for this work is a grounding in classical psychoanalysis.

2. The work done is, however, not psychoanalysis, since the work is done in the original subjective atmosphere of the first contact. The analyst in doing this nonanalytic therapy cashes in on a *dream of the analyst* that the patient may have had the night *before* this first contact, that is to say on the patient's capacity to believe in an understanding and helpful figure.

3. The aim is to go all out in the first, or first three, contacts; should further work be needed the case begins to alter its character and changes over into a psychoanalytic treatment.

4. In fact, the main part of the treatment in these cases is carried by the child's own home and by the parents, who need to be kept informed and supported. They are only too willing to do this if they are able, which is another way of saying that parents do hate the loss of immediate responsibility which they sense when a child starts a psychoanalytic treatment and when the treatment is going well, and the transference neurosis is in full spate.

A corollary of this is that children who have no supportive background or who have parents who are themselves mentally ill cannot be helped materially by this quick method.

5. The aim is to unhitch something that is holding up the parents' management of their own child. It must be remembered that in the vast majority of cases the parents succeed in their

treatments by management and do not need help; neither do they consult a psychiatrist. They do in fact see their children through phases of difficult behaviour, and they adopt complex techniques which are part of parental care. What they cannot and must not do is this psychotherapeutic work with their own child in which a layer is reached which is held in reserve from the parents, and which makes contact with the child's unconscious.

Interview. I saw the child without first seeing the mother who brought her. The reason for this was that I was not at this stage concerned with taking an accurate history; I was concerned with getting the patient to give herself away to me, slowly as she gained confidence in me, and deeply as she found that she could take the risk.

We sat down at a small table on which were small sheets of paper and a pencil, and a few crayons in a box.

There were two psychiatric social workers and a visitor present.

First Ada told me (in answer to my question) that she was eight years old. She had a big sister, aged sixteen, and also a small brother of four and a half. Then she said she would like to draw, "My favourite hobby." She drew flowers in a vase (Fig. 1); a lamp, which hung from the ceiling in front of her (Fig. 2), and the swings

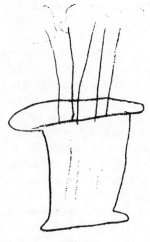

Figure 1

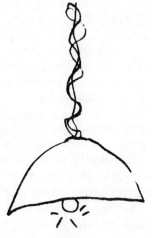

Figure 2

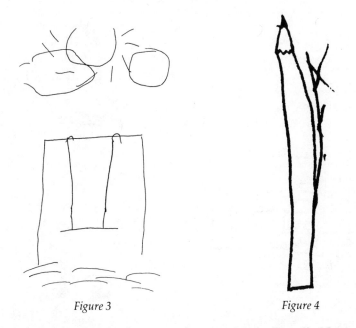

Figure 3   Figure 4

in the playground, sun out and some clouds (Fig. 3). Note the clouds.

Comment. These three drawings were poor as drawings, and they were unimaginative. They were representational. Nevertheless the clouds in the third had a significance, as will appear towards the end of the series.

Ada now drew a pencil (Fig. 4). "Oh dear, have you a rubber? It's funny, there's something wrong with it." I had no rubber and said she could alter it if it was wrong, and she did, and said "It's too fat."

Comment. Any analyst reading this will already have thought of various kinds of symbolism, and of various interpretations that might have been made. In this work interpretations are sparse and are reserved for the significant moments, as will be illustrated. Naturally one had in mind two ideas: An erect penis, or a pregnant belly. I made comments, but no interpretations.

Then she drew a house, with sun, clouds and a flowering plant. (Fig. 5. Note the clouds.) I asked if she could draw a person. Ada

Figure 5   Figure 6

replied that she would draw her cousin, but as she drew (Fig. 6) she said: *"I can't draw hands."*

I was now growing confident that the theme of stealing would appear, and so I was able to lean back on the child's own "process." *From now on it did not exactly matter what I said or did not say, except that I must be adapted to the child's needs and not requiring the child to adapt to my own.*

The hiding of the hands could be related either to the theme of stealing or to that of masturbation – and these themes are inter-related in that the stealing would be a compulsive acting out of repressed masturbation fantasies. (There was a further indication of pregnancy in this drawing of the cousin, but the pregnancy theme did not develop significance in this session. It would have taken us to the mother's pregnancy when Ada was three years old.)

Ada rationalized. She said, "She's hiding a present." I asked, "Can you draw the present?" The present was a box of handker-chiefs (Fig. 7). Ada said, "The box is crooked." I asked, "Where

did she buy the present?" Then she drew the counter of John
Lewis, a leading London store (Fig. 8). *Note the curtain down the
middle of the drawing.* (See Fig. 21.)

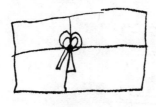

Figure 7

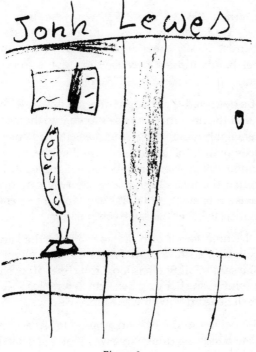

Figure 8

Figure 9

I now asked "What about drawing the lady buying the present?" Undoubtedly I was wanting to test Ada's ability to draw hands. So she drew Figure 9 which again shows a lady with her hands hidden because the view is from behind the counter.

It will be observed that the pictures are drawn with a stronger line now that the imagination has entered into their conception.

The theme of buying and giving presents had entered into the child's presentation of herself, but neither she nor I knew that these themes would eventually become significant. I did know, however, that the idea of buying is regularly employed to cover the compulsion to steal, and that the giving of presents is often a rationalization to cover the same compulsion.

I said "I would very much like to see what the lady looks like from behind." So Ada drew Figure 10. This picture surprised Ada. She said "Oh! She has long arms like mine; she is feeling for something, she has on a black dress with long sleeves; that's the dress I have on now, it was Mummy's once."

Now the person in the drawings stood for Ada herself. In this drawing the hands are drawn in a way that is special. The fingers reminded me of the pencil that was too fat. I made no interpretation.

Figure 10

Figure 11

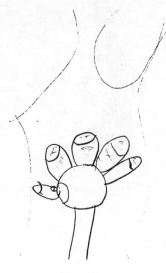

Figure 12

It was not certain how things would develop, perhaps this was all that I would get. In a pause I asked about techniques for getting to sleep, that is, for dealing with the change from waking to sleeping, and the difficult time for children who are having conflicting feelings about masturbation.

Ada said "I have a very big bear." While lovingly drawing it (Fig. 11) she told me its history. She also had a live kitten in bed with her in the mornings when she awoke. Here Ada told me about her brother who sucks his thumb and she drew (Fig. 12) a picture showing the brother's hand with a supernumerary thumb for sucking.

Observe the two breast-like objects where there were clouds in earlier drawings. It could be that this picture includes memories of seeing her baby brother on her mother's body, and near the breasts. I made no interpretation.

Our work together was now hanging fire. One could say that the child was (without knowing it) wondering whether it would be safe (i.e., profitable) to go deeper. While she was thus engaged she drew "a proud climber." (See Fig. 13.)

Figure 13

This was the time of the climbing of Everest by Hillary and
Tensing. This idea gave me a measure of Ada's capacity to
experience an achievement, and in the sexual field to reach a
climax. I was able to use this as an indication that Ada would be
able to bring me her main problem and give me the chance to help
her with it.

I made no interpretation. I did, however, deliberately make a
link with dreaming. I said "When you dream, do you dream of
mountaineering, and all that?"

There followed a verbal account of a very muddled dream.
What she said, talking very fast, was something like this:

"I go to the U.S.A. I am with the Indians and I get three bears.
The boy next door is in the dream. He is rich. I was lost in
London. There was a flood. The sea came in at the front door.

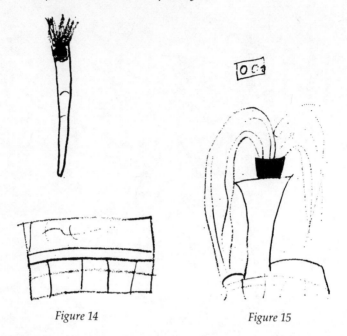

Figure 14   *Figure 15*

We all ran away in a car. We left something behind. I think – I don't know what it was. I don't think it was Teddy. I think it was the gas stove."

She told me that this was a very bad nightmare that she once had. When she woke she ran into the parents' room and got into her mother's bed, where she spent the rest of the night. She was evidently reporting an acute confusional state. This was perhaps the centre point of the interview, or *the essential reaching to the bottom of her experience of mental illness*. If this be true, then the rest of the session could be looked upon as a picture of recovery from the confusional state.

After this Ada drew several pictures. I forget what the first one (Fig. 14) represented.

Then she drew an aspidistra which she thought of while talking of spiders and other dreams of stinging scorpions "walking down in armies, and one big one in my bed" (Fig. 15); and a muddled picture indicating a mixture of house (fixed abode) and caravan (movable home, reminding her of the family holiday) (Fig. 16); and finally a poisonous spider (Fig. 17).

Figure 16

Figure 17

The spider had characteristics that link it with the hand; it is likely that the spider here symbolizes both the masturbation hand and also the female genitalia and orgasm. I made no interpretations.

I asked what a sad dream would be and Ada said: "Someone was killed, mother and father. They came all right again though."

Then she said "I've got a box with thirty-six coloured pencils." (Reference to the small number supplied by me and, I suppose, my meanness.)

Here we had reached the end of a middle phase; it must be remembered that I did not know whether anything more would happen. But I made no interpretations and waited for the working of the process which had been set up. I might have taken the reference to my meanness (pencils) as a sign that her own stealing impulse would be appropriate at this point in the interview. However, I continued to make no interpretations and to be waiting in case Ada should wish to go further.

After a while Ada spontaneously said "I had a burglar dream."

Figure 18

The final stage of the interview had started. It will be observed that Ada's drawings became much more bold at this point, and to anyone watching her draw it would have been clear that she was actuated from deep impulse and need. One felt almost in touch with Ada's unconscious.

Ada drew and said "A black man is killing a woman. There is some kind of thing behind him, with fingers or something." (Fig. 18.) Ada then drew the burglar, his hair sticking up, rather funny, like a clown (Fig. 19). She said "My sister's hands are bigger than mine.

"The burglar is stealing jewels from a rich lady because he wants to give a nice present to his wife. He could not wait to save up."

Here, at a deeper level, appears the theme represented earlier by the woman or girl buying handkerchiefs from a store to give as a present to someone. It will be seen that there are shapes like the

Figure 19

Figure 20

clouds of the earlier drawings, and these are now like a curtain, and *there is a bow*.

I made no interpretation, but I found myself interested in the bow which, if untied, would reveal something.

These curtains and the bow reappear in Figure 20 which is a drawing of the present. Ada added, looking at what she had drawn, "The burglar has a cloak. His hair looks like carrots or a tree or a bush. He is really very kind."

Figure 21   Figure 22

Now I intervened. I asked about the bow. Ada said that it belonged to a circus. (She had not been to one.)

She drew a juggler (Fig. 21). This could be thought of as an attempt to make a career out of the unresolved problem. Here again were the curtains and the bow.

I now thought of the bow as symbolical of repression, and it seemed to me that Ada was ready to have the bow untied. I therefore said to her "Do you ever pinch (steal) things yourself?"

This is the place where the subject of my study appears in this description of a therapeutic interview. It is for this detail that the reader has been invited to follow the development of the process in the child who has used the opportunity for contact with myself. There was a double reaction to my question, and here is represented the dissociation.

Ada said "NO!"; and at the same time she took another piece of paper and drew an apple tree with two apples; and to this she added grass, a rabbit and a flower (Fig. 22).

This showed what was behind the curtain. It represented the discovery of the mother's breasts which had been hidden, as it were, by the mother's clothes. In this way a deprivation had been symbolized. This symbolism is to be compared and contrasted with the direct view depicted in the drawing (Fig. 12) which contains a memory of the baby brother in contact with the mother's body.

I made a comment here. I said "Oh, I see, the curtains were mother's blouse, and you have now reached through to her breasts."

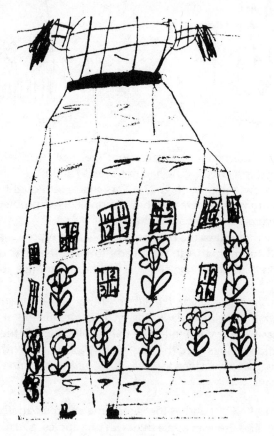

Figure 23

Ada did not answer, but instead she drew another picture (Fig. 23). "This is Mother's dress, that I love best. She still has it."

It dates from the time when Ada was a little girl and indeed it is so drawn that the child's eyes are about at the level of the mother's mid-thigh region. The theme of breasts is continued in the puff sleeves. The fertility symbols are the same as in the early drawing of a house, and are also changing over into numbers.

The work of the interview was now over, and Ada wasted a little time "coming to the surface", playing a game which continued the theme of numbers as fertility symbols. (See Figs. 24, 25, and 26.)

Ada was now ready to go, and as she was in a happy and contented state I was able to have ten minutes with the mother who had been waiting an hour and a quarter.

In this brief interview I was able to learn that Ada had made satisfactory development until she was four years nine months old. She had taken the birth of her brother in her stride when she was three and a half, with some exaggerated concern for him. At four years nine months, the brother (then twenty months old) became seriously ill, and remained ill.

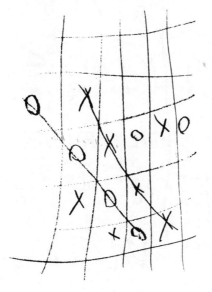

Figure 24

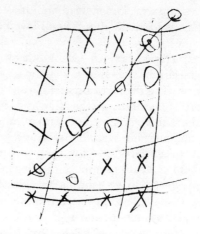

Figure 25

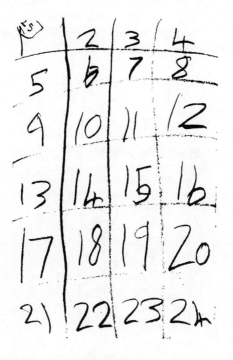

Figure 26

Ada had been very much mothered by her older sister, but now (when the brother became ill) this older sister transferred her attention absolutely to the small brother, and so Ada became seriously deprived. It was some time before the parents realized that Ada had been seriously affected by the change in her sister. They did all they could to mend matters but it was two years or so before Ada seemed to be recovering.

At about this time Ada (seven years old) started to steal, at first from the mother and later from the school. Recently, stealing had become a serious matter but Ada could never own up to it. She even took stolen money to her teacher and asked her to give it out to her slowly, thereby showing that she had not dealt with the full implication of her stealing acts.

Along with this compulsive stealing Ada's schooling had become affected by a lack of ability to concentrate when working. She was always blowing her nose, and she had become fat and ungainly. (See Figure 4 – "pencil too fat – something wrong with it.")

In short, Ada had suffered a relative deprivation at 4.9 years, though living in her own good home. As a result she had become confused, but as she started to rediscover a sense of security she had developed stealing as a dissociated compulsion, which she could not acknowledge.

Result of psychotherapeutic interview

The interview was evidently significant for although Ada was stealing right up to the interview she has not stolen since, that is, in three and a half years. Also her school work quickly improved. (The nocturnal enuresis did not clear up till a year after the interview, however.)

The mother reported that Ada came out of the clinic with a new relationship to her, one of ease and intimacy, as if a block had been removed. This recovery of an old intimacy has persisted, and it seems to show that the work done in the interview was a genuine re-establishment of contact which had been lost at the time when the big sister suddenly switched her mothering from Ada to the ill brother.

Here is an example shown in detail of the *dissociation* to which I am referring. Ada could not own up to stealing, and when in the interview she was asked: "Do you ever steal?" she said firmly "No!" but at the same time she showed that she now need not steal because she had found what she had lost – symbolic contact with her mother's breasts.

Summary of case

A psychotherapeutic interview is given in detail, showing the resolution of an eight-year-old girl's compulsion to steal.

At the critical moment the child denied that she ever stole, and at the same time she reached through the barrier and reached what she had lost, thereby making her "No!" into a true statement. In other words at this moment the dissociation ceased to be operative.

In this case there had been no attempt to make the child own up, that is to say, to move from the dissociation into an area of intellectual understanding and integrating. At the deeper layer at which the work was done it was possible for the interview to produce a result, not conscious insight, and not confession, but a true healing of a dissociation.

Sources of the papers in this volume

April) 1963; (2) Timothy Raison (ed.) *Youth in New Society*, London: Rupert Hart-Davis, 1966; (3) *Adolescent Psychiatry*, New York: Basic Books, 1971; (4) Partly in 'Adolescence' in *The Family and Individual Development*, London: Tavistock Publications, 1965.

18 'Youth Will Not Sleep' in *New Society* (28 May) 1964.

19 'Correspondence with a Magistrate' in *The New Era in Home and School* (January) 1964.

20 'The Foundation of Mental Health' in the *British Medical Journal* (16 June) 1951.

21 'The Deprived Child and How He Can Be Compensated for Loss of Family Life' in *The Family and Individual Development*. London: Tavistock Publications, 1965.

22 'Group Influences and the Maladjusted Child: The School Aspect' in *The Family and Individual Development*.

23 'The Persecution that Wasn't' in *New Society* (18 May) 1967. Review of Sheila Stewart, *A Home from Home*, London: Longmans, 1967.

24 'Comments on the *Report of the Committee on Punishment in Prisons and Borstals*', unpublished.

25 *Do Progressive Schools Give Too Much Freedom to the Child?*
'Contribution to Conference at Dartington Hall' in Maurice Ash (ed.) *Who Are the Progressive Now?* London: Routledge & Kegan Paul, 1969.
'Notes Made in the Train', unpublished.

26 'Residential Care as Therapy', unpublished.

27 'Varieties of Psychotherapy', unpublished.

28 'The Psychotherapy of Character Disorders' in *The Maturational Processes and the Facilitating Environment*. London: Hogarth Press, 1965.

29 'Dissociation Revealed in a Therapeutic Consultation' in Ralph Slovenko (ed.) *Crime, Law and Corrections*. Springfield, Illinois: Charles C. Thomas, 1966. Also in *Therapeutic Consultations in Child Psychiatry*. London: Hogarth Press, 1971.

Name index

Subject index

military and naval, in adolescence,
150; *see also* control
disintegration, 105, 129, 198, 258
dissociation, 126, 256–82
disturbed children *see* antisocial
tendency
disturbed parents *see* abnormal
doldrums, adolescent, 145–55
dramatization, of inner psychic reality,
89–90
drawings in therapy, 264–80
dream(ing), 95, 128, 185, 187, 188, 218,
240, 263, 271–73; day-, 30, 95, 243

early nurture *see* environment
eating: and not eating, 111; one's cake,
139, 144; primitive loving and, 95–6,
97, 104, 109, 139, 140
ego: character disorder and, 242–50;
defence, breakdown of, 110, 245;
distortion, in character disorder, 247;
distortion, in psychosis, 245, 261;
and fusion of drives, 129;
independent of mother's 102; and
integration, 100, 242; and intellectual
area, 258; maturity, determining
antisocial tendency, 129, 249;
maturity and ability to keep alive a
memory, 124; maturity, and ability to
mourn, 132, 134; -needs, 127;
organisation, as achievement, 102;
organisation, and denial, 262;
-relatedness, 130–31; -support, early
environmental, 105, 127, 131, 244,
245; -support, in therapy, 247, 248
emotional development: and
adolescence, 145, 151–55, 157; and
ambivalence, 102; basic theory of,
214–15; continuity of, 190, 211; and
creation, 111, 116, 125, 177, 186, 194;
and deprivation, 127–28, 169–70, 198,
245–46; and environmental failure,
110, 138, 175–76, 190, 191, 245; and
environmental stability, 115–17; and
establishment of me/not me, 98, 99,
102, 193; and failure of adaptation,
127; and fusion of drives, 126; and
good-enough environment, 173–74;
immaturity in, and psychological
disorder, 234–35; and integration,
102, 109, 119, 137, 138, 191, 192, 195,
198, 237, 242; and innate morality,
106–07, 109, 111–12; maturation

processes basis of, 101; and
omnipotence, 129; and
psychoneurosis, 234–35; and
psychosis, 234–35; and
psychosomatic life 102, 192, 237; and
reaction to loss, 132, 134; and
relationship to primary love-object,
216–19; and sense of reality, 118; and
stage of concern, 100–05, 119, 134,
136, 137–38; and therapy, 118,
236–40; and triangular relationships
(Oedipus complex), 101, 119, 146;
and transitional objects, 185–86, 192
emotional stability *see* stability
environment: and ability to survive,
227–28; in adolescence, 146; diagnosis
in terms of early, 178–79; evolution
of, 215; facilitating, 106, 214, 245, 260;
good-enough, 101, 173–74, 191, 245;
good internal, 117, 223; and holding,
191, 225–26, 237, 239, 248;
importance of in early development,
190; 'let down' in, 127, 157, 236, 246;
–mother, 103–05; reliability of,
224–25; specialized, for antisocial
child, 1, 117, 118, 121, 177, 179–81,
238, 255; and stability, 10, 125, 183;
tantalizing, 185, 225; testing of, by
child, 51, 71, 115, 129; *see also* home;
management; setting
environmental conditions for therapy,
223–28, 236–37, 239, 247–50; *see also*
management; setting
environmental failure: and
deprivation, 173–77, 181–82, 235,
236, 238, 245, 247, 260; and
maladjustment, 195; and psychosis,
193, 234–35, 245, 260
environmental framework, 115–16, 125;
see also home
envy, 141–42
erotic drive, 101
European Congress of Child
Psychiatry, paper to, 241–55
evacuation: and antisocial behaviour,
40–3, 45–6, 56, 73; and billets, 33, 35,
46, 47, 53; and billets, failure to settle
in, 54, 56, 57; Cambridge Survey,
22–4; and delinquency 2, 56; and
deprived children, 3, 12, 42, 57; and
foster-parents, 39–43, 45, 47, 52; and
homecoming, 44–53; and hostels for
difficult children, 2–4, 52, 54–72, 73,